Praise for Chad Faries

"Like some improbable love-child of Dorothy Allison and David Sedaris, *Drive Me Out of My Mind* is a gritty, unflinching memoir about growing up on a forgotten frontier of broken American dreams—Michigan's brutal Upper Peninsula—that is also an uproarious comedy about a childhood spent in houses pollinated by drunks and users and poets and lovers and madmen. . .and one unforgettable mother."

— Adam Davies, author of *The Frog King*

"I loved this grave, manic, kickass, drug-addled, sex-drenched, visionary memoir. It starts as a tale of rootlessness and slowly becomes the opposite of that: the story of a constant love between a troubled boy and his unhinged mother—the portrait of an iron chain. It's mesmerizing."

— George Dawes Green, author of *Ravens* and founder of "The Moth"

"Chad Faries' *Drive Me Out of My Mind* is a story of dilapidated, transient 1970s America, of grotesque and haunting experience gnawing the innocence of a visionary child perhaps only William Blake could fully comprehend. From the seats of motorcycles, Greyhound buses and hundred-dollar cars, this child watches one house after another disappear behind him into a vortex spun by adults on the perpetual run from themselves. How did he become the man capable of telling this tale? Often, I could bear to keep reading only because somewhere over the road's horizon, beyond all these addresses, an extraordinary spiritual self-reliance—a home of his own making—was obviously waiting for him."

— Johnathan Johnson, author of *Hannah and the Mountain*

DRIVE ME OUT OF MY MIND

24 HOUSES IN 10 YEARS

by

CHAD FARIES

Barbara,
Thanks for
supporting books and
the U.P. Art scene!

EMERGENCY PRESS
NEW YORK

Printed in the United States of America
First Edition

Interior design by MaSovaida Morgan
Cover Design by Audrey Raudabaugh

Photo credits:
Front Cover: Matthew T. Perry and Holly Harvey (house)
Back Cover: Andrew von Goellner (background image and author portrait) and Matthew T. Perry
Inside title page: Andrew von Goellner

Faries, Chad
Drive Me Out of My Mind: 24 Houses in 10 Years
ISBN 978-0-9830226-2-6
1. Biography and Autobiography—General. 2. Biography and Autobiography—Personal Memoirs. 3. Biography and Autobiography—Literary.

Emergency Press
154 W. 27th St.
#5W
New York NY 10001
emergencypress.org

9 8 7 6 5 4 3 2 1
First Printing

DRIVE ME
OUT OF MY MIND

Dedications

Above all, this book is dedicated to Mom. Unconventional parenting apparently works, and I love her for it. And of course there are the other fantastic, resourceful, and resilient women—Gramma and my three aunts. Basically, everyone alluded to in this book—this is for you. Regardless of story or actions, everyone deserves dignity and that is what I tried to give them here. Efforts were made to change the names, but obviously those who know my story intimately will also know the characters by association. And let's not forget the Man Worth Mentioning, Greg, who never left my side. Thanks for not killing him with Pandora's Box, Mom.

Sister Jazmine, though you were born after all the events that took place in this book, you will have a central role in part two and a much greater dedication!

Beyond those mentioned in the book, there were many that helped bring this story to fruition. Special thanks to the Hungarian Fulbright Commission and all my fellow "Fulbrighters" in Budapest where this book started taking shape: Alex, Haleh, Tyler, and the whole crew. Thanks to The Bard Room and Treehugger Dan's in Budapest where I first unleashed these stories.

Thanks to my buddies Jonathan Johnson, George Dawes Greene, Adam Davies, Robert Firth, Jayson Iwen, Aaron Hunter, and others who gave me direction and reminded me about the importance of STORY. Becoming a raconteur for the Unchained Tour also helped.

In Savannah, I have to give extended thanks to Matt Pricket and the Savannah Book Festival, Joni at the Book Lady, all my colleagues at Savannah State, and the creative team that brought the book and trailer (check it out online) to life: MaSovaida, Audrey, Mike, Matt, Josh, Andrew, Ashley, Beck, Noah, Jeff and his Impala, and the wonderful parents that trusted me with their children on a motorcycle. And LaShawn "Lone Star" should be thanked for her patience and sweetness.

And then there is the dark haired girl who is behind the shadows on every page. Sometime she is called Ruby, Star, Eurydice, Suzy, etc. I finally found her walking across a street in high-heeled boots in a foreign land where people speak a language delivered from aliens. For better and for worse, the other central dedication must go to Gingike. *Things like this drive me out of my mind.*

What makes a house grand
ain't the roof or the doors.
If there's love in a house
It's a palace for sure.
Without love . . .
it ain't nothin but a house,
a house where nobody lives.

from "A House Where Nobody Lives"
– Tom Waits

DRIVE ME OUT OF MY MIND
24 HOUSES IN 10 YEARS

Foreword

Behind City Market.
Iron River, Michigan

Has he lost his mind?
Can he see or is he blind?
Can he walk at all,
or if he moves will he fall?
Is he alive or dead?
Has he thoughts within his head?
We'll just pass him there
why should we even care?
from "Iron Man"
– *Black Sabbath*

At five years old it was hard to get me off the top of Barbie. When you're the first boy born to a family of three aunts, a single mother, and a middle-aged grandmother on husband number four, you don't have much say about what gets handed down, but you do have a say about use. Every afternoon I would take Barbie to my bedroom for her nap. I would undress her and place her plastic body softly on a pillow, take off my second-hand mismatched Garanimals, and mount her. Since my body hid her face from me, I stared at the poster of the Dallas Cowboy Cheerleaders over my bed and picked a different girl each session to focus on. My favorite was Suzie

Holub from the 1976 roster. Her hair was dark, and her smile even darker. In her brown eyes was a distance I wanted to travel, a distance that would fly me east over an ocean to a larger city on a larger river where Suzie would be at the bank, parting my hair and speaking the language of aliens. It was natural that her breasts were adorned with stars because she was of another universe. This supernova love was painful. My pee-pee was half the size of Barbie's body so I just rested it there like a rocket on a launch pad until the boosters kicked in. And then I launched a thousand expeditions in minutes, and my rocket often got damaged in the atmosphere, but I figured if I did it long enough I would reach love.

It wasn't supposed to be right for a little boy to play with Barbies, but it felt so . . . heavenly, in a Carl Sagan sort of way. I wasn't playing with Barbie; I was nurturing her. I stole Grampa Duke's moustache comb and ran it through Barbie's hair. I washed down her body with my tongue, a damp sock, and undiluted Mr. Clean. With baby oil libations, I squeezed her through the love-tunnel of my grasped hand. I carried her in my back pocket and untucked my shirt to hide her.

I treated her well, and everyone knew it and was getting a little worried.

Aunt Molly was the first one to walk in on us in my new bedroom in the alley house behind City Market. My Spider-Man underwear were at my knees, and my ass travelled to and fro in the dank air of dirty socks, broken Crayons, and asbestos. She was 15 then, seven years younger than Mother and ten years older than me: silk-black hair, gap-toothed, busty, tushy, and already letting boys mount her like I did Barbie. She never made eye contact and "really liked praying" is what Gramma would say sarcastically. Maybe she was always just looking for the Lord, and I didn't know much about that either so to me, he was just something like a superhero—Spider-Man, the Green Lantern, or even Ragsy, the mutt across the street.

"Jesus Christ! What the hell are you doing?" she screamed after she entered my room without observing the "Chad's Domain" sign. "Oh my fucking God!" she said drawing out the vowel in "God" in a sharp ascending pitch. I was bummed because I had to look away from Suzie and my rubbing rhythm was all off now. Molly started running in place as if she were trying to escape something she clearly could not. All I saw were her breasts shaking freely under her Warhol Rolling Stones tongue shirt. In a half laugh/half scream she called for Aunt Ally to come and look. Molly and Ally were always visiting Mother in her new house because they were free to smoke cigarettes and meet boys there. I really dug them most of the time because when they babysat me we'd go to Ben Franklin's dime store and steal art supplies for them and action figures for me so I could have some toys for boys. But nothing beat a naked Barbie and her breasts cutting the waves of excited adolescent shrieks, and a poster full of flat bellies and blue stars.

I made eye contact with Suzie again and got my rhythm back.

"Chad's fucking a Barbie, for Christ's sake!" It sounded so crude and base. I was trying to fill her with love, albeit unsuccessfully. It was the process of removing her clothes, combing her hair, licking her clean, and rubbing her down that really counted.

I tore my eyes again from Suzie and looked back over my shoulder at Molly there with her hands on the doorway jambs. I didn't know what to do, so I didn't stop. I just kept pumping her and pumping her while Molly laughed and ran and ran without going anywhere, still yelling for Ally to come, "Oh Lord, Holy fuck! You gotta see this Al!" I looked Molly right in the eye and kept giving it to Barbie because I remembered that is what I saw Ragsy—my buddy LittleMan's mutt—do when he was giving it to Gramma's Fox Terrier, Lady. I had walked into the backyard on Roosevelt because Lady was whining. I let out a scream when I saw Ragsy mounted on her rear-end. He just glanced over his shoulder at me with a really dumb look. I guess he was confused that I was disturbing him and not leaving. And that is exactly what I felt; why would Molly stay, all exposed in the doorway like that? Maybe she could have hid in a closet and observed in order to learn something, but to just gawk on like that was really strange.

Then Ally finally responded, the only one in seven generations of family to be a member of what Gramma would call the Itty Bitty Titty Committee. At twelve, her body was nearly fully matured just like the other women in the family had been. Her bitty-titties had no hope of growth. Her hair was as long as Molly's with no bangs, but lighter, reds and blondes like the color of a sunrise, which fit her well because most of the time her thoughts were in the sky. "Spacey" is what Mother said, and I thought that's what I wanted to be;

to me, "spacey" and "heavenly" were the same. She was the most petite in character and stature, but when she had her mind made up about something, she painted it with loud, dark language and a glare from her icy eyes.

"What? I'm painting clouds," she said in her spacey-tone from somewhere in the distance. She was really eating her stash of Kellogg's Corn Flakes with Tang.

"Get your little tits in here and check this out!"

And so the loud painting came, "I said I am fucking painting clouds, slut-face! I'm coming now. Happy?" she said in a way that boomed from some deep, animal place. Seconds later the busty and the bitty were both there staring at me and laughing, like I was a scene in a cartoon that they had always wanted to see. "Wow," is all Aunt Ally could say with her orange lips, and that could have meant she was really proud of me, or that I had disgusted her beyond words. It was always like that with her. So I just thought of Ragsy and kept going until I was so excited that I peed all over Barbie. That yellow was always my weakness, and I would manage to piss in every place I lay my head for ten years. A puddle formed on the pillow and overflowed to the linoleum floor and streamed toward Molly and Ally's bare feet. They didn't notice until the liquid heat touched their toes. They looked down, then at each other briefly, screeched "gross!" drawing out the vowel in "gross"—this time in a sharp descending pitch, spun around in opposite directions, accidentally knocked their foreheads together—and left me alone.

I had never given it to Barbie like that before and I'm not sure if she liked it. The only thing I got was a heart beating really fast and the shakes. If anything, I lost something, and that would have been my breath, I guess.

Nevertheless, there were benefits to Barbie fucking. Somehow people knew I wasn't naïve about humping and petting. I got a little more respect and people laughed and joked about me admiringly. I sat up late at night thinking about what they would say:

"Dat Chad really knows how da give 'er tarpaper," Toivo Takala would say shaking his head, smiling, and staring at the ground with a beer in his hand, trying to picture it all and reframe his own childhood. It made people feel good about themselves and their youth to know I was screwing Barbie.

"Holy wah!" Vain might say, "What a character. Dat Chad is all right." He was saying this from the arms of my Aunt Molly who he practiced with in the backseat of his car parked out at Cannon mine.

Barbie was my tool for practicing. I was just trying to figure things out, how a prairie dog knows his hole from all the others, what is flotsam and what is jetsam, am I a grown-up acting like a child, or a child playing "big." People never stop trying to figure these things out. Mother was still working on figuring things out, and that's why we had moved again.

* * *

Depending on the slant of the Earth's axis and Mother's inclination, we would roll up or down the hill that separated Iron River from Stambaugh in Michigan's Upper Peninsula—U.P. for short. Had it been 60 years earlier we would have been able to take a trolley with an interior decked out in Mahogany. And we would have seen miners, red with ore dust coming up right out of the Riverton, Beta, Caspian, Buck, Fogarty, Berkshire, Seldon, Paint River, Mastadon, Nanaimo, Isabella, Baltic, Homer, Crystal Falls, or Hemlock mines. There was just one mine of over a hundred still operating, but the open pits right in the center of every community were a constant reminder of a better time, even though the whole county was now a toxic waste site.

So, the emotional tilt of the axis rolled us down the hill again and we came to a halt behind City Market. City Market was still pure Main Street U.P. and had the soul of that better time. It was no bigger than a living room and had one of everything you ever needed stacked in a metrical pattern that composed a song of processed food, saggy asses, and large guts. There was a butcher too. His name was Butch, and like any good butcher had a white fresh bloodstained apron with tiny animal hairs crusted into the fabric like shaggy scabs. He smiled a lot and was considered quite handsome by the over-40 conservative helmet-hair housewives who had voted for Nixon. They wore polyester pastel colors and white pumps—smoked cigarettes with fake ivory holders. My Gramma kind of looked like this, but didn't care much for politics—liberal by nature, not by choice—and had an authentic ivory holder. Her preferred drink was a Bloody Mary and for a long time I believed that blood was the ingredient and never thought much of it. It matched her character, and anyway, all the women in my family were constantly bleeding and complaining about being "on the rag." At five, you know that blood comes from somewhere, so you figure things out on your own—the women in my family drank too many Bloody Marys.

None of Butch the Butcher's admirers worked, just shopped and flirted with him. They kept houses in order and food on the table. The prescription seemed to work well since there was nothing else to do other than Friday Fish Fry and Polka. But Mother and my aunts never read the instructions, and Gramma wasn't a very good teacher, so they made up the expectations of women. Even after Eddy—Mother's experimental half-a-year husband that divorced her and the entire U.P. for a life below the bridge back in Battle Creek—she wanted someone to expect something from her, still. All the women did for that matter, but you'd never know it if you heard one of their conversations:

"I said fuck that, I'm not putting up with his shit about wanting a good woman at his side when he rolls over in the morning with nothing more than a spent roach and a pocket full of blank applications. Get a real job and buy a proper bed that's not stuffed with hay and maybe a good woman will appear. Wash your prick twice a day with laundry detergent too; it stinks from being stuck under your ass."

If you wanted a man for more than a couple of days, this talk didn't work. Nevertheless, it was fun to learn new vocabulary and I started to respect the boldness of speech, even though I would never want Barbie to treat me like that.

* * *

Mother was growing and growing like an umbrella plant in good light—not up or down, but out. She was trying to fill her stomach with meats and chocolates to satisfy her hunger for wanting to bust out of Iron River. Her lips, breasts, and hips had already been full since she was twelve and men had often remarked "she sure doesn't look twelve" while they secretively envisioned licking those lips while licking their own. And Mother—for reasons sometimes sexual, but most of the time not—would grab her FF breast—most of the time for real, but sometimes not—take aim, and squeeze it as if she were shooting a bullet out of her nipple.

She was doing a lot of "speed" is what everyone called it, and to me it was like the spirit of a U.P. Championship Rodeo Bronco condensed into a little pill. Our love had a distance and I never got close enough to figure out the reason we would move 24 times in a decade, but I followed her and tried to collapse that distance and always stumbled. Sometimes, though, I took the lead. Maybe each house was an hour in a day that had a deadline for figuring something out. And maybe she was trying to figure out how a seemingly random and fleeting emotion on August 15, 1970, like wanting to feel a man "explode inside of you" is what I had heard the women say, could lead to your child writing it all down years later. But then, "years later," after all the stories of all the hours in that "day" had been written, I learned at "Randy's Hole in the Wall"—when she was too drunk to drive and I brought her home—of another one of her seemingly random and fleeting emotions: the desire on May 6, 1971 to be a mother at 17 and not give me to the family that had been making arrangements for months to take me into their story. "Can I keep him, Mom?" she asked Gramma.

And after her second daughter Hope's botched illegal abortion 15 months earlier in a New York City hotel room, after her implicit cover-up of Mother's being molested by her step-grandfather, Gramma took a nervous puff from her ivory cigarette holder, shed a tear, and exhaled, "Of course you can. That's my first grandson." And in that odd moment they lay down the pathetic legacy of rapes and beatings and denials for something far more stellar and perhaps not random at all. Gramma and Mother embraced chaos—a determined future, nevertheless, unpredictable.

"And that's my story and I'm sticking it to you," is what Gramma would say, draw a long puff, throw her arm down to her side, stare in three-quarter profile up at the sky, and then blow a smoke cloud as if she was creating a weather system. The saying was a concoction of clichés synthesized into something that made a perfectly fresh sense. There was no escaping the story. If you were in the presence of it, it adhered to you.

Though wild, and knowing she would ultimately throw anyone, at night Mother still wanted someone to ride her. She had all this energy with no direction, no plan, and if only someone could break her we might stick around for a while. She'd wake me up around midnight and we would walk a couple of blocks down Main Street past the old City Hall which was one of the few old brick buildings that was kept up. The others had either been torn down or abandoned because since half the population had left over a 50 year period on account of almost all the mines shutting down, there were a lot of empty rooms. The City decided that an empty lot was better than an empty historical building so there were tons of places to park in West Iron County, but not enough cars to fill the spaces. The City planted trees and put picnic tables around the perimeter of the lots to attract people to come and park, but this didn't work either. Finally they just stopped tearing down the old buildings and left them as some representation of an ancient mining civilization "that on_e endured in t_ese gre_t lan_s of sweat and toil," is what the plastic sign with missing letters said in front of the Iron Country Museum.

Walking at night with Mother, sometimes I would stumble in my partial slumber over the uneven slabs of pavement that the winter frost had unsettled. I stumbled in front of the Jack-O-Lantern bar where black strippers from Detroit danced on the weekends, and scabbed my knee on memory—once LittleMan and I had sneaked out of our houses and met by the trash cans in Roosevelt alley and rambled all night down back street wonderlands, puffing on old cigars the whole way with stars stuck to our eyes. We were off to see the "chocolate" that his older brothers were always talking about. I had seen a lot of breasts, even LittleMan's sisters', but never anything the color of a Hershey's bar. I knew somehow that food used to describe people seemed a little funny, but Mother, after all, would be eating men.

I didn't have any brothers or sisters, but LittleMan did—a whole constellation of them: two younger sisters, Tracy and Elaine; and three older brothers, Pete, Jimmy, and Marky. In the sky of Stambaugh they formed something like a sickle that cut its way through the checkered flannel fabric of a traditional family. Naturally, I turned myself into a star and often resided, dwarfishly, in their cosmic field. LittleMan was a year older than me and a little more "badass" is what Aunt Molly would say. We shared yellow hair, lake blue eyes, bedwetting, and lack of breath. He would often take his left hand and squeeze his jugular vein and wind-pipe with his thumb while the fingers held on to the back of his neck for a good grip. Holding back that blood and air made him a little dizzy and spacey.

He called it "nuthing" because it was the same feeling as huffing, but with no glue or spray paint. My lack of air came in the form of panic attacks.

We climbed on top of the trashcans in the back of the Jack-O-Lantern and peaked through a crack in the window that had been painted black. Indeed the women were dark. We first saw the whites of their eyes and then drew the rest of the wild curves with our gaze, which, at five, was respectful, though ignorant Their nipples were like the tips of markers with aureoles resembling a scribble of storm cloud banks. Their teeth were brilliant like bleached white construction paper on which I drew pictures that I worked hard on and wanted to last.

The darkest people in Iron River were the full-blooded Chippewas and some of the Italians, but the African-Americans never settled up here, and it's no wonder; the way the men inside the Jack-O-Lantern screamed at those girls would have sent me running home right away. But the women pretended to like it, probably because they had no say in the matter, and knew they didn't have to stay forever locked to the sick magnetism of West Iron County. I thought it would be easy to fall in love with one of those women, but to the screaming men they were no different than the "food" in the pictures LittleMan's oldest brother, Morrie, had stashed between his mattresses.

Mother caught me before I planted my face in the sidewalk and put me on track. I shook the memory off and we took a left and ended up at The Dinner Bell all-night café. It had the only neon sign in town, a blue coffee cup that looked more like an elephant scratching the back of an ear with its trunk. It was right next to a parking lot so it made the perfect truck stop. Those truckers were like weathered and worn superheroes to me and I really dug them. They had a way of hunching up their shoulders so their necks would disappear, as if they were always hiding from their past of fighting dangerous villains and saving maidens from the clutches of husbands that beat them. Under their eyes was black shadow that hadn't been wiped away by sleep's dirty kerchief for a long time. It didn't look bad, really—it was just part of being "on the road." I guess after staring at blacktop long enough, it soaks into your eyes and you just can't wash it away, no matter how many filthy gas station bathrooms you stop at. And belt buckles. Everybody likes a belt buckle as big as a TV screen. In that late night café I saw eagles, Peterbilt semi-trucks, Indian heads, turquoise stones, Harley Davidsons, and a lot of text, like "keep on truckin," and "gear jammer" all riding above a crotch, cinching diesel-stained jeans to a solid ballooned-gut of landscapes that they had been feeding on.

After midnight everyone at the Dinner Bell looked like a different strain of human and I guess we weren't excluded. The wait staff and truckers knew us pretty well there, and it never seemed weird that we showed up in the earliest of morning that was still night to me. There was no sense of time in a 24-hour café. The people who worked there never slept and worked continuous shifts so there were always the exact same faces greeting me. Don was the owner and had some kind of accent, maybe Italian. His eyes were like an Orangutan's—like big benevolent, sad pennies.

"Hey Kate! How-a the hell are you?" and then a kiss on each cheek. "Oh Chad, come-a here," then a kiss on each cheek and Don would give me some crayons that he stole from the new Big Boy across the street that would ultimately put him out of business.

And then there was Mary who was definitely on speed, like Mother and Aunt Hope, but her recipe must have been different. She clicked her teeth all the time as if she wanted to eat me, and I was frightened, and I thought about how bad it was to think of women as food. She talked really fast, even faster than Aunt Hope, and even faster than Alvin of the Chipmunks. I didn't understand a single thing about Mary. Her hair was a foot high and she wore gold fishing lures with baby-blue dyed feathers for earrings. From a distance, Mary could have been a looker, but up close her hips blurred into her breasts and her shoulders into her head—she had no knees or elbows, just tubes for legs and arms. Perhaps she was something Don made in the backroom one night with pasta dough and chicken parts when it wasn't too busy. Maybe he just ordered her and added water, a couple of breaths, and a lot of coffee. She seemed low maintenance because she never slept or changed. Maybe she wasn't even really there. Maybe she was some kind of trucker construct made to make sure they always had something to come back to. But they surely could have done better. I finally came to the conclusion that Don grew her between the three trees on the grass island in the middle of the parking lot. He put coffee grounds and egg shells over the soil until she sprouted. Then he salt and peppered her for three weeks. When her mouth formed, he fed her farina and goat milk.

I had a problem with Mary; she wasn't a mother. And I couldn't be sure about any of the above, because we never went to the café in the day when I was coherent. Even when I walked by The Dinner Bell in daylight, I couldn't tell what was going on because the nicotine-stained curtains were drawn. Only at nightfall would Don pull the string in unison with the last hour clang of the church bell at 9 p.m. before it went silent for the night so workers could get a good rest without being reminded of the presence of God on every hour.

Gary Taggit often showed up around 4 a.m.—ready to ride—after his night shift at the Coleman Company where he twisted wires for AMC automotive on an assembly line. He was from the South and talked differently too, and when he and Don got to talking it was really something. Don was always adding extra syllables, while Gary Taggit was stretching them out.

"Howww Yaaaall Dooooooin,'" Gary would sing in his placid drawl that tweaked Mother's ears.

"Ah, Gary! It's-a good-a to see you," Don sang. Mary cracked a smile too, revealing a bobbie pin she plucked and stuck in her hair. There were hugs and handshakes and dead animals smiling on the wall, wondering at the hours and days on plastic beer clocks that needed their batteries changed, and dated yellowing calendars with a coat of fur where dust from the five years they had hung there stuck to multiple layers of grease. It was another festive night at The Dinner Bell.

Everybody was always just "doing" and "being" and most of it was good. People talked for hours about what seemed like absolutely nothing, but the whole gamut of emotions was still covered by simple inflections. We all drank coffee together and ate hash browns and eggs with frozen sausage links that Don brought out from the kitchen where something cooked the food. And Mother grew a little more with every bite.

* * *

Mother was so hungry she started eating men. If she didn't get enough food she would often bring Gary Taggit back to the house with us which was convenient because I was usually sleeping in a booth by the time we left and Gary was strong enough to carry me all the way back to my bedroom.

Mother would pull back the sheets and Gary dropped me in as if he was putting dirty clothes in a hamper. If I was awake, I was too tired to move, but I could hear Mother feeding on him. The sound was like the tiny skull of a hamster being chewed and sucked dry by a cat. In the morning I would run into him in the kitchen and we would eat cereal together while Mother rested up for another late night.

"Where are your wounds?" I asked him, man-to-man.

"You mean this purty ole thang?" and he pulled up his shirt and showed me a big scar shaped like a canoe. I couldn't believe how fast he had healed. I started to fear Mother.

Craig Kalavala, a volunteer fireman, was the first I actually saw her try to swallow. I saw her on her knees in the living room in front of an overstuffed chair one night when I was sneaking a glass of water from the bathroom because Mother was trying to prevent me from bedwetting so I hadn't drank any water since noon. Her feet were tiny and her toes were curled so that their knuckles rested on the carpet. Her back was to me so all I could see was Kalavala's huge hands on her head like an ugly hat. I thought he was trying to warm her up by placing her between his legs and putting a hat on her. I smiled. It was nice when people treated Mother well. Soon the wet skull crushing began again and Mother was swaying her head all over as if she was grooving to the Grateful Dead. She even put her shoulders into it, and wiggled her hips as much as she could while on her knees, feeding on Craig Kalavala's legs while he relished in the pain. When Craig finally contorted his face and pinched his eyelids shut as tight as he could, I saw Mother expand another inch. Then she lifted her head and I saw her profile. She wiped off her mouth with her forearm and left Craig Kalavala there all exposed, and I saw his profile—top and bottom. I wasn't naïve anymore about what she was feeding on. And now it made perfect sense to me given the relationship I had with Barbie. I figured it would do Barbie good if she could feed on me.

* * *

Since there was never balance in her nights and days, Mother wanted to celebrate stability when it occurred naturally so she planned an autumn equinox party and invited everybody we had brushed into in Iron River. The cast of characters included all of the above, and then some. They can't be excluded and it is impossible to give them the attention they deserve. This is one of the effects of a nomadic life that equated "proximity" with "family" superimposed onto a decade of liberated love; this is one of the effects of living in 24 houses riddled among over a dozen cities. That said, the staples that fed my family story and cinched it together were Gramma, her daughters, and a slew of would-be dads sometimes masquerading as animals and superheroes, or an effeminate "Man-Worth-Mentioning." All the others simply aided the women in their processes of figuring out the chaos, equally impossible.

Gramma came with Grampa Duke, husband number four. He had moved all his kids from a previous marriage up with him: Brandon, Bud, Martin, Shel, and daughter Jennifer. Aunt Hope and her husband, Bruno, came up from the Lower Peninsula and Mother's best friend from Battle Creek, Melody, caught a ride from them. The Dinner Bell must have shut down for the night, because for the first time ever I saw Mary and Don outside of work. Some of Mother's snacks came: Craig Kalavala, Gary Taggit, and bad old Big Tom. The three of them wore the same type of ripped knee bell-bottom blue jeans with square-toed buckle boots and drank beer with cocked elbows. The frayed threads hung from their knees like trembling tendons as if they had just been scrapping in the alley and won. That was their way of showing what they were like on the inside. No emotion, just raw meat. But the three were just different flavors of the same ice cream to Mother. They never took their eyes off of Jensen, the Indian, who also had received an invite from Mother. He didn't have holes in his knees—because he had cut his pant legs right off and came over in a stained muscle shirt and cutoffs. He was being really quiet all night on purpose. But I knew he wanted to make small talk, maybe even play with me. And then again, maybe he was "anti-speeding" is what Aunt Hope called it. Downers is what everyone else said, but Aunt Hope hated being down. The one trait she and I shared was being down for no reason whatsoever. Maybe Jensen had this too.

Mother was trying to seek some purpose in Iron River, and she felt that inviting everyone she had at least a minimal connection to would possibly make her feel "at home." In a world of bartending, dealing pot, and exchanging plastic welfare coins for cigarette money there didn't seem to be a lot of room for purpose beyond satisfying men who didn't give a shit about you. And if they did give a shit about any of the women in the family, the girls would run them out of town anyway. But there was a lot of possibility to dream. And that is what I did with Mother in that living room on that night. Dream.

The house was decorated with candles and dried grass. The few antiques that she had acquired from Jack Hartley, Gramma's third (and dead) husband prior to Grampa Duke, were polished with lemon oil. In each ashtray was a cone of patchouli incense. Silk scarves batiked with suns and moons hung from the mirrors. In the corner of the living room a card table was set up with a fishbowl turned upside down stuffed with dried trilliums that looked like white tongues, next to a pack of old Tarot cards she got in exchange for a couple of joints when the town went dry and Ella Vogel was parched. The house smelled like a rainbow farm and LittleMan was spending the night to keep me occupied so we could watch the harvest and wonder at all the colors of 1976.

Tony Tarnovsky and his brother Hairy Jerry showed up with a couple of the strippers from the Jack-O-Lantern and things really got going. The women were parting the smoke with moves and figures U.P. women could only dream of. The women of my family were among the most beautiful in town, and also had all the moves. That is why people flocked to the party. None of my family was actually from the U.P. We weren't provincial Yoopers. All of us, including me, were born below the bridge, just like the Jack-O-Lantern sisters, and we dreamed ourselves class acts. Mother and family danced freely with the strippers and, because of proximity, they were too now family. That was that.

Molly and Ally were the DJ's and had Mother's albums scattered all over like a tiled dance floor. They were both wearing orange and brown striped halter-tops and tie-dye bellbottoms that masked their feet. The comments were all the same:

"Those girls sure look like dey could jerk a bobber," Toivo mumbled with a plastic cup full of green liquid in his hand.

"B.J. said the one with the little titties ain't even a teen yet, but her ass looks like a Michigan apple. How the hell did she end up with little titties in a family like that anyway?" Craig Kalavala said with his head cocked back and to the left staring at Ally bending over a Led Zepplin album, and Mother's breasts in the distance that were pressed into the side of Indian Jensen as she whispered something into his ear. "Hey, B.J.," he yelled across the room to Gramma, "what do those letters stand for?"

"What do you think?" she yelled back, and continued bumping hips with the strippers.

"I get the shifty one with the big tits and big brown eyes to match," Big Tom said, his thumbs tucked behind his Peterbilt belt buckle.

"I get the shy one," Gary drawled.

Under his breath, Craig Kalavala mumbled, "You wish, you fucking redneck."

"Yous' guys go ahead because I'm gonna pank me some jungle rump," said Hairy Jerry, "Let's go dance with all those apple-knockers, Tony," and they walked off toward the record-cover floor Ally and Molly had created.

LittleMan and I were being cute by sipping drinks and everybody got a kick out of that. I was talking shit too and it went over pretty well with the company as they descended deeper and deeper into the bowels of the rainbow.

"Hey Butch," I yelled over Janis Joplin, "check this out," and I made a face by stretching up my mouth with my thumbs and pulled down the tiny bags under my eyes with my pinkies.

"Hell! That looks like the skinned face of a rabbit!" he said genuinely impressed. Then I tried to show him something else but he started chatting-up Gramma. LittleMan called me into the kitchen where he was working the crowd.

"Look at this stuff! It's like a mad-scientist's lab!" and we gazed at the bottles of Schnapps, Kahlúa, Ouzo, JD, and countless cheap wines—T.J. Swan, Lambrusko, Mad Dog—spread out all over the kitchen. We mixed them into plastic cups. I pulled Barbie out of my back pocket and used her leg to stir. There were some old cookie tins in the corner that we grabbed for trays and placed the plastic cups hastily down, spilling a bit. We walked into the living room and served the guests, but not before we tasted what we had made.

Bruno was getting paranoid and telling stories about something called "Nam" to the macho guys while Melody provided the soundtrack by singing "Summertime" a cappella for the girls. Gramma was tying knots in cherry stems with her tongue.

"Girls, let me teach you something; this is how you make men happy. If you can do this with their pecker, they'll never leave you. I'm not sure if they'll like it, but they won't dare to leave you." Her hair was always done up like cotton candy, and her lips were full and bright red. Beauty-wise, she had all the best characteristics of her daughters.

Catfish are jumping, and the weather is hot

"Can I have a sip?"

"You wouldn't believe the grass in Nam, high enough to hide behind, but better to fire up. The buds were like roses, I am telling you. Not the kind you buy in the flower shop, but the small wild ones you find out by Camp Lake with the round heads and firm petals. The ones that won't even let you pick them they're so potent. Well that was Nam: A bouquet of buds to fan yourself with. And if you fondled them too much they would make you bleed."

Hush baby, baby, no, no, no, no, no, no, no don't you cryyyyy.

"Can I have a sip?"

"Ally, give me that fucking album; don't let anybody stand on that one! That's a classic. Look at the cover. That's The Moody Blues for fuck sake. *On the Threshold of a Dream.* I'm gonna paint that fucker ten times bigger and hang it over my bed."

"Huh? What did you say?" Aunt Ally replied, more interested in studying the pictures on all the albums.

Aunt Hope was talking really fast—like usual—to Grampa Duke's boys. Her preferred drug was usually speed and then she would adjust the velocity with weed and alcohol so she wouldn't get too anxious and panic. She sounded something like:

"Damn, Duke raised some reallygoodlookin' boys. ShitShel, take your eyes offof Melody and lookoverhere. How tall are you Martin? Is your dick reallybig? Bud, I love those curls, your whole body's like pubic hair," then she'd laugh like a mad lamb, "a big cock! Letmelickyou." And she ran her tongue across Bud's cheek and her husband Bruno couldn't really do anything but be confused because it was sort of her brother and Grampa Duke was sort of her father so it wouldn't be good to start anything with sort-of-family.

Don't you cry.

"Can I have a sip?"

Don and Mary were decked out in lime green polyester. Plastic gold and pink beads the size of walnuts dangled lazily from Mary's neck. Don was sucking on them in a corner and I was even surer that he had created her with kitchen scraps and his bare hands. I had never seen him be affectionate with her, but now he treated her like a gourmet meal. She wore butter lip gloss and had an egg white manicure. Her hair smelled of mayonnaise and beer. Outside, in the fluorescent lights of The Dinner Bell with some sips of brightly colored tonics in my stomach, I realized it didn't make any difference whether Mary had a human mother or a vegetal mother, she was loved. In a time of little thinking or evaluating in a little town at an insignificant house on an insignificant alley, the only ideas we had were of love, and in that vagueness slowly we would figure things out.

LittleMan and I met in the corner. "How many sips did you get?" he asked.

"I got about ten! Did you get anybody to try the drinks we made?"

"Yeah, your Uncle Shel with the Harley and braid. He drank something that I put a little dish soap in."

"What did you do that for?"

"Well I needed more color! You used up all of the green melon stuff, so I just put in a little of that green liquid by the sink. It smelled exactly the same. Anyways, look at him, he loves it. He's all over Melody."

"I want to talk to those girls from Detroit. I think they dig me. They keep looking at me and pointing when I sip someone's drink. I think they like the way I bring the glass to my lips. I bet they think I'm hot."

"You're crazy man. We're kids."

"But don't you know? It doesn't matter what you look like. Look at Toivo over there. Go talk to him. He talks like a little baby with his 'Tank yoos' and 'How she go' stuff. Molly and Ally are fighting over what records to play and pulling each other's hair. Butch the Butcher is all stiff trying to dance sexy and smashing Molly's records under his feet. It's all messed up, LittleMan! It doesn't matter how old you are here. So these chicks can dig me, because in this room with a plastic cup in my hand, I am a man. Watch this," I said confidently.

The only thing I managed to say to one of the strippers was "I like tobacco." And she didn't know what the hell I was talking about, but she smiled and ran her long finger across my lips. I spun on my heels and came face-to-face with LittleMan who had a full tray of drinks.

"We're really talking now! What do you say about some more sipping? Let's see who can get ten more sips first," I said to LittleMan.

And with that we spun around the room. Each sip burned like hell at first until the heat was distributed evenly from head to pee-pee to fingertips to toes.

The three macho men in jeans had Mother's tarot cards in the corner and were trying to play poker by designating death as the king and so on. Craig Kalavala got a pair of cups and a pair of Grim Reapers. The candles dimmed from a brief gust of wind as Arnie the neighbor showed up at the front door with a big red nose and a monkey on his back that bit you if you tried to touch it.

"Arnie, how the hell are you?" Butch the Butcher said as he shook his booty and trampled over Mother's Rod Stewart album. Arnie looked about 80 and was really slow with his speech and movements. He moved his head up for ten seconds and then down for ten more before opening his mouth to respond,

"I'mmmmmm goooood." Any delay that he had, the monkey on his back made up for in a hurry. It was a little spider monkey that could fit into the palm of your hand. Arnie had the leash running from his neck to the monkey's so it wasn't apparent who was in control of who. As Arnie made the slow rounds, the monkey began masturbating out of nervousness and tossed his tiny wads of semen into the crowd. It was no different than the sweat flying off a forehead. LittleMan and I held our stomachs as we chuckled and couldn't talk the rest of the night. All we had was laugh left in us and we did it until it hurt. And the music played on.

Yeah, fairies wear boots and you gotta believe me;
Yeah I saw it, I saw it, I tell you no lies.

"BANG!" Grampa Duke yelled—just like that, for no apparent reason—to derail conversations and get people to lose track for a while. He had a big arm around one of the black strippers. Butch the Butcher was next to him shooting the shit with the other stripper at his arm. When he yelled "Bang," the strippers hit the floor and Bruno screamed, but only with his eyes. They swelled up as big as the vinyl 33's Ally and Molly were spinning. It was as if that expression summoned in a new mood, and all of the sipping started to manifest itself in a slow mirror where images were delayed to the brain, and by the time they got there, the light had already changed so there was no point in evaluating the present because it was already passed. A glass falling to the ground was already broken so no need for wasting the energy to move suddenly across the rooms to catch it. It was no different than looking through a telescope at the Orion Nebulae whose reality we see is actually already thousands of years old.

Mother appeared from the kitchen with a tray of brownies filled with pot, "Who's hungry?" With the strippers on the floor and Grampa grinning, everyone was a little tense and ate them right up and asked no questions. LittleMan and I managed to get our paws on some too. We gave some to the strippers to help them get back on their feet, but not before tasting a little, which made staring into the slow mirror even more interesting. LittleMan leaned against the wall and started doing "nuthing" with his hand on his neck, rolling his eyes. We watched the reflections of the strippers as they rose, transformed, and taunted the monkey by lifting up their shirts and showing their nipples. The monkey screeched and swatted at them as if it had no interest in ever nurturing again. It preferred to suck on Arnie's hairy earlobe, which—if sucked hard enough—produced wax drawn out from the canal, which the monkey rubbed on its lips like a mother-balm.

Yeah fairies wear boots and you gotta believe me
I saw it, I saw it with my own two eyes,

At this time of night, most of the light was coming from candles, or tiny lamps situated in corners with blue or red flower patterned bandanas thrown over them. The light was even darker given my sipping. People were talking again, but not just about the monkey, they were talking about me and LittleMan too. I knew they must have thought we were cool again, at least the guys.

"They're tanked!"

"Holy Cow, Kate, look at dat kid! I tink he's fucked up!"

Aunt Molly glanced over where she sat next to a pile of records, "Goddamn! His eyes look like two festered assholes!"

"Hey sugar," said one of the black girls tickling me under the chin. I put her fingers in my mouth and sucked them. She pulled them out fast and acted like she was disgusted, but immediately laughed and slapped her full hip. The monkey mimicked her, slapping his own hip as he sat on Arnie's head now, like a really fucked up hat. Molly was playing the drum sequence from Black Sabbath's "Iron Man." I moved right in to doing my psychedelic rendition of the robot. It was customary that I did a spastic interpretation of the robot to this section as I often did at the parties she and Molly threw when they babysat me. It was an incredibly fast section, but tonight it was syrupped, sweet and slow, like my breath.

People had brownies smeared all over their faces which distorted in the body heat of a naughty monkey and strippers, and two little kids grasping each other's hands and spinning slower than expected. The slow mirror was not only slow now, it was warped so that you could see what people truly looked like before they had time to fix up themselves for the present. Heads were misshapen and stretched wider than the shoulders. People had no necks and no hips in a warped mirror. All my life I longed for people to look like this, like cartoons; but when it really happened all around me, an actual carnival sounded a little better because the people were supposed to look freaky there. But here, with weed in my stomach, trying to spin as fast as possible and managing to go slower than the second hand on a clock, I wanted a little distance; a carnival with cages would have helped the anxiety. The faces were getting a little frightening. Somebody was shouting "monkey" and laughing deep and slow, and they weren't talking about the monkey. It was Big Tom doing his bad math, figuring the strippers looked no different than the monkey.

"Fucking monkey bitches" he started saying, and the slow laugh blanketed the crowd. Gary Taggit chimed in and those men had that strange bond I would often witness in the future that drew me away from my U.P.

Thankfully there were gentleman I learned about, gentleman who didn't just wipe the tip of their dick with a square of toilet paper after they pissed. These gentlemen were in direct opposition to the men that treated women like bad objects who deserved to be punished, or even worse—rotten food. U.P. gentleman treated women as good objects that should be placed on a shelf next to stuffed fish and guns, which I suppose was a little better. Butch the Butcher was a gentleman. And he was big. Grampa Duke was a Lower Peninsula gentleman—and not so old for a Grampa—not even fifty. He was big, 6'4" with a lean, movie star face whose only imperfection was an under-bite, but only when angry. Now he had an under-bite. He yelled "BANG" again, but in this time progression it sounded like something thick poured out of a bottle, "Baaaaaannnnnggggggg" and his arm came around from behind his back like the slow arm of a record player until it settled into the groove of Big Tom's mouth. The momentum was transferred to Big Tom as his torso twisted backwards while his feet stayed planted as long as they could until they gave into the momentum too and spun into the air, launching off a little like a failed rocket. His arms opened up from the centripetal force so that at a point in his spinning, about 90 degrees, he struck a perfect Crucifixion pose. The liquid from his burnt orange drink LittleMan had mixed up cascaded into the air like the flame from his rocket fuel and splashed stigmata on his hands. Big Tom had been transformed into Rocket Jesus. And all of the slowed voices were like deep groans and I incorporated the rhythm into my Black Sabbath robot dance routine, panting, and dodging the body as it fell.

Butch the Butcher was in the corner in love with my adolescent aunts feeling "chivalrous,"—a word I learned earlier in the week after reading about King Arthur—and responded similarly to the way he responded to dead meats. He made a fist, and rather than swinging it around from the side, he raised it above his head and came down on Gary Taggit's head like a hammer on a carnival anvil. All of the slowed motion was the closest thing I had ever seen to a ballet. It was beautiful the way everyone had memorized their moves and executed them with perfect precision. Just like in the *Wild Bunch* when all those cowboy guys and Mexicans were blowing the hell out of each other, and it looked like they were smiling, almost enjoying it as they pranced through the air on a descent down to death. Gary fell to his knees with his back perfectly erect, and then forward onto his face, keeping the perfect posture.

Since she had ran out of brownies, Mother was in the bathroom eating Jensen when she saw the thick sound seep under the door. She patted the sides of her mouth with her wrist and excused herself from Jensen's table. When she got to the living room, she took her left breast into her right hand, cocked it, and surveyed the room. The breezes of bodies had blown out most of the candles. There was the antique lamp in the corner and a yellow streetlight outside that lit up the room like a lighter lights up the palm of a hand in a dark night when the wind is blowing. Here we all were in a cupped hand like failed action figures and Barbies that nobody wanted to buy. Nobody every wanted "Suzie Stripper" or "Indian Jensen;" "Butch the Butcher" or "Toivo the Yooper." So whoever's hand held us must have either really cared, or was just plain bored. Perhaps there was a closeout sale on Seventies sub-culture heroes.

And with that, the subculture's all-time headliner, Jesus—not Rocket Jesus—JESUS, appeared at the door with wire rimmed glasses. "Peace!" he said calmly, "What's happening? Am I late? How is my Goddess?" he said to Mother. He had a big brown beard and wild long hair in ringlets. Behind him from the street the angelic headlight rays of a red 1964 Plymouth Fury cast a golden aura on his skinny frame. I was sure Aunt Molly summoned him with all her "praying." Had I been coherent I would have known it was the Man-Worth-Mentioning mother had met at the Shamrock Bar. Had I been more coherent I would have known that this could possibly be one of the few men that cared about me.

Tonight no one was boring. We had celebrated and liberated. No one cared much that Big Tom and Gary Taggit were laid out on the floor or that LittleMan was puking at age six off the front porch. With brightly colored alcohol and chocolate Marijuana in our stomachs, ages were collapsed. Grampa Duke and I were peers. No one cared that the monkey started throwing shit rather than semen. We were all "throwing shit." The drum solo from "Iron Man" was playing over and over. Full of nervous laugh, I still couldn't manage to speak. I kept dancing and dancing, doing the robot with slow, jerky, movements trying to mimic something of artificial intelligence. If I did talk at that moment, I would have only been simulating some emotion. So I straightened my hands and tweaked my head and hips. I malfunctioned and started spinning on my heels, stuck in a rotating pattern. I spun until the few light bulbs burnt out and everything went black except for the headlights of Jesus' Fury outside.

I fell into his arms.

I woke up in the back of a 1960 Ford Falcon station wagon sleeping on top of twelve cases of beer with Barbie at my side. Mother turned the ignition.

And then we moved.

Orchard Place.
Battle Creek, Michigan

There's a chance peace will come in your life, please buy one.
For sometimes when I am feeling as big as the land
with the velvet hill in the small of my back,
and my hands are playing the sand.
And my feet are swimming in all of the waters,
all of the rivers are givers to the ocean
according to plan, according to man.
from "Peace Will Come"
– *Melanie*

The first house was yellow, and the wood smelled of it. That's all I really remember, if that. In 1971, a house full of women—one widowed and already a grandmother at 37, one with an illegitimate child—on a middle-class street couldn't be trusted. Gramma B.J., Aunt Molly, Aunt Ally, and Aunt Hope welcomed me home from the hospital, a nine pound and some ounces red-haired, blue-eyed boy. The 7:32 p.m. sun had painted me ugly, especially in the eyes of the neighbors. My head was already a sunset on the first day. As Mother stood at the door of the yellow house with my red head at her chest, together we stepped over the threshold into an open field of brilliant descending color and in her arms I inhaled the stories:

Clayton Johnson, Mother's stalker of five years had been here. I could still smell his cheap cologne and nervous sweat. He had sneaked into Mother's bed two years earlier and raped a friend of the family at knife point, mistaking her for Mother—who was sleeping at a friend's house—and threatened her to not say a word because he knew Orchard Place was the house of women on a block where it didn't belong:

Earl Luck had been here. I could still smell the Triumph exhaust in his motorcycle jacket. He had shown up looking for Mother's friend, and Mother offered her sweet 16 year-old self to a 28 year-old drifter instead under a tree in the backyard, just once, after taking portraits of her in hats, posing against the backdrop of the garage door:

Jack Hartley had been there, right behind that garage door, and never, ever left.

How can 24 houses in 10 years be anything other than a jumble of coming and going? Sometimes all there can be is a name, like Clayton Johnson, and then he's gone. But the stories of all these men, and some women too, affix themselves to these five women living under the roof of what would be the most beautiful house ever lived in from the outside. But from the inside, in the guts, it wasn't that different from the belly of a beautiful beast—full of blood and excretions, yet driven by a heart and wonder of the complete mammalian organism. This is where my story, maybe the first significant story ever told by a male in this family, began to shape itself. And since I was only five days out of the belly of a beautiful beast, the house was familiar to me. It had been grazing on wonderful grasses.

Guests were coming and going all day. At five days old, with no reason, everything is a simple emotional blur of color, a steady movement of subtle light on grasses of the field swaying in a Lower Michigan spring breeze. Like a white puff of pollen tinged with red sun-blood, I drifted from grass to grass in this Orchard Place.

Aunt Ally was Wall Barley, found in country lanes huddling up at the foot of walls, but not very often growing out boldly in the fields. When I was in her eight year-old arms her bristly spikes were quite sharp.

Aunt Molly—her older full sister—was Barren Brome, growing in bleak places where few things survive. It's rarely found in the States. In her arms

I felt a certain kinship and somehow I knew my light did her good. In a wind her sway was always a bit rough. She couldn't look me in the eyes, so I just mimicked her gaze and learned about the stains on the floor, the loose threads on the curtain, or the muscles on a man.

Molly and Ally's father, different from Mother's, had shut himself up five years earlier in the garage and turned the ignition switch on the Pontiac. He was dead and all over this house as I gazed with Molly: The old roll-top desk; the oak table with five leaves; the bone-china; the mahogany scars on Mother's shins from his beatings, and all the other antiques he had kept in immaculate condition, just like his body. His memory was the reason we would soon leave this house. Gramma was finished with her shock treatments that were administered after Jack's death. Her field was in order and she had husband number four lined up.

Mother and Aunt Hope shared the same father. His name was Boyd and he was around before Jack. The seed of the man never really mattered in our family, though. It could be said that the men were Meadow Soft Grasses. They had smaller seeds than the majority of grasses. So small were they that, by weighing and then counting a small number, it is calculated that it would take nearly two million of them to weigh a pound.

Aunt Hope's arms felt the most like Mother's, but she was closer in character to Wall Barley. She was both Meadow Barley and Floating Meadow Grass, growing in open fields instead of hiding away at the foot of walls. And loving the river banks, often growing right up out of the water itself, sometimes bending over and floating on its surface. Commonly found in ditches too.

And then there was that extended family, stretching over the hill and past the horizon. These were the blurs. They were all my mothers: Laura Jane, Sweet Scented Vernal Grass with yellow flowers; Chris Kip, Reed Canary Grass smelling like a river; Melody Nelson, Purple Molina on a wet moor. I drifted all evening from female to female wet with thick paint of sunset and the gentle strokes of exquisite grasses until I found Gramma:

Orchard Grass. The tallest of all. This is the grass that hares and rabbits are so fond of, for not only are they nourished by it, it's high enough for them to hide in, especially when dusk descends and zero hour approaches incessantly.

And then we moved.

711 Roosevelt Street.
Stambaugh, Michigan

Everytime I look at you I don't understand
why you let the things you did
get so out of hand.
You'd have managed better
if you'd had it planned.
Now why'd you chose such a backward time
and such a strange land?
from "Superstar"
– *Murray Head*

Mackinaw Bridge. There was a lot of blue and a certain floating sensation on the bucket seats in Mother's lap as I crossed my first bridge. Her legs were soft and supple like bulky pillows stuffed with strong clouds. The sunset was gone from my hair and she parted my new blond bangs with her beautiful chipped fingernails. At 17 with full breasts and hips she glowed off and on as the pillars of the bridge broke the rays of autumn sun shining in our blue eyes. Who needed a father with a cradle like this?

Gramma's new husband, Duke, was at the wheel of the cobalt blue Pontiac station wagon. He had chosen Gramma, even after he had second thoughts and disappeared for two weeks while he moved his ex-wife and five adolescent teens to the U.P. where he would work as a right-of-way agent for the pipeline. But when Gramma finally called and gave him an ultimatum, he kicked out the wife, drove down to Battle Creek with a bag of chips, a liter of pop, and a six-inch statue of a pregnant girl inscribed with "I should have danced all night" across the pedestal for Mother, and threw us all into the station wagon, with the Chief Pontiac hood ornament leading the charge. Although I had a biological grampa somewhere, blood wasn't as thick as Grampa Duke's huge arm with its large hand and splayed fingers reaching into the back seat to massage my stomach. And Gramma, in the passenger seat with a cheap dress and fingers full of diamonds, massaged his upper thigh. From the backseat Mother tapped Gramma's shoulder to ask her for a cigarette. In a circle of single touch we all crossed the bridge and drove into the woods of the Upper Peninsula and headed west.

Mother lit her cigarette and rolled down the window. The smell of lake and soil was all over us and it was good.

My three young aunts, Hope, Molly, and Ally, were in the boot of the station wagon peeking over Mother's shoulder watching me suckle her as she suckled a Merit Ultra-Light. They were fighting over an Etch-A-Sketch, and the awkward cubist pictures they had drawn of my mouth and her breast were erased over and over as the gray screen jostled. There were voices from every direction that I couldn't distinguish from the broken muffler and cheap Delco radio.

Mother's shirt was drenched with milk and sounds. With her nipple in my mouth I sucked and sucked, my belly swelling under Grampa Duke's hand. Through that nipple came a vision of Mother in a hundred hats. A man at a camera. And her back against the inside of the garage door, a hand like a full field of grass over her body and her laying into it. I sucked out the smell of motorcycle on a patched jacket. I sucked out the fear of Clayton Johnson stalking her, step-grampa molesting her, and step-father Jack beating the shit out of her. I drew in the twists of her dishwater-blond braids tucked up under her bandanna and was dizzy. I drew in the cloud pillows from all over her body and was fat with sky. I sucked and I sucked so hard that I couldn't suckle again because Mother had to wear some special patches over her teats after that. Though full of clouds, I never felt as clear as I did that day driving in a new land toward a new house in the sway of a station wagon, and neither did Mother.

* * *

At four months, 711 Roosevelt was a blue-gray two story monolithic smudge to me. Nestled between an Elm and an apple tree, it might as well have been a pile of fresh loam waiting to be seeded.

The world was turning and pictures were flying off the walls. Mother and her sisters wanted freedom in the guise of boys. Gramma wanted to get away from the smell of carbon monoxide in the Orchard Place garage and the stench of electricity at Battle Creek General where she memorized Shakespeare while doctors shocked the past out of her system.

A cool north wind moved in from Canada that month as I continued to drift from one grass to another until everything went white. The last thing I remember about that house is reaching up to the window sill and standing on my own two feet looking at the apple tree covered with a skin of snow. Wondering what happened, I let go of the window, turned, and walked across the room for the first time, trampling the green shag carpeting with every step. I walked right out the door toward the tree and found a low branch weighted with snow. I stuck it in my mouth and started sucking and sucking until blossoms came.

I wiggled my toes. I think.

And then we moved.

Gennesee Street.
Iron River, Michigan

A woman left lonely will soon grow tired of waiting,
she'll do crazy things, yeah, on lonely occasions.
A simple conversation for the new men now and again
makes a touchy situation when a good face come into your head.
And when she gets lonely, she's thinking 'bout her man,
she knows he's taking her for granted, yeah yeah,
Honey, she doesn't understand, no no no no!

from "A Woman Left Lonely"
– *Janis Joplin*

Driving down Stambaugh Hill to Iron River was no different than the quick trip down the canal and out the womb and into the arms of someone you would grow accustomed to.

The staircase on Gennesee Street was the first I learned of geometry. Driving through the alley we stopped, backed up a bit, and stopped abruptly again. My forehead bumped the passenger window. I snapped awake and had my first vision that I understood—a fantastically constructed network of treated pine stairs that scaled the back of the house, winding up three endless levels to a tiny door near the peak of the roof. And I had a sudden urge to spend the rest of my life climbing toward that door.

"This is it," somebody said, and I understood again. "It" was everything to me—wonderfully vague like the brown shapes I finger-painted after mixing all of the colors together:

"Look at it," Mother would say, "It is beautiful."

"It is god-awful ugly," Molly said.

"I think it is weird," Ally said.

"Shut your mouth or I'll break your neck," Gramma would say, although I didn't understand that yet.

"It" was all these things—my Charlie McCarthy puppet, snow, a Johnny Jumper, a bright light, a braid of pot smoke, a rotting apple in the backyard of Roosevelt, my pee-pee—and now I was looking at it, wanting to surmount it. To Mother, "This is it" was quite clear. "It" meant a forced independence. A bud picked from a tree and discarded in the grass.

With one of Jack's antique lamps under one arm and me under the other, we climbed the stairs. Mother kicked the door open and the smell of ammonia and stale cigarettes painted us. I cried because we hadn't climbed enough. She cried because at 18 she'd gone too far. In a distance, the station wagon beeped and fled and Chief Pontiac was gone.

* * *

That month we never left the house. Mother gathered her tears in a big glass pitcher etched with flowers that didn't exist. She mixed the brackish liquid with baby formula and I drank it for a month, licking my salty lips until they were raw like pure emotion. She ached on the plaid couch and rubbed her thighs together—sucked down cigarettes with a single puff and sweat adolescence until the couch was wet with it. I climbed up the couch and straddled the elbow rest so I could massage her temples with my tulip fingers, which existed. I tried to push thoughts of multi-colored flowerbeds and cold milk into her swollen head.

After two weeks, enough spring dust had gathered on the windowsill to fill two saucers. We made a table out of empty milk crates and sat down to a meal. Embroidered light shined through the yellow nylon curtains and lit Mother's softly parted lips as she uttered my name.

"Chad," she looked into my eyes and fed me strawberry cake and Neapolitan ice cream with her gaze, "Happy Birthday." And she meant it. I knew she meant it because she licked the tip of her pinky, stuck it in the saucer, and rubbed my chapped lips with the dust Iron River had created. I tasted Red Breasted Robins and freshly cut grass; bee pollen and Friday night fish fries. There was a whole different world outside our three-story windows that we started to let in, particle by particle. She reached into the tight shallow pockets of her bell bottoms and pulled out a red plastic lighter with white letters that spelled *Speed's*. She lit it and brought the flame near my lips. "Blow it out," she commanded, and I did.

* * *

The last two weeks I walked around the cheap blue utility carpet from window pane to window pane looking down at the street and pissing my diapers happily. Peering out the window, everything was still blurred in baby ecstasy. The F-stops on my eyes were opened too wide and everything near and far blended into one intoxicating depth as excessive light poured in. I was star flesh riding in a red licorice trolley car with purple puppies and Howdy-Doody puppets that took to nibbling my feet with their wooden jaws. The oak tree was littered with apples and turnips that kept launching off toward flying caterpillars and grounded snowbirds, which I could almost grasp if I got a little closer. And in the distance, a Green Lantern lit the whole scene. It was all so giggly and I pissed myself a little more as I found happiness at the top of the stairs with a single, legitimate mother who came and swiftly swept me up in her arms before I fell out the screenless window. She ripped off my Pampers and then picked me up under the arms lifting me up over her head and held me like that in the frame of the window, airing us both out from a month of stewing in our emotional nectars. I tried to swim a bit higher and kicked out my knees. How funny and fortunate it was that our house had the only exterior stairs that led to the peak.

Our smells were all over. Janis Joplin was playing on the radio. We lit the mildewed couch on fire with my birthday lighter and fled and twirled to the bathroom to wash away the stench that had suppressed us for a month. Mother drew a bath and squirted some turquoise dish-soap under the tap to make some bubbles. She undressed without ever having to put me down and we climbed into the lukewarm water, the two of us thoroughly stuck together. She patted my lips with hot water until the salt-water scabs were soft enough to remove. I knew that in her arms I would never break.

I guess that month Mother just couldn't take "it." But with a couch on fire and us safe in our medicinal bath, she didn't give a shit, at least for the moment. And what prompted this feeling was the sense that she could leave this situation. Somehow different scenery and a new couch would make things better, and she never, ever forgot this wonder.

"We're leaving, Chad." And our happy cow eyes glossed over with the dazzling burn of smoldering fabric drifting in from the living room.

And then we moved.

Third Street.
Stambaugh, Michigan

I am on a lonely road and I am traveling
traveling, traveling, traveling
looking for something, what can it be?
Oh I hate you some, I hate you some
I love you some.
Oh, I love you when I forget about me.
from "All I Want"
– *Joni Mitchell*

Mother and I headed back up Stambaugh Hill after her independence initiation in the geometry house. Third Street was completely tunneled out of Elm branches and we lived at an opening, our apartment half in and half out depending on the direction of wind and which of the four rooms we felt like settling in. My room was almost always in the shade because of the thick trunk that ran past the window. On some evenings night bears crawled up and scratched at the window with their claws and I let them in to part my hair.

Mother was not only a mother now, she was a sexual being again. She was loving off and on like a lighthouse spotlight briefly shining on an island of screaming gulls. She'd thought she'd lost the magic of a full hip sway and pouting lips, her heavy blue eyes full of love letters. She soothed her stretch marks with my baby oil. She'd rub us both down every evening, preparing me for bed and herself for lovemaking. Since I couldn't see the sun, I counted the days by the comings and goings of men. Lying in my oil slicked sheets, I was lulled to sleep by the chiming of the door bell and the beats of boots clomping up the stairs to the living room where a man would be greeted by a scratchy Joni Mitchell album and a high-pitched pucker from Mother's sea-ship lips that often floated down my arms to the tips of my ecstatic, waving fingers. And that is what I imagined as I lay there, knowing it was night because another man had come. I held my arms up in the dark wondering what my hands were holding, then floated off to sleep.

"I want you," is what woke me up most of the time. I understood that. It drifted in from the next room. I thought she was calling for me, but tonight it was Big Tom. I saw him once in the daytime as I was looking out the window when I was supposed to be napping. Through the branches I saw a beam of sun striking his big red truck and his silver belt buckle. The light from the buckle struck Mother's cheek and illuminated her dimple that was nestled in a drop of shade. I was happy she was smiling. I was happy I was smiling. That simple stretching of the lips seemed to soothe my crooked teeth that just couldn't manage to come out right. She was saying "I want you" then too, but without words and I saw a brief semblance of what might be called love. Then a bird flew into the tree and I thought about that, and a red tricycle. I fell asleep with my chin resting on the windowsill.

I don't know if Big Tom was a good man, or if any men were good. And I didn't know what she wanted him for. Did she want to feed him or give him a bath? What usually followed "I want you" was confusing sounds of what I came to know as some sort of ecstasy, which at one-and-a-half years old could only equate with jumping up and down in my Johnny Jumper until the elastic was about to snap and I was out of breath.

With Big Tom the sounds came again, but much heavier, like the wind that had pushed open the vertical window a little bit and frazzled my hair. In this ecstasy it sounded like she was hurting. Her breath was so heavy I confused it with the wind. It whirled in under the door and warmed me a little but wasn't enough to pacify my concern that she was really hurting and needed me. She whimpered like the wounded puppy I watched get struck by a car out the same window that was opening wider now, like a huge mouth. Things got really loud and I began to think that all the men had been secretively beating her and she kept taking it, while I just lay there wondering. I started to get really hot and itchy. My ears swelled so big that I could hear Gramma and all my aunts being beaten from across town. I was waiting for the night bear to come and itch me a little, part the hair from my eyes. I thought that if she would just come and cuddle me that the bear would part her hair too.

One itch for each sound manifested somewhere on my baby-oiled body until I couldn't take it anymore and let out the biggest fucking bear roar I could possibly muster up. And I understood what a fucking roar was. So here we all were in the house with four rooms, situated in a schizophrenic shade, in a city with four-thousand women screaming, and roofs lifting off at the moon like rockets. Everything was clear in the moonlight and I twisted out of bed, full of itch and oil, and slid into the living room to make some sense of ecstasy.

And there she stood, naked, radiating moonlight. It was the way her shoulders shook and what they were shaking for.

"Go back to bed honey, everything is all right," she said without a trace of sorrow.

"What the hell does he want?" Big Tom boomed.

"Fuck you!"

"Sorry!" he exclaimed.

But I was still roaring, and hot, looking at Big Tom without his belt buckle. I itched my sea-dream arms until they bled salt water and oil slicks.

"Oh my God!" Mother panicked as she stared at my arms.

"What the fuck's a matter with him? Are you all right kid?"

"Fuck You!" I said, falling in love with language. She rushed over to me and examined my arms.

"Some kind of bites?" Big Tom said.

"I don't fucking know. Put your clothes on," she told him. A gust blew in from my room. "Oh honey, you're so hot."

"But it's freezing in his room—is the window open?"

She picked me up and we entered my room where the window's big mouth was panting wide open and the wind rustled in the trees where birds pretended to sleep, silently watching. Big Tom trailed behind, stumbling as he tried to put his pants back on, his buckle chinking against his zipper.

"Bugs!" Big Tom said, "That tree's full of them I bet! He got eaten alive!"

I still roared, and would continue to roar until Big Tom fastened that magic buckle and descended the staircase, taking back the footsteps that had lulled me to sleep hours earlier.

"Oh shit," Mother said to herself as she bobbed up and down with me hot in her arms. "Don't worry honey, we'll call Gramma . . . I said put your fucking clothes on and get out of here!"

She held me in one arm and picked up the phone with the other. Big Tom left. The plastic phone dial wouldn't turn fast enough. I quieted down a bit when I heard the red truck fire up. I got lost in the sound of the engine idle while Gramma finally answered, rescued from her own screaming.

"Chad's all hot and full of bumps! I don't know what happened—I think the window blew open and there were some bugs in the tree that ate him up or something. I don't know. I don't know what to do. Can you come?"

I don't know what Gramma was saying on the other end. The roofs had come back from the moon and settled in their proper places and my hearing was normal again as I rested limp in Mother's arms. She took me into the bathroom. Those spots were all over me now. She put me in the tub and hosed me down with cold water to break my temperature. I was in love again, a good love, like when lemons and matches are in your stomach. I just sat there a while, not talking because it felt right. The itch subsided under the stream of cool liquid and I imagined a water slide that led out my window and down into the street. I slid down it. I imagined running back up the stairs, and sliding down again. I imagined it faster and faster until I was just a circular blur of entering and exiting.

"Chad!" I opened my eyes to the women. "Look at him! I told you! What the hell is it?" I didn't pay much attention to anything.

"Well it sure the hell isn't bug bites," Gramma said, "It's Chicken Pox."

* * *

My first disease wasn't so bad, really. I was slightly dazed and ate a lot of soup. And the men stopped coming around for what seemed a couple of weeks, but it was hard to tell since their presence had been the factor that determined time. We stayed a while, I guess. My body scabbed up and I kept opening the wounds to draw out the salt water. I wanted some lasting memory of the night Mother fell in love with me again. I finally got the pockmark scar that I wanted above my left eye and then let myself heal. The whole scenario of the house on Third Street was all a bit complicated for Mother. She had found brief ecstasy, but failed to find romantic love, so she turned once again to loving me and anointing us with oil each night. Now she slept with me and played the Doobie Brothers, which was my favorite. Some song called "Black Water." Well I built me a raft and it's ready to float . . . . She dreamed of the bugs crawling in-between the cracks in the window frame. With a big black platform shoe she beat them until they blended in with the carpet. After she killed five, ten more appeared, and finally she made a decision to leave Upper Michigan. But she had already been bitten and didn't even know it. And we slept a long time while the arm of the record player kept lifting and settling the needle into a groove, again and again.

And then we moved.

A Basement Under a Doctor's Office. Battle Creek, Michigan

Why, why some people break up
then turn around and make up,
I just can't see.
You'd never do that to me (would you, baby),
staying around you is all I see
(here's what I want us to do).
from "Let's Stay Together"
– Al Green

A little looser with some real men under her six-inch-wide belt that cinched up her hips, Mother tried to escape the U.P. and hopped in a Greyhound bus and ran with it all the way back to Battle Creek, with me on her back, holding on to her belt with one hand and slapping her flanks with the other the whole way to give her a little oomph.

Mother met Melody there, and that's that. Melody's eight-ball black hair poured its black streams all over my baby-oiled body. She sang Bessie Smith to me and I knew I had found an additional mother. From this point on, with Melody in my ear, the mothers in my life added up until I couldn't distinguish between a female and mother.

I descended the stairs with a mother in each hand. We ducked through some hanging beads; the room, though dark, lit up with a purple carnival light that never left. There were pictures on the wall that glowed as if sunsets and cartoons were shining through them. I walked to one and lifted up my arms to touch it. It was hairy like caterpillars. I pulled up a wicker chair to stand on and placed my cheek to that black light velvet fur. Mother and Melody put on a record. Melody pulled out a plastic baggy full of weed and some pink strawberry-flavored papers. I crawled down and walked to a blue glass table, picked up the papers and smelled deep. They smelled good, and tasted even better when I licked them. So I stuffed a bunch in my mouth and ate the stiff cotton-candy in our new sub-carnival world.

"Give him a hit!" one of them said, and I took the paper that was on fire and full of weed and sucked it like I had sucked the snow off an apple tree branch back on Roosevelt Street. I had no concept of lungs or getting a good "buzz" is the word I heard, so I just let the smoke seep out of my mouth as if it was the embodiment of this basement amusement park dream, complete with lava lamps and the scent of patchouli. A ray of sun refracted through the glass block windows near the ceiling. And doctors paced to and fro above our heads, administering tests and anesthesia to the needy while my mothers coughed and giggled, and we all hugged each other and spun on a carousel of dogs and bears with Spider-Man, somewhere in the distance, casting a phenomenal web.

* * *

We managed to get out into the world a little in Battle Creek. I began to recognize more and more. We hitched rides all over town in big cars full of gas and always ended up at Speed's, a burger joint with a good jukebox that I stuffed full of dimes. There were a lot of mothers there too—Strawberry, Chrissy Kip, and a bunch more. I was always the only little kid around and I never paid much attention to that position. Sometimes I would crawl up on the red padded booth and look over the back at some kid sucking down a malt with a man and a woman on either side. The scene never measured up to the group of late teens I had all around me, full of smells, feeding me French fries dipped in chocolate malt. They talked about everything in front of me and my vocabulary showed it. I knew about nice asses and something called a "pill" and a "period" and all about foxes, pricks, and assholes. A typical conversation would go—

"Did you get a look at that gas station guy with the tight jeans and nice ass?"

"Holy shit he was a fox."

"No way. You really think so?"

"Oh hell yes, right on! I'd love to get me some of those black curls and wrap them around my finger."

"Gross! He was all greasy and shit."

"A working class man is something to be!"

"He drives a motorcycle you know!"

"No shit!"

"Yeah! That's why he's always wearing that white bandana."

"You mean greasy brown bandana."

"Get outta here, he's hot. You're just jealous because frat boy can't fuck and won't go down on you. You need a good grease monkey down there."

"Fuck you!"

"Fuck you!" I interjected, and they all laughed and stamped their feet and shook their heads frantically, shaking their cigarettes in the air and exhaling a thick braided smoke into the deep fried air of Speed's. I knew who they were talking about that time. They were talking about Fast Eddy. He looked just like the guy on the strawberry papers I used to eat—The Zig-Zag man. A head drawn with a thick black line and no shading. The Zig-Zag man was the late-20th century Bohemian wanderer complete with pirate earring, bandana, and full beard. The black lines hovered in a white space and I often thought that maybe it was the white that was painted in and the thick black lines were just empty space. I thought he was something I could draw in the dust or sketch out on a dirty window, but it was possible that his jaw line and ear lobe were just the presence of absence on the canvas of Battle Creek, 1973. Regardless, him seeming like the Zig-Zag man was enough magic for me. He was the first young guy I ever really paid any attention to.

There were about five of us in Chrissy Kipp's Ford Fairlane and we pulled up to the pump and he came out twirling a white hanky. I was on a mother's lap in the back near the passenger window. He bent down to remove the gas cap and noticed me.

"Hey little guy," he said tickling me under the chin, "What's your name." I don't think anybody had ever asked me that before.

"Chadillac," I said.

"Right on," he said as his eyes shifted to the car full of chicks. "Right. On," he repeated, slowly placing special emphasis on the consonants. With his full beard rubbing against the half-rolled-down window, he looked right into Mother, who was on the other side of the car. "And what's your name," he asked to her in a low tire tone.

"Mom," I interjected.

"Chad, shut up," she interrupted from the other side of the car. She looked into Fast Eddy's eyes, "It's Kate."

"This little guy's yours? What's he doing over here?" Eddy asked.

"Mom," I interjected again, pointing to Chrissy Kip; "Mom," I said, pointing to Strawberry; "Mom," I said, pointing to Melody; "Mom," I said, pointing to Kim something. I was staking out my territory in my wonderful world of mothers, and that's what they were to me. I said "Mom" out loud but that was only an uttering of a primitive monosyllabic chant that embodied the written picture of M-o-t-h-e-r.

"So," he cleverly asked Mother via Chadillac, "Where's your Daddy?" I don't think anybody ever asked me that before.

"He's a sugar daddy working a real job downtown which is more than I can say for your sorry ass," Chrissy Kip retorted.

"Get out of here, Chrissy," Mother interrupted, "She's full of shit. Don't listen to her. It's just me and Chad and that's that."

And I guess that's what it was. Something factual that needed no explanation. It was a good answer. Something like when I asked Gramma what the speed of light was and she walked over to the switch on the wall and flicked it off so we could feel the darkness a little, then switched it back on and said, "That fast." I didn't ask any more questions. And either did Eddy for that matter.

And shortly after that and a couple of more gossip sessions at Speed's with my mothers, she met Eddy—the guy who asked questions nobody else would—again and she said "I do." And we did.

* * *

The marriage went something like this. She kissed him so much until he had little hickey marks that spelled "I do too." Their bodies were hot love stories. A grape skin bruise on the shoulder and teeth marks under the arm. I saw that some love was painful. Confusing too, with all of those shrieks and slap movements on the stained mattress they pulled out of a dumpster and threw on the basement floor. At 3 a.m. I woke up to "I want you" again, and she was feeding him her breast and I knew that Eddy must have loved her as much as me. I watched from my beanbag bed in the corner by candlelight and incense embers. Their bodies together, all naked, white, and twisted, were like a fist of sun rays that had collected on the cement floor after shining for months through the glass block, looking for somewhere to manifest themselves and make some ultimate good. Sound came again. It wasn't only Al Green singing "Let's Stay Together," it was a sound like a spider moaning when the silk of its web is destroyed and then at the end of the day it is all repaired by rubbing its skinny legs all over it, weeping with joy. At two this is a good sound, and it's loud. I stared into the light and sound they created until sleep came into my eyes, yet they never closed.

* * *

He tied her hair back in the morning and she wore dresses like she never wore before—flower dresses that blended right into her copper skin. She started to dream in threes. There could be simply a house, a car, and a table set with matching plates. At least that is what she thought she wanted.

Eddy showed me how to piss properly by standing me up on a stack of old *Playboys* in front of "the John" he called it, and how to wipe the mushroom tip of the shaft of my pee-pee with a piece of toilet paper so it wouldn't drip into my Snoopy underwear. He said that was how gentlemen behaved. And he had other strange warnings, "Chadillac, you gotta watch that yellow stream and make sure it doesn't splash the sides of the John; it'll sap your power." I didn't really understand, and then he started telling me about the Green Lantern, this "cat" who had no fear. But I didn't get it. He wasn't really a cat, he was a fearless superhero, and the only thing that could hurt him was the color yellow. And it was all really "trippy" he said. Standing there with our pee-pees hanging out, he reached into his cut-offs pocket with his free hand and pulled out, well, nothing. But he held that nothing like it was really important—as if it was unlike nothing else, that nothing was. He put his thumb and forefinger in front of my face, as if he were holding "nothing" the diameter of my finger. "You see this, Chadillac?" I didn't see shit, but yet at two, the empty space between fingers, coupled with sincere attention from a grown-up seemed like a page from the best pop-up book you could ever imagine. "This is an invisible Green Lantern ring. I am gonna put it on your finger. Is that cool?" Without answering, and still holding my pee-pee in one hand, I raised my other hand toward nothing and the ring slid down the tiny pole of my finger and spiraled down slowly over my knuckle.

I could feel it. And I closed my eyes and saw a dark-haired girl and a bridge and a sapphire light on the horizon swallowing stars. I was so comfortable in that space that I pissed again all over the toilet bowl and Eddy didn't even care so much.

"Just beware of the yellow, my man. It'll get you," Eddy said. We giggled together and all this talk of "johns" and "cats" didn't mean much to me, but the sound alone of Eddy giggling was really something.

Mother was with Melody in the other room sucking hash oil smoke through a straw, listening to the piss streams and Eddy's words of wisdom. She was thinking of another word that I never used, "father." That was the vocabulary that I never learned from all those mothers. But after we came out of the bathroom and the four of us disrobed and went streaking around the basement, in our garden nudeness I noticed that I had more in common with Eddy, and at some point I might realize that all men were my fathers.

Mother began to think of family again and the itch from the bite she got in the U.P. was bothering her. Stoned in a basement under the aura of ether hovering above in the doctor's office, she imagined things could be even better if she could get a bit higher. So she imagined due north again, and her mother nearby. She thought all of this in one continuous inhale until she let out the hash smoke all over us and we collectively dreamed of driving across a bridge on a motorcycle with the smell of lake and soil all over us. Eddy would be at the handlebars; Mother, resting her back on the bitch-bar; and me nestled somewhere in between, wondering about "nothing."

And then we moved.

6

Late Fall 1973

Lincoln Street Across from the Cemetery. Stambaugh, Michigan

On you, I see the glory,
from you, I get opinions.
From you, I get the story.
from "See Me, Feel Me"
– *The Who*

We were driving on reserve with water in the fuel, the plugs missing, and pipes sputtering all the way until the motorcycle died at the cemetery on Lincoln and we moved into the first house we saw when our windy eyes cleared.

Lincoln Street house was between two cemeteries, one for people in the front, one for geology in the back. The monuments in the back were much bigger. In the distance beyond the arc of the meadow, a gutted ore-colored monolith with shot-out windows jutted up 150 feet. It had something to do with a "mine." I didn't know too much about that, but it had to do with digging and people going underground. Mother said the people in the cemetery went underground too, but they could never dig their way out.

Off the front and back of Lincoln Street house were two identical screened porches. When the noon sun was shining directly over the house and my stomach was full of spinach and cream carrots Gramma had brought over,

I would take my juice bottle and head for one of the plastic hobby horses that were located on either porch with the intent of rocking myself to a lucid sleep. We had bought a pair of them on the second day back in the U.P. at the Salvation Army thrift store on the corner, along with a record player and a set of plates—some with little fish, some with little flowers—whose round shapes and cherry colors resembled each other enough that they almost matched. The horses were both yellow and had dents around their muzzles where someone had beaten them, but I could never understand why because their rock was absolutely heavenly. The paint had completely flaked off so I colored them the best I could with some fat crayons. I had only seen a horse in cartoons so I colored one completely purple—eyes and all—and the other a kind of pink.

With the sun directly overhead and no shadows, a full stomach and a full bottle, I often confused the identical porches and simply wandered out of one of the doors and mounted a horse. I was in the front staring at the people cemetery, but thought it was the back. A procession of people in soot black was wandering through the freshly cut grass. Miners returning to tunneling, I thought. Others in smaller groups—sometimes alone—were surveying the terrain and when they found a spot they liked, put a flower or tiny flag to mark the spot so they could come back and, I guess, dig for something. Rocking there on my purple horse, I imagined all the dark clothes were once white, but because of the digging they had become literally soiled. With the nipple of a bottle to my lips and a hand on the horse's plastic mane, I flung my weight around and laughed at all the playing and digging the soil-people were doing and wished I was part of their happy tunneling lives.

In my juice bottle confusion, I decided to switch porches and stumbled across the house through a maze of cherry blossom wallpaper to mount the kind-of-pink horse I had colored. The mine that wasn't a mine appeared much livelier than the people cemetery that wasn't a people cemetery out back. There, no one would ever exit the monolith except for squirrels, rabbits, and pigeons, at least that's what I figured since all these animals made their way to the backyard and had to come from somewhere. Indeed this was the place where people couldn't dig their way out. Under that gently arched meadow where a thousand grasses fondled a fleeting warm current to ward off a slow death were people sucking soil in pure darkness and I think they wanted to leave. And if they could, they would take to beating the rabbits, squirrels, and pigeons whose roaming they envied.

My bottle was finished and I started to whine a little. The sun had tipped and shadows were stretching out all over town. I blamed the horse and slapped its ass, creating yet another dent. I dismounted and headed for the center of the house to get my bearings and sat down in the middle of the rag rug between the kitchen and living room and went to sleep for a couple of months.

* * *

The torn seams of the cherry blossom wallpaper were dazzling when I opened my eyes. Lifting off into evening iridescent lit living room with the hues of the television helping out and Woodstock on the record player, all scratchy and worn, the blossoms flew at me in little pieces that I puzzled back together. And something else was really loud.

It occurred to me as I looked through the doorway and saw Mother and Eddy naked, running back and forth in the kitchen, that they had discovered one another's full flesh too quickly. I stood up and rubbed my eyes but the blur of bodies flashing across the doorway wouldn't clear up so I filmed the whole scene in soft focus.

We forsake you
gonna rape you
let's forget you, better still.

It starts like this with Eddy, close-up on his lips:

"You were the one who dragged me all the fucking way up here," and then he walks out of the frame. Then a still shot on the kitchen sink tap dripping. In the background The Who strums a couple of chords that signals the introduction to "See Me, Feel Me." They sound like the sun downing after it's been tapped of its fire and only a hollow memory echoes.

Enter Mother. She lost her flower dress and had put on a little weight in the past months. Only her belly and breasts are in the frame—and the tips of her lips that move frantically, as if they are the little goldfishes that we brought home from the carnival in a plastic baggy and transplanted into a Mason jar full of tap water from the leaky faucet. Eddy won them by squirting water into a clown's mouth. We hadn't changed their water and they sat in the window for days trying to tell us something until they gave up and tried swimming on their sides to pass time. Soon, Mother too would be on her side, floating on the pale blue kitchen linoleum, passing time because no one would listen to her when she asked for some help.

"Fuck you and your tight jeans. You just followed me for a piece. You don't give a shit about me, this house, Chad—all you do is smoke weed and fuck, and you can't even do that good anymore." Now her hands periodically entered the frame as she swung them frantically for emphasis while the drums of "See Me, Feel Me" kicked in from the living room over my shoulder and I remembered seeing Roger Daltry in his fringed white leather shirt, swinging his microphone in a full circle when Mother brought me to the movies for my first time.

Listening to you,
I get the music.
Gazing at you,
I get the heat.

My beady eyes lit up and I tilted my head in some sort of toddler awe.

"I can't take it! I can't take it! I can't take it!" she kept saying. She drifted out of the frame. What was "it" I wondered, as I stared at the dripping faucet. Then the two crescendoed into each other with their chests at the center of the frame and Eddy grabbed her wrists and she sang, "Let go of me you prick! Stop it. Fucking needle dick!" And her voice was an aria now and my toes were licked by indolent waves as they danced and the record played. Release. Out of the frame. Body crescendo.

Release. An empty frame. And in my soft focus I again locked my sight on the flayed wallpaper seam launching blossoms into the air as if it were breaking it. There was a cymbal smash, then another shower of petals everywhere, some little fishes on the floor too, fluttering their tiny gills, gasping to recite the lyrics of the record when I realized I was witnessing the splinters of plates exploding on impact as they were hurled out of the frame of the kitchen at the hallway walls. The almost-matching plates that we bought along with the horses and the record player were now dying breeds of blossoms wilting and little red fish flapping on the scratched hardwood floor. Everywhere fish were flying above the horizon in a flower-meadow-fragile air that broke with each note sung by Mother and Roger Daltry.

Following you,
I climb the mountains.
I get excitement at your feet.

"Prick! Prick!" she bellowed and her tears fell with the tap. She got softer in the distance as she fled even further from the perimeter of the frame. She must have been near the window now where my paper cutouts I had made with Aunt Molly would be in the panes putting on smiles. "Prick," she hummed, and her tune carried.

Enter Eddy from the other side of the kitchen into the center of the frame as the last plate shatters at the wallpaper seam. His dick is hanging out and rising with the record momentum. Staring at his nudeness now I knew indeed they had discovered each other too fast and didn't take the time to start with fingertips and massage each other's cuticles and know the blossoms in those seams too, at the very edge of the body where all skin begins.

Right behind you,
I see the millions.

With his hips facing me, and his torso twisted toward my mother, he reached out his hand and simply said, "Come here," without any singing. And for a moment I was reminded of all the holes under us—how we would probably never be complete, and I was O.K. with it, really. The truth was almost all the mines were abandoned, and there wasn't any difference between back and front anymore. Mother once again entered the frame. Crescendo. And Eddy and Mother settled to the floor, right above a hole and laid there on their sides together as the music wound down and they fell into each other.

See me.
Feel me.
Touch me.
Heal me.

"I fucking love you," he said, panting over the top of her, "I fucking love you."

"Me too."

On you,
I see the glory.
From you,
I get opinions.

Their rock was absolutely heavenly. They rocked until the air stirred so that it rocked the horses on either porch. I stood up from the rag rug where I had lain for two months and walked delicately over the blossoms and fishes, making my way toward the basement steps, off to find a mineshaft and dig a little to comfortably burrow myself in.

From you,
I get the story.

And then we moved.

Lincoln Street on Top of the Hill. Stambaugh, Michigan

Satellite's gone up to the sky,
things like that drive
me out of my mind.
from "Satellite of Love"
– *Lou Reed*

On top of the hill is where I first folded into the crease of freedom and was stuck there like the text of a love letter that's stuffed in a back pocket of a soldier walking in a foreign land. Mother and Eddy had rolled out the door in the Lincoln cemetery house and stopped at the crest of the hill before they rolled down and hurt themselves.

There was Lisa Lantini across the street in pigtails, sucking on a Pixy Stix full of purple sugar. Her tongue looked like a big bruise when she stuck it out at me from across the street. She knew our house was old and my shoes were plastic. Her house was big and blue with aluminum siding and a garage. Ours was big too, but had old gray asbestos siding with fake wood grain. We didn't mow our lawn much either so the grass was high and shabby. After a good rain ducks in love would often settle there under the big elm tree, mistaking the landscape for a secluded marsh. Mother and Eddy had taken to streaking so much that the shades were always drawn and it appeared that maybe no one really lived in that Lincoln Street house at the crest of a hill where the only direction to go was down.

I walked across the street and grabbed Lisa's pigtails with each hand until her tongue popped out of her mouth, and I looked right at it and said, "I want you." She ran home crying and at three years old I knew she wanted me too, even though she didn't know it.

I figured she was going inside to a nice lunch of Wonder Bread with perfectly square orange cheese and a perfectly circular slice of bologna. The sandwich was surely cut into two perfect triangles. Maybe her father patted her head while she was eating her geometry and said, "Don't cry; Daddy's right here."

I went home, opened up a can of tuna, and peeled an onion with my teeth. I grabbed the broken saltines out of the pantry and the mayo from the fridge, made my way into the living room and sat down on the floor with a paper plate since most of the glass ones had been broken. I grabbed a tattered Green Lantern comic book I had found tucked in with a bunch of Eddy's *Playboys*. Once when he was playing "father" he read a little to me. With those memories and those pictures in the strips, I could make out the story pretty well. With my tiny fist stuck to a picture of the lantern itself, I powered up my imaginary Oan power ring and was an intergalactic policeman for the next 24 hours. And there was the dark-haired girl. Eddy told me her name was Carol Ferris and if her last name was any closer to mine we would be married. Her waist was the opposite of Mother's. It was cinched up like the tie in a balloon. Her breasts were about the same size though. Alone in the living room, with brightly colored paper I had no anxiety and could breathe freely without an artificial heaviness in my chest. There was a bump sound and I looked up at the ceiling. Mother and Eddy were napping upstairs in the dark with the music playing loud to drown out their sleep-talking. They were listening to "Satellite of Love." And in my stellar state, I liked that song:

Satellite's gone way up to Mars,
soon it will be filled with parking cars.
I watched it for a little while.
I love to watch things on TV.

I loved to watch things on TV too so I clicked it on, but with no volume so I could listen to the rest of the song. *Sesame Street* was on and Big Bird was with

Mr. Snuffleupagus, a big hairy mammoth with droopy eyes. Only Big Bird and I could see him. Anytime someone else would come into the picture, Snuffy would discreetly leave and Big Bird would have to argue for his existence.

Satellite's gone up to the sky
things like that drive
me out of my mind.

I wanted to see Lisa again. I bet she was finished. I bet she'd have on different clothes too. Probably some long pants because it got a little chilly in the spring. There was really nothing to worry about in Stambaugh other than the weather. The only crimes around were those of ecstasy, and as long as you stayed out of its path you were safe. The women of my family were fast becoming criminals....

At seventeen Aunt Hope married the first man that she saw with dark skin and sunglasses sitting behind the wheel of a Chevy Impala. Bruno had just got back from fighting in some war. As far as I could tell he was a good man because he let me steer the car in a big flat parking lot with modern apartments one time when they had taken me away to another city for a weekend. Molly and Ally had taken to breaking the law with Grampa Duke's sons who followed him up from Lower Michigan. There were four of them: Shel, Martin, Brandon, and Bud. And one daughter too, Jennifer. She was about thirteen with a lot of freckles and used to practice her kissing on me. She was doing illegal things with Uncle Bruno's younger brothers, Chris and Corey. In 1974, there was a lot of ecstasy in the U.P. It smelled like patchouli and something Bruno called napalm.

I wiped the tuna fish oil off the corners of my mouth with my hand and stood up. I was off to check out Lisa's pants. As I walked toward the door, there was a knock. I stood on my tiptoes and looked out the plexi-glass window of the front door. It was Winston, another guy who had been in that war with Bruno. He was with his girlfriend whose name I could never remember, and hair I could never forget. Long like a horse's tail, tied at the back of her head with some dried flowers in it. In my world of binary oppositions, her dark river-water skin was love, and Winston's warped and torn smirk was hate.

"Come on, let us in," he commanded, so I did because I was getting out of there anyway. "Jesus Christ it's fucking dark in here. Man, open the shades or something," he said as he tossed a paper bag on the Formica tabletop. "Where's Kate and Eddy, kid? Upstairs again? Christ, listen to that music. Hey!" he screamed, "Come on down, you fucking rabbits!" I said bye to the girlfriend and left the house full of sound.

* * *

Lisa was across the street on her tire swing that hung from a thick branch, pumping her feet up in the air trying to touch the leaves of the oak tree with her patent leather shoes. Standing there in my tall grass, I imagined to her I must have looked like a smear of chalk on a green blackboard. I wondered what she thought I spelled out. Probably something like "silly boy," or "naughty boy." I was O.K. with either. I just stood there for a while as a smear of illegible text until her sweeping arc became less and less. Then she stopped and read me clearly as she swayed across the street, knowing she was about to break the law.

We walked around back together and turned on the tap that stuck out of the house and took turns putting our mouths under the stream of water and drinking until we were silly. We spun around on our heels and confronted a lapse in the landscape.

"Let's go down that hill," I said, and we would. The hill in the back of the house was really wild and full of old car parts and barrels. It was a dumping ground for broken branches neighbors had collected from their yards after great spring storms. All the energy from those wild winds and fat raindrops was concentrated in that scene. The Weeping Willows laid long sheets of shadow over everything. As Lisa and I stood there together looking down at the expanse, we hooked our pinkies together and walked on, looking for a corner of a sheet where we could sit Indian-legged and act like we were disgusted of each other's presence.

We walked into the even taller grass, over some rusty engines, and sat together on an old rotting branch and looked out over Stambaugh like we owned it. There was Nelson Field at the bottom of the hill across the street. On the weekends the West Iron County Wykons would play football there and the sportscaster's voice booming from the loud speakers would carry up to our house. The words seemed more like directives than information on the football game. At the very bottom of the hill was a brick Catholic church. It still had a bell that someone would ring manually around 6 p.m. For sure it wasn't the priest, because by six he had a shiny nose from drinking blood all day and was in no mood to pull a chord and turn on the light of God. If the wind blew hard enough the bell would ring on its own and the whole town would get confused about time.

"Do you want to sing a song together?" I asked.

"Why?" she said.

"Because I think it would be fun."

"What kind of song?"

"I don't know. We could make something up."

"That sounds kind of dumb. We don't even have any music."

"We can just sit here and wait for the bell to ring," I suggested, so we did.

The smell of burnt cake was thick in the air and I knew that bell hadn't rung. The Scandinavian grandmothers still had faith in the bell's ability to clang at a consistent moment and would regulate their baking accordingly. But tonight, with no clapper clanging, the cakes smoldered in overheated ovens and smoke filled the households. Children were hungry.

"I don't think the bell's gonna ring," Lisa said.

"We don't really need it. I have a song now," I comforted.

"What is it?"

"Do you like stars?" I asked.

"Yeah, but what's that mean?"

"It just means do you like stars?"

"Yeah."

"O.K. then," I said.

"Well, where's the song?"

"I'm thinking. It's kind of about stars and stuff."

"What kind of stuff?" she asked, again and again.

"Like cars, and Mars, and love."

"Really?" she said, all confused and sort of disgusted at a dirty tuna fish boy's ramblings.

"Yeah," I said and sang, "*Satellite's gone up to the skies. Things like that drive me out of my mind.* Now you sing it with me." And she did. We sang it over and over and I poked her belly and she giggled. In our tall outback grass littered with dead cars, houses ceased to exist and we watched it for a little while.

"What song is that?" she asked genuinely interested now.

"It's called 'Satellite of Love.'"

"What's that?"

"What's what? A satellite?"

"Everything," she said firmly.

"Well a satellite is like a big thing in space that goes around the world really fast over and over."

"And love?"

I didn't really know. "I think it comes from Paris," I said. "People kiss there a lot, you know." She didn't ask any more questions. I grabbed her hand and licked the back of it.

"You wanna get naked?" I said bluntly.

"Why?" she said.

"Because we can! Mom and Eddy do it all the time."

"Who's Eddy?"

"He's like my dad."

"Is he your *real* dad?"

I didn't know how to answer. "I have a lot of dads, and moms."

"No you don't."

"Yes, I do," I said and took off my shirt and Big Bird shorts. "Now it's your turn."

And she took off her white jeans that had sunflowers all over them first and then took off her shirt. The wind of all the past storms passed over our bodies from the gnarled sticks and we were tickled. Then we forgot our nudeness.

"Can we go in a satellite?" Lisa asked suddenly.

"I don't know," I said, "but we can go on my Big Wheel. We can go really fast I bet, maybe even all the way around the world." We were so amazed at the possibility. I'm sure we were, regardless.

We left our clothes and took our nudeness and amazement with us to the front yard and I pulled my Big Wheel out of the grass. I rolled it over to the very top of the hill with one hand and led Lisa with the other. I sat way up front on the seat so she could fit right behind me. Her skin was all over me.

"We're gonna have to go real fast to make it all the way around the world," I said, "so you better squeeze me really tight."

"I'm afraid," she said, and she really meant it. I could feel something moving in that belly I had poked as it pressed against my spine.

I held up my hand and looked back over my shoulder. "Do you see this?" I asked her.

"What, your hand?"

"No, the ring."

"I don't see nothing," she said. Her voice was still a little shaky.

"That's because it's an invisible Green Lantern ring. I've got no fear and you can't either. Now hug me." I put my feet on the pedals that were attached to the big front wheel. I was Eddy on his motorcycle with Mother on back. I started pedaling like I never pedaled before and we fled past my own voice screaming from inside the house. We fled past the Elm in my front yard and ducks in love flew off into the dusk as Winston came out on the porch bleeding from fingernail scratches to the cheek; his girlfriend at his side with black clouds in her eyes while Lisa's parents screamed across the way over the sound of a ringing bell for her to come home, but everything was drowned out by speed and the plastic wheels tumbling along the cracked and uneven pavement as Lisa and I sped faster and faster down Lincoln hill, fleeing an inevitable night.

* * *

There was no Big Wheel. There was no nudeness. The sun had set. Inside the house on top of Lincoln Hill, Winston bashed in the face of his river-water girlfriend. The distant loudspeaker at Nelson Field said in a dead pan voice, "Winston, it is time to stop. Stop Winston. It is time." I was in a corner screaming, smoothing memory into a shape without blunt edges. Here I was, watching Eddy wrestle Winston to the ground, yet the whole time I was imagining I was back at one, crying because Molly and Ally were antagonizing me by strangling my Charlie McCarthy puppet. His wooden jaw was limp. His mouth was opening and closing, but all of his language was gone. He was supposed to make a noise, just like that fucking bell. Molly was tugging on his puppet string harder and harder, blistering her hands, but the clapper must have been broken because he wouldn't ring. So this is how I managed to be three, by blurring myself back to a seemingly less significant time so I could forget the present. But it didn't always work. And then I would just have to rewrite the story. There was a Big Wheel. There was nudeness. The sun was setting.

* * *

I kept pedaling. And I realized that in Stambaugh, a day was a really long time and you could push the darkness away with a friend if you had the right muscles in your tongue. I reached my arm back over my head with my superhero hand to stroke her pigtails, but they had unraveled. Instead I felt wisps of hair and the spray of tears. I patted her head and told her "Don't cry. Daddy's right here." And she squeezed me tightly and I knew I would never escape that type of touch again. She pressed her cheek to my back and closed her eyes.

"I can see Mars," she said.

And then we moved.

Sometime in Spring 1974

Lost Chapter for the House Behind Heartbreak Hotel. Iron River, Michigan

I've got tears in my ears from lyin' on my back
in my bed while I cry over you.
It's been so many years, my sacroiliac
feels as though it's been soaked through and through.
from "I've got Tears in My Ears"
– *Harold Barlow*

Everybody who lived in that house got divorced. There was really only the massive confetti of ripped up jeans and tie-dye t-shirts lifting off from the windows animated by the breeze, trying to catch a cloud and then failing on the lawn like flat sheets of hand-made paper laid out to dry with an invisible yearning to be sketched upon with stories. *If you don't want to go to fist city, you better detour around town, cause I will grab you by the hair and spin you around.* If I remember anything it was a porch and the sound of a wounded jukebox drifting across the street from Pike's bar: *I forgot to remember to forget you; Slippin' around afraid we might be found. Well, here I sit, while tear drops fall and wonder why I care when you don't care at all.* The house was a sick ideal of ecstasy that always failed beautifully. Daddies were on fire and mommies were broken like the loves in the country ballads.

Last night all alone in the bar, I met a girl with a drink in her hand. And I was almost persuaded to strip myself of my pride; Don't let those Geisha girls get your heart in a twirl. Don't forget your sweetheart while you are away back home in Heartbreak, U.S.A.

Heartbreak Hotel itself was a dumping ground for washed up WWII veterans that rocked in broken wooden chairs on a cement slab porch covered with four layers of asphalt shingles. Their dreams were more broken than their chairs and the men sat there perpetually and stewed in their own piss. Mother didn't want me turning out like them so she stuck flowers in my hair and taught me the peace sign. She spent a whole afternoon with me on the potty reading to me and telling me how grand it would be to be a big boy. But what I saw in the back of my head was Eddy in his bib-overalls, miserable as hell and unsatisfied. *If the river was whisky and I was a duck, I'd swim to the bottom and never come up.* If that's what it was to be a big boy, I wasn't having any of it. "Chad, you're such a big boy and I'm gonna be so proud of you! Big boys use the potty and not their pants." But what about those old guys, I thought. How come it was O.K. for them? "Let's read a book while you sit on the potty!" Damn I was bored, and those stories sucked. It was so much better to listen to the breezes from Pike's bar, or watch the sunset get pulverized by the fists of trees and muscles of hills as the sun attempted to go down on Iron River's hardened body. So, I got so bored I just peed right there on that damn "potty" and Mother was ecstatic! So ecstatic, she forgot to put my diaper on and just had me wear some thick underwear. With some quarters in her pocket we went to use Pike's pay-phone to call Gramma and tell her I was a big boy. Out front of Pike's we ran into one of the heartbroken WWII vets.

"Hey there big boy!" he said to me while staring at Mother.

"Yes he is! He uses the potty now!" and she was so uncharacteristically happy that she now started to bore this poor old man to death, but he hadn't received this much attention from a woman in years so he just kept listening while staring at her tits. All this just really made me have to go, so I did, right there in front of Pike's bar with the sky turning purple and ballads bleeding out the front door. *Where does the good times go, where does the river flow, where does the north wind blow?* It was all here, right in front of Pike's bar with mom gibbering, and the old veteran looking out the corner of his eye at the pool of yellow at my feet. With his eyes and an inconspicuous finger he pointed at the ground until Mother's eyes locked with his and followed them to the disappointment. She stopped talking, never made the call, and dragged me back to the house. Then, finally, she remembered to put my diaper back on and I could be a big boy again rocking on a front porch with wonderful memories of love.

It was so easy to forget this house, but impossible to disregard the emotion. Everything that happened at the house behind Heartbreak Hotel was in black and white. The siding was grey asbestos and the trim longed to be white again, so much so that it split under the pressure of five layers of asphalt shingles. If you asked me, that house wanted to die. The last house on the left on a dead end meant no one paid it much attention and after people gave up on living there it just sat getting grayer and darker. And over the ridge was the river that fed off perpetual sunsets that sat bruised in the sky. *There's a ceiling of blue above and the tree as peaceful as a dove, it's a wonder people love*...Iron River.

The house is still there, though no one has lived in it for years. Mother says I am a man now because I got educated, you know? And I didn't know it until I stumbled out of The Northern Getaway—Pike's new name—on Halloween, in a new Millennium, that the house behind Heartbreak Hotel was the most significant house of all because of its persistent emotional gnawing. Looking at that house, one could feel the erotic teeth of infatuation at the throat. Speechless, I knew that the erection in my pants was not from having to use the potty, it was from wanting that love fix—the same fix the evergreen needles shot into sundown every night, turning it into an ache that only ecstasy and orgasm could quell, but never cure. *Come back to me when roaming days are over. Go have your fling, go dance and sing, and get it over.*

I have knelt before as many women as Mother had men, and after all these years, I'm still a fucking little kid manipulating with tears and whining in an effort to get a hug or a fuck. *One of these days and it won't be long I'll rejoin them in a song, I'm gonna join the family circle at the throne.* I don't know any more now than I did at three or four when I contemplated shades of gray and the absence of light. As much as the house wanted it, spring never came. Everything and everyone came except spring and the house was really sore about it and just shrugged its shoulders and sagged. The two windows off the front sagged in opposite directions like the sad eyes of a beagle. When the front door of the house opened, it whimpered a pastiche of song lyrics and fragments of chuckles, grunts, ecstatic screams, and sobbing. *The harbor's empty, my love has gone, with aching heart I face each heartbreaking dawn.*

And then we moved.

Eddy's Sister's House.
Battle Creek, Michigan

Well, if it rains, I don't care, don't make no difference to me,
just take that street car that's goin' up town.
Yeah, I'd like to hear some funky
Dixieland and dance a honky tonk
and I'll be buyin' everybody drinks all around.
from "Black Water"
– *The Doobie Brothers*

I hugged too much and swallowed too many green apples on top of the hill at Lincoln Street. I drew the whole story with a lethargic sweep of a crayon on a whitewashed plaster wall that stretched the expanse of the back staircase, where a single plate-sized window looked out over the vertiginous hill out back that was all busted up with memories of storms and driving fast, overheating the engine of morning. Right before we left Lincoln I was already drawing a car and put some other father in the driver's seat. There was a Man-Worth-Mentioning, a man worth stumbling down the steps of certain houses and shuffling the narrative for. He was the last man that I remember before Mother packed up again to give her home town, Battle Creek—and her marriage—one more try.

* * *

Mother, Eddy, and I were at the Shamrock Bar in Gaastra eating pizza and drinking beer from plastic cups on our way out of town. Gaastra was one of the "Quad" cities—Stambaugh, Gaastra, Caspian, and Iron River—that each sat on its own hilltop of iron deposits whose magnetism consistently drew those who fled through the forests of Northern Wisconsin and across the table of the Great Plains—or across a lake, or a bridge, or an ocean—back to the peak of a slowly eroding hill. The hills of Upper Michigan were once bigger than the Himalayas. Some of the oldest rock in the world can be found there. Magnetism was the only power this iron had left as it sat dormant inside the hills because almost all the mines had closed down before I was even around. Specifically, we were trying to escape the two Lincoln Street houses that had huge deposits under them. I discovered one while digging in the basement at Lincoln Street cemetery house. It was two days before anyone noticed I was missing, at least in my perception of time:

"Where's Chad?" Mother had asked.

"Why would you be afraid when you knew I was with a father?" I responded when she found me. She was really confused. So was I, but regardless, it was really comfortable down there with a red glow that really wanted me. She pried me away, and I was screaming something about finding the birds and the rabbits. "I fucking know they are here," I said, and she put some soap in my mouth that time. There were certain periods where mother would jump on the "responsible parent wagon" and punish me for things she figured it was traditionally right to punish kids for. But there was no consistency in it, and she often got it wrong. For example, this time it was bad soap. Gramma said it had a "solvent" in it. We called some special number on the telephone and then Mother hung up and ran to the kitchen to get a quart of milk and made me drink the whole thing.

"I'm sorry, I'm sorry," she kept saying and hugged me a lot. I didn't know if she was sorry for not leaving me in the basement or for censoring me. It didn't matter much anyway because I was comfortable.

I was comfortable here at the Shamrock too, sipping a Shirley Temple and eating a cheese pizza in the presence of stuffed freshwater fish and dead mammals. I plugged some quarters in the jukebox and played some Doobie Brothers. Bowling balls crashed in the other room and I felt the rumbling in the ass of my chair. There was always the possibility that at any given moment the land could just give way like an old porch hanging crooked off the front of an old estate. And that was the Quad cities, a porch hanging off the old estate of Iron County, Michigan, longing for repair and something to quench the rumbling. The bowlers used Blatz and Old Style to pacify their rumbling and it worked most of the time.

The Man-Worth-Mentioning was behind the bar serving drinks. He had a magnificent head of hair, all curly like the fat buds of marijuana on the silver tray inside the roll top desk right next to my crayons. His hair was too big for his body, but not his nose, so I guess he balanced out pretty well. He was all earthy looking: brown hair, brown eyes, brown tinted glasses over his brown eyes, brown corduroys, brown Jesus sandals, and a brown plastic hair-pick sticking out of his back pocket.

Eddy was taking a piss like a gentleman—wiping the tip of his shaft with a single square of toilet paper—when Mother stole the Man-Worth-Mentioning's pick as he was bending over to get a bottle of Kahlúa to make Mother's White Russian.

"You want it back?" she said with a big smile. The Man-Worth-Mentioning giggled nervously and stuck a couple of cherries in my Shirley Temple. He made sure to not look into her eyes which were much more powerful than mine, and instead looked into my eyes, which he perceived as safer. He asked me what my name was, just like Eddy had done when I first met him at the gas station, but somehow I felt this man sincerely wanted to know, and it had nothing to do with Mother.

"Chad," I said really sure of myself.

"Do you like to draw?" he asked.

"Yes," I said, "I really do, and I think I am pretty good." He turned around again and I noticed Mother was watching him just as closely as I was. Eddy had finished in the bathroom and was straddling the barstool, but I don't think he noticed a thing. The Man-Worth-Mentioning turned around with a handful of pens and some paper placemats with big green frames already drawn in. He placed them on the bar and told me to draw the most interesting thing that came to my mind. I told him I wanted to do it like my Aunt Ally and instead picked the most interesting thing that "came to my eyes" so I could run my pencil around the paper as a blind person does their hand around a stranger's face, and get a feeling of how the object was originally created by the hand of something more divine, so I drew him. I started by scribbling tight circles over and over until I had a full bud of hair. Then I drew a big nose, probably too big, but it felt really good to drag my hand across that placemat. I put a pair of glasses on him and colored in the lenses so you couldn't see his eyes. Then I made his torso all real-like with muscles and everything, though he didn't really have any muscles and was a lot skinnier than Mother. The legs were difficult to draw so I just made a couple of sticks and drew in some kneecaps and a pair of sandals on his feet. It was a good picture, but I didn't have any color. I took one of the cherries from my glass and squeezed it right where his cheeks were so he could have a little warmth.

It must have taken me an hour to draw that thing. In the meantime, the Man-Worth-Mentioning had gone to the bathroom, and so had Mother. Eddy was sitting next to me bitching about the U.P. and how he was glad to be getting the hell out of there. He was telling all this to some old miner who looked like he belonged in the ground. Mother, on the other hand, was telling the Man-Worth-Mentioning that she would be back for sure and that she wanted him, and if he wanted his pick back, he'd better want her too. I know because I had to pee, and I saw them in the back hall near the bathroom. He was really happy to see me. Mother was holding him up against the wall, but he didn't look comfortable. She had a breast in her hand and was aiming it at him. When he asked me if I'd finished my picture, Mother looked over at me and let go of him so fast that he almost fell into me.

"Come on, I'll go to the bathroom with you," he said relieved. So we did, and we crossed streams together and laughed. I got a little on the floor and he told me not to worry because he'd clean it up later, "The goddess doesn't care too much about things. It is natural."

"Is the goddess Star Sapphire?" I asked.

He was really impressed with the words I knew, "Well if she has a name, I bet that is it!"

"Is her hair black?"

"I don't know—she is just pure energy." Then I thought about Suzie Holub jumping up and down, or Star Sapphire trying to sap the power from the Green Lantern, and knew the answer to my own question.

When we got back into the bar, people were complaining about not having drinks, but the Man-Worth-Mentioning still took a second to look at my picture. He saw the spotted cheeks and told me that was no picture, it was a real painting. And I knew he was good enough to be a father and was sorry I had to leave the sound of the Doobie Brothers and bowling balls crashing into pins. Mother and Eddy finished their drinks and the three of us spun around on our bar stools a couple of times and headed back across the bridge.

* * *

As we left Iron River on a motorcycle, I looked out at all the empty train tracks that led into the forests of sticks. My eyes were blurry and I fell into a Quad City reverie that I kept in my back pocket to remind me of languaging and loving in the U.P. And the reverie—all busted and rusty like abandoned train cars—could be seen lugging down the tracks. A track looked something like this:

Johnson Lindwall. Johnson Lindwall was one crazy motherfucker with really big boots and a mustache to match. He was a welder and small engine mechanic living on the cusp of Caspian and Gaastra. Mother said he was a Taurus like me and that's why he was always hot tempered, like the time he shot bullet holes in his ceiling trying to kill a squirrel that had been stealing his cat's food. He shot about four holes in his ceiling until he couldn't hear the thing moving around anymore and droplets of blood fell from one of the holes. He went upstairs and tripped over his cat's head, which he had blown clear off. So he surrendered and adopted the squirrel and fed it all the cat food it wished. He used to come to our house with "Little Prick" in his parka and let me pet it. Its jerky and manic movements were just like Aunt Molly's. And then, as the bike shifted to third, I noticed another set of tracks:

Aunt Molly. Molly had taken to stadium bands and dressing like a groupie. Her brown eyes were still shifty and rolled all over the Quad City hills when she talked. I guess the blue in my eyes was just too bright for her. She also had a lazy eye. If she went cross-eyed, one of her eyes would get tired and drift off toward her ear. It really freaked me out. Now her moves were shifty too, and slinky. She was what Mother called "a rocker," which was like a Hippy, but angrier. I liked the music she listened to. Black Sabbath's "Iron Man" was my favorite: *Heavy boots of lead, is he real or is he dead?*

"Oh My God! That's Fucking Excellent!" is what she'd say as she fidgeted a cigarette and tapped her big shoe on the black top as she stood in front of her boyfriend Vain's green emerald Chevy Nova with a green shag carpet interior—like in Gramma's house—to match. The gas pedal was shaped like a big bare foot and the back seat was littered with eight tracks. He had it all: Supertramp, Triumph, Uriah Heep, Nazareth, Aerosmith.... Molly loved to study the art on the psychedelic paper labels of those eight tracks and that was her excuse for driving all over town with him. She was a real artist and painted her blue jeans on every morning with midnight blue acrylic paints that Vain would awkwardly lick off with his 16 year-old tongue which could hardly speak, let alone erase such a masterpiece. Her younger sister, Aunt Ally, was always watching in the distance, learning with her own paints; but she was painting landscapes. Another set of tracks:

Aunt Ally. Ally never made her own pictures—just couldn't trust her mind, I guess. She copied pictures so she could feel with a sweep of her hand how the scene was originally constructed. Maybe she was always trying to recapture the emotions she had for her pet rabbit that Grampa Duke fed to her when it froze to death. She was intuitive enough to know that completely different scenes constructed with totally different materials and created using a different medium could kiss your eyes and lick your lids and sockets and massage your eyebrows with the exact same sentiment—a sentiment that touched your brain before sinking into the heart. And she did it all while washing down sugared cereal—her only good memory of Battle Creek, cereal city—with Tang. More tracks:

Aunt Hope. Things were really coming to me now as Eddy shifted into fifth gear with his Redwing boot. Aunt Hope had full lips, but it was her brown eyes that smiled. She had full breasts just like Mother, but she didn't use them as weapons until years later when she would finally leave husband Bruno and take her brief turn at letting men run their fingers through the chestnut hair of the only sister with curls before jumping into another long marriage that would ultimately leave her a widow. The men who dated the women of the family often met a certain disaster—be it death, or just the inability to let go, and I often wondered what would become of me.

Cousin Jason was in the world, Hope's first child. She no longer had to treat me like her own child she had lost at fifteen in a New York hotel to the hands of an illegal abortionist. When she wasn't talking fast and biting her fingernails, she was working on mothering and trying to do "it" differently than Mother and Gramma. I'm not sure any of the women in the family would know what "it" was. But whatever "it" was, "it" seemed to work best when not trying.

I would often stand over Cousin Jason and try to steal his breath for fear of losing my own. I was no longer the only grandchild, or the only boy. I'd like to present myself as something sweet, something that an adult woman could read and think, "He was really something;" a tragic hero that endured. Maybe Orpheus—*deprived, put asunder, darkness, fatherless, casting spells*—singing so beautifully that sticks and stones refused to hit me because of my song, yet struck with lightning by Zeus for sharing secrets of the gods. Already, with my four year-old song, I could charm birds, fish and wild beasts, coax the trees and rocks into dance and even divert the course of rivers, but I just never knew when to keep my mouth shut. And that's probably why I would lose Star Sapphire, Suzy Holub, a handful of Lisas. Euridike—*she whose justice extends widely*—they were all Euridike. I was supposed to be able to soften hearts with that music. But that's really bullshit. Orpheus could have just as easily been a coward who wouldn't die for his love, and ultimately killed by women. So far, in 1975, I was just living, and that was that.

The broken boxcars of reverie faded down the tracks. Out past Chicaguan Lake I saw real horses for the first time in a snow-dusted meadow. Their manes were just like I had imagined, like the hair of Winston's girlfriend, but a bit looser and less afraid to blow freely. I sang to those horses. They were nuzzling away the snow to get at the grass. It was the same thing I was doing when passing days and years in the U.P.—trying to get to the meadow green of that first living room that I entered through a sunset. If something bothered those horses, all they had to do was gracefully wag their tails and sweep away the discomfort.

I shuffled my ass a little on the motorcycle seat and got comfortable. I nuzzled Eddy's back to warm my nose as Mother sat behind me, fencing me in with her arms that were big enough to hold both him and me. Eddy decided to take a shortcut and galloped down the last tracks I noticed before I fell into another sleep, travelling toward the underworld.

* * *

The sun in Upper Michigan was always lower and fled faster. Paradoxically, if you wanted to stay in the light a bit longer you would have to go below the bridge where things were shadier. In late 1974, the fabric of everything was inside-out. To be in the shade of a bridge meant to be in a heavy shaft of light, and to be in the sun meant to be veiled. So Mother tried to turn on the light of her youth one last time in Battle Creek beneath the bridge in a bright, blinding shade, while I stood on the sky, nulled by the tenebrous sun.

We were totally broke when we arrived and had to stay a couple of months with Eddy's sister. Our groceries were purchased with play money and plastic coins that were sent to us in the mail by the government. It was hard to take that money seriously when it was the color of candy. And people who didn't use these "foodstamps" couldn't take the people who did use them seriously either. We were just useless, insignificant people playing around with life rather than working in an accepted profession making an acceptable sum of money, like manning a Fruit Loops machine at the Kellogg's Factory.

Battle Creek, or cereal city, is indeed international headquarters of the factory. The successful half of the family that wasn't on welfare—mainly Gramma's brothers—worked there and received real money that had passed through generations of ardent hands.

The food stamp money was only in circulation once and had no history, the same predicament as our family. It went from a machine to the palm of a needy hand, into a cash register, and then into some paper shredder, I guess. This was the welfare system: Mother would trade Eddy's sister two bills of play money for one bill of real green so she could buy cigarettes and the sister could get twice the amount of food and everybody fared well.

To be honest, I don't remember shit about the sister. Back in Battle Creek

I even started to forget Eddy, and he started to forget us. There were no more tales of superheroes and gentlemen. Shooting pool was his new hobby, and apparently he was pretty accurate. He was working at a gas station again and spent one of his paychecks on a two-piece cherry cue. The Zig-Zag man looks were still doing him well and he filled up many cars full of gas and bullshit as he flirted with flower dress girls who sat behind the steering wheels of really big American cars. Then they would meet at the pool hall where he would take out his cue, screw the skinny end into the fat end, and chalk the tip by resting the butt of the cue on the ground and spinning the whole stick into the concave of the red chalk with his foot, accurately.

In 1974 with everything being inside-out and all, my bad became good and vice versa. I had taken to torturing cats because I loved them: I cut off their whiskers and sizzled the strands over a candle flame to show them how much. When I saw my Mother from across the room all brilliant and flushed, I longed for her arms around me: so I threw a fit, spit, and stomped my little feet on the ground. Mother and Eddy were fighting more and more and it was like my favorite cartoon complete with POWS! and people falling down stairs and getting back up like nothing ever happened.

Eddy's sister's house had a flat rubber roof that jutted out from the center of the peak. We all hung out there smoking joints and grilling processed meats. "Give him a hit! That's so fucking cute." We wrapped up potatoes in aluminum foil and stuck them into the coals. Those were good meals. Good smells I remember, like burnt flesh and refined metal. And after our bellies were full we all reveled in being lost, mistaking it for peace. I walked over to the railing, climbed it, and jumped on a cloud and stood on the sky looking back down at that house. I was stuck there. A blue toy glider was arching over the peak of the roof launched by a blond child with a plastic and rubber band crossbow. An omnipotent mother was puffing a cigarette, her breath a braid of smoke.

This day was somebody's fourth birthday. There was a strawberry Mickey Mouse cake down there with cream cheese frosting. It tasted of sugared air I bet—anything but strawberry fruit. You see, the flavor had to be that of a red gumball from the glass globe machine outside of Pour Gene's back in the U.P. It had to be that of the pre-sugared Kool-Aid I ate with a spoon; something utterly artificial and welfare-coin-bright, something that would stain my tongue and make others jealous. Beer tabs were popping and I could almost mistake the sound for the tips of a goose's wings brushing against one another as it fled south for more light, just like we had done.

"What a shitty fucking cake," Eddy said, and from my vantage point on top of a cloud I knew that meant the cake was good. Eddy took his full hand and scooped off the layer of cream cheese frosting and rubbed it all over his face. All the sweetness was gone from his life and I understood he just wanted it back. The guts of the artificial strawberry cake on the black rubber roof were like an ore spot embedded in black earth, but without any magnetism.

And I remembered and I fucking remembered. Voices were drifting in and out and time was obliterated. All I had was a knot of language and memory that I tried to unravel so I could use the line to get back down to the party, to that smell of the Kellogg's factory—to Great Aunt Mavis showing me the dent on her leg from when an oat-toasting machine fell on her.

Then that glider landed on the roof and stuck there. I didn't unravel the knot in time and everybody left the party except for the blond kid. I saw him down there and knew it was me. All that "bad and good" confusion had finally manifested itself into a punishment. Something had taken that glider from Chad on purpose, and he wanted it so he could ride it to the place where the other Chad was—on top of the sky. So there was me out there hours after the party in a spring storm, half stoned with wind and lightning, crying with my hands stretched in the air, waiting for a gust to boost the glider just a little more so it would be mine again; and there I was also nestling inside of a cloud now, sheltering myself from the elements, trying to unravel the knot until the tips of my fingers bled and it rained red, and I was reminded of the cheeks of the Man-Worth-Mentioning and smiled.

The moment I figured out the knot, a gust came and knocked down the glider. All of the Chads were content for a time at a house whose interior I never even noticed.

And then we moved.

Merit Street.
Battle Creek, Michigan

So please play for me a sad melody,
so sad that it makes everybody cry-y-y-y.
A real hurtin' song about a love that's gone wrong
'cause I don't want to cry all alone.
from "Somebody Done Somebody Wrong Song"
– B.J. Thomas

Mother and I were alone again and she was about to give up living below the bridge in the Lower Peninsula. It was so shady under there that I couldn't really see a thing. I could feel the mugginess thick on my knees and elbows, but they looked bone-dry to me. Mother and I hazed the day beautifully.

The street we lived on was named after Mother's cigarettes that she used to send me to the store to buy with real money she had exchanged for food stamps. Back in '75, shopkeepers didn't care how old you were when you bought cigarettes even though I always told them my age because at four years old I was proud to be so independent. Mother's Merits came in a white pack with a big yellow stripe I feared. They tasted like shit. I preferred the taste of the pot that I periodically hit when all my mothers came over and sat in a circle in the middle of the floor around homemade candles. One time when I was holding a roach, Chrissy Kip took off her bra from underneath her tie-dye shirt and lit it on fire. The flame was a brilliant green. It melted just like a candle and Mother caught the thick liquid in her empty snifter and stuck a paper match in the center of it so that when it solidified we had another candle. That really smelled bad, worse than the Merits.

Although I never caught what everybody called "a buzz," I think the closest I came was when I opened up Mother's nail polish remover one night and took a big whiff from the bottle. We were at the Laundromat because we never had the machines at home. Those were the best times I had with her. The tumbling clothes and warmth always pacified me. It had something to do with the consistency of time and motion. I enjoyed the dryers most. A dime was ten minutes and about 250 revolutions. It was something I could count on. I would press my cheek to the glass and warm it ruby red while I counted the revolutions and watched the clothes rise and fall.

Mother let me paint her nails if I removed the old polish. When I whiffed that stuff in the Burbie's Wash-o-rama around the corner from Merit Street, my hearing went all funny and it was as if I was in one of those big dryers with a cat that was in heat. That cavernous rumbling catcall was really distant and echoed for a little while. I was all dizzy for a moment and then came to. I realized Mother was weeping, the sound too like a cat in heat. She was weeping because she had lost something again. She had lost our Eddy. But I had always thought that he lost us. We were easy to forget because we always hovered in the shadows of what was acceptable: I had shoes, but didn't always wear my socks. I crawled out of my clothes-dryer buzz and massaged Mother's wet knee that was blistering in the Laundromat heat. I figured it would help her move around better and make a decision to walk away from the situation again. I didn't mind another move. If we stayed I might remain four forever.

* * *

At Merit Street we lived on the second floor and had plenty of windows for a change. Mothers were visiting often. They brought us a lot of plants, mostly spiders and philodendrons that hung from macramé hangers that Melody and

Mother made. The ropes were fascinating and twisted like curly slides down from a single hook on the ceiling. If I could, I would have slid down them into the thick forests of the foliage. We created our own paradise with furniture that neighbors put out onto the curb for the waste disposal people. Mother had a knack for reupholstering stuff with tie-dye sheets and recycled fabrics she purchased from second-hand stores. She never made any curtains though, because there was no reason since Eddy was gone and she left her clothes on. We sucked in as much light as we could through empty Pixy Stix straws we bought with our purple plastic welfare coins.

During naptime, I would drag the pillows Melody had made from two garbage bags full of old lingerie the widow next door had thrown out after her husband "expired," is what Mother would say. Most of the fabrics were real silk so the pillows were even softer than goose feathers, inside and out. For the pillowcase, she cut a bunch of squares out of underwear and took the cups out of bras and used the straps for a decorative border. She found an old garter and tied it in a half-knot so it looked like a bow. That pillow had more love in it than any house I would ever live in. I carried it with me everywhere I went. I even tore open one of the seams so I could get at the stuffing that was made of complete pieces of lingerie, not all cut up like the outside. I never pulled a piece all the way out—just enough for me to wrap it around my index and middle finger. Then I would lie on the pillow and rub the silk on my lips for hours, and when I drifted off to sleep I would naturally put the silk right into my mouth.

Our whole house was made of the shadows of others, and we sucked that gray light into our guts to push the total darkness away and claim everything as our own. Mother would say we were making beauty, but we were really redefining beauty. She never thought enough, and maybe that is why everybody loved her so much, but for such a short time. Because when the newness of a fresh run wears off, you have to think. You can't just lick each other's gums and cuticles; you must talk. And even I knew I must talk, so I did. Too much probably, but I didn't want to be left because I was boring, or living in the shadow of empty euphemisms and clichés. People liked it when you talked shit, especially at four. I mean good shit, like about what you heard in songs—like "Tush" and "Boots of Lead."

Regardless of how many new people I could woo with my advanced vocabulary so they wouldn't leave me, whether they were adults, pets, or peers, I was the one who ultimately had to leave, something that never really changed. With Mother and Eddy, I couldn't figure out who wanted to leave who. So finally, I just thought of "leave" as some ecstatic "release;" but this was bullshit, just like the sweetness between Eddy and me, because everyone knew that we beat cats and spit a lot.

All the light, gray and white, was sucked out of the Merit Street house completely one night and the pale siding couldn't be seen from the street. Only intuition could find our house in the darkness, and Eddy, even though drunk off his ass, had it still. He also was confused about leaving and being left alone. He didn't perceive the definition as something ecstatic like I did so he wasn't sure if he wanted it to happen.

* * *

I was sleeping and didn't hear his motorcycle pull up on the grass and tip over. He didn't even take the time to put the kickstand down. I did hear him yelling "Kate" and so did everyone else. Windows were waking up everywhere.

"Kate," he kept saying, "Don't leave! Don't leave!" She was snoring so loud that she was the only one on the block that couldn't hear him, and he was so drunk he never thought to use the door and come in and tell her to her face. I got out of bed and ran to Mother's bedroom window at the front of the house, pushed it open, and saw the bike and Eddy's pee-pee. After every "I love you" and "Don't leave," he had removed an article of clothing. He must have been very assertive because he was totally nude now. I shook Mother a little, and then a little more.

"Eddy's back," I said frankly. For the first time in my life, I couldn't figure out if something was good or bad. It was more complicated this time. I was really thinking now, and really tired on top of it, so it never occurred to me that I had made my own bridge to hide under that spanned my good and bad.

"What?" she said

"Eddy's here. I heard him yelling outside but I guess he can't find the door."

"Oh shit," she said and hopped out of bed and threw on one of the negligees that Melody had rescued from the neighbor. The silk looked really nice draped over her. I smiled lackadaisically in my 2 a.m. stupor and wandered back to bed to observe my hands that I floated in the black air and stared at them. This is what they showed me:

Mom ran down the hallway stairs and tripped on the last step, but didn't fall to the ground. She caught herself with the doorknob, which she conveniently twisted and proceeded to glide right out the door and then fell in the manicured lawn that the landlords kept up for us. Eddy's bike was tipped over and still idling in the grass. The back tire was spinning because the bike was still in gear, just like him, under her bedroom window with his head in his hands crying for Kate. All the windows in all the houses were awake now. The wind caught Mother's negligee and her ass was exposed a bit. In unison with the wind, Eddy turned his head toward Mother and caught a glimpse of her ass and ran for it like a bull to a cape and knocked her down on the ground. The grass was totally wet with dew and the air was still sticky. They made love right there for a while, at least she did, because I indeed heard that, even in my slumber. I don't know if that sound was good or bad either.

In the light of awakened windows, the grass was purple like the belly of an earthworm, and just as smooth. Mother dug out tufts of grass with her fingernails that she would keep dirty for days in order to hold onto the memory and ward off the leaving. Eddy got more aggressive. They wrestled in their love clutch and rolled toward the door. They managed to make love all the way up the stairs. "Making love" to me at four meant pressing naked skin together as tightly as possible until enough perspiration was generated to stick bellies together. When I heard them at the top of the stairs I stopped looking at my hands in the dark and ran to peek out the bedroom door. Eddy and Mother were indeed stuck together, just like my good and bad. Their sodden bodies slithered down a short hallway to her bedroom. Sounds were really loud now. The house was full of the distant hum of an idling motorcycle, wrenched bed-springs, strained vocal chords, and a lot of wind blowing in from a curtainless window I forgot to close. My bed was covered with a big blanket and I ran to it in order to seek some shelter from the wind of Mother's confusing mating calls. I was becoming more and more convinced that once again she was hurting. Eddy's voice and movements were deeper than before, resembling the gray ambiance of our dark house that Mother forgot to illuminate with candles. None of this was expected so I feared it.

I didn't like what my hands were showing me so I grabbed my pillow and tore open the seam a little to pull one of the negligees out. I wrapped the silk around my two fingers. I put the silk in my mouth and suckled it. It tasted like perfume, must have been the widow's. There was old love and midnight on my taste buds. I ran my tongue around the purple paisley prints and knew the contour of the widow's childbearing hips. I sucked her nights of lovemaking right into me and I saw her on a different bed with an old man—maybe her husband and maybe not—at her ankles. He kissed his way up to her knee and then turned her over on her stomach so he could lick the backside. Her healthy smile was swollen with rosehips. With her mascara-smeared eyes she took in his whole history of playing as a child and loving as an adult. She wasn't what Mother called a "floozy." She was a real woman who could spit a phlegm ball, yet massage away any doubts a man might have about being drawn to her like a magnet is to steel. I pulled that negligee right out of the pillow and wrapped it around my ears and stuffed the lace fringe in my mouth, trying to swallow someone else's life.

But you can never escape sound. Its waves pour all over you and penetrate right into your blood. The spiral vibration of the bedsprings bore a hole right into my guts and I keeled over sideways with all the wind knocked out of me. I rocked there under the blanket in a ball until I made my own bedspring vibrations and then I fucking twisted right off that bed that came from some curb around the corner. It wasn't big enough for the steel frame it sat on, so when I rocked off the bed, I smashed my collarbone on one of the sidepieces. I landed on the floor and screamed really loud hoping that my vibrations would make their way to Mother, but somewhere in the center of the hallway between our two worlds, the waves from her room and mine collided and my sounds flat-lined against her waves which arched from the ceiling to the floor. My waves were just a long, drawn out intestine. I lay on the floor with a negligee wrapped around my head and a broken collarbone, realizing I was defeated. For Mother and Eddy it was a draw and they left it at that.

* * *

I never saw Eddy again. He was gone before morning and left his motorcycle idling in the grass. After the gas ran out and it stalled, Mother and I buried it right there. It was still dark. When we were digging the hole, Mother noticed I wasn't using my left arm much.

"Do you hurt?" she said.

"What do you mean?"

"You're not using your arm."

"I don't know. I think I fell off the bed and hit my shoulder on the way down. That bed is too small for its holder," I said.

"Frame—It's too small for its frame," she corrected me.

"I thought frames were just for pictures."

"Frames hold stuff together."

"Well that frame is holding the bed all right, but it's too much for the mattress and me." She took of my shirt and used it to wipe the dirt away from my shoulder so she could get a better look. It was apparent that the stick in my shoulder was snapped and splintered under my skin.

"My frame is broken?" I asked

"Yes," she said, "but we don't have to throw it out. We'll get rid of the bed, and the house for that matter, but we'll keep you." She smiled, "We'll take care of that arm right now."

The sun came up and it was purple all over just like my shoulder. We left the motorcycle half buried and went to the free clinic. The doctor said there was nothing to do but put my arm in a sling for a couple of months and it would take care of itself. He gave me an ugly blue sling that I hated. My shoulder ached and I threw a fit and cried for my silky.

When we got home I headed for the tie-dye couch and she went upstairs to observe the bed. She saw the purple paisley negligee with fringe on the floor and had an idea. She ripped it down the seam so it was just a big flat piece of fabric. With a tiny pair of scissors from her manicure set she cut out a big square.

"Chad," she called, "come up here, we can take care of something." I left my couch-sulking and rode the waves to my bedroom. I saw the negligee dead on the floor and was frightened. She looked me in the eye.

"Come over here," she commanded and then opened her arms really wide, enough for 100 Chads, and hugged me while I looked over her shoulder at the discarded memories of the widow. Mother slid her fingers up my sling, and traced my collarbone delicately with her fingertips. She slid the ugly blue fabric off my shoulder and threw it across the room.

"We don't need that shitty thing. I think this is better," and she picked up the silk. I guess she changed her mind about that old floozy who had lost her husband because she saw the value in her silk memory as she cradled my elbow in the fabric and tied it over my shoulder. Then she parted my hair.

"What's up with Eddy?" I said.

"Well, Eddy is just Eddy," she said, "and that's that. We're going back up to Gramma's."

"Above the bridge?"

"Yes, above the bridge"

"I understand the light up there."

"What?" she asked.

"I like the light, the way it frames everything. You know, like when it shines really late in the summer and holds the trees and Aunt Molly's bucked-teeth out in the open before the dark comes."

"I guess it's a strong frame then." She was really thinking now, and I was happy for her. "The U.P. makes a good bed." And that is what she had to hold on to in order to justify yet another move.

* * *

We packed up a couple of things and threw all of the furniture back out on the curb. Melody was back living with her mother, a piano teacher, and had a phone so we went over there to call Gramma. Mother told her about burying the motorcycle and how she wanted to go back home so my arm could heal. She started to cry and I realized there wasn't a lot of difference between four and 21 years old. While she was crying, I was looking around the room for images to latch on to. Melody's mother's house was full of things that matched, like bound leather volumes of books, Tiffany lamps, matching plates, and Maple dining room chairs. The sense of order in her positioning of objects is exactly what I was looking for. The walls were bleached-bone-white and full of sort-of-colorful pictures that didn't resemble anything.

Somebody didn't care much about what the painting was supposed to be. I felt comfortable confronted with them, just like when I was confronted with the world going by the car window as we drove back and forth over the bridge. In the blur of speed I could choose my visions—buttercup fields full of brand new Huffy bicycles, one hundred Lisa Lantinis swinging over my head, neon grasses poking through a snow that would never melt; and somebody waving and smiling, calling me to play, or even paint. And I liked to see bad things too in the blur—neighbors with severed hands who wade in their own red and purple body juices; dogs grazing on porcupine quills, all foamy and bleeding out of their noses and muzzles. We all see these things, yet slide the lever of our personal plastic viewfinders to change the scene on the circular cartridge; but we can never get rid of the negative, only skip over it. At four, you don't really know that you can skip over these scenes. You're still practicing, and nobody really wants to show you how to deal with those images because then they'll have to confront their own defeat. So every day I felt the thrust of people shunning seemingly disturbing visions, but I sure didn't have the language to articulate any of that stuff other than to just think "holy shit" to myself.

Melody's mother was in the other room practicing the piano, which provided the perfect pathetic soundtrack to Mother's conversation with Gramma. I heard things associated with Eddy like "asshole," "womanizer," "I love him," "divorce," "rape," and a whole range of other themes one can find in pulp novels. There were just too many emotions again and not enough thinking. But that piano was really thinking—Melody's mother was really hitting the keys. The sound helped me figure out the paintings. It helped to just look at the paint and not search for figures. A sweep of green—plastic horse mane; a solid block of burnt orange—Mother laying in the sun; a black squiggly line—the absence of Eddy. By now I was spinning around the living room like a weed in the wind, going from color to color.

At a point the teeth of the piano latched on to my toes and shook me around like a dog shakes a rubber squeaky toy. I was beaten back and forth against benevolent waves. The piano ran me all the way back over the bridge past all the scenes, be it Mother tending flowers in a tornado, or a woman with the back of her hand pressed to her forehead screaming for the kittens to come home. On the way across the bridge, the notes dunked me and I was afraid I would drown, but it was just a lick to wake me up. I watched everything equally in my viewfinder, just like the artists who had painted those pictures.

The next day, the piano became a simple Greyhound bus and all I saw then in my personal painting of dizziness was Mother and I eating peanut butter and jelly sandwiches at the back of the bus. She was staring out the window. Thinking. I was proud of her, whatever that meant. We would never live in Battle Creek again.

And then we moved.

10

711 Roosevelt Street.
Stambaugh, Michigan

Ah, yeah, it makes life a drag.
Baby, since I've been loving you,
I'm about to lose,
I'm about to lose, lose my worried mind.
from "Since I Been Loving You"
– Led Zeppelin

In Roosevelt I started making friends out of the drifts of snow and rotting apples in the backyard. I did pretty well, even with my arm in a sling from the accident back below the bridge where I fought with a bed frame and colossal waves of sound. I put enough spit and love into one of my snowfriends that it came to life, and I named it LittleMan.

LittleMan lived on the corner of Roosevelt and 11th in a big white duplex everyone called the Indian house. I don't know why really, I guess because an Indian family lived there once and made a lot of noise. They had been filthy dirty too, and there were still cockroaches crunching inside the walls and scurrying at the sight of light. But LittleMan's family was also filthy and noisy, so I don't think it had to do with Indians. Maybe it had to do with the energy stuck up inside that house. 711 Roosevelt had some good stuff in it, "good medicine" Gramma would say, because it was clean most of the time.

That house liked to groom itself at night with the help of Lady, a little Fox Terrier.

I told LittleMan I figured he was an Indian just to start something.

"What's an Indian like?" he asked. I thought about it for a while.... Mother dated a couple of Indians, still has pictures of them. I didn't even know they were Indians until she told me. There were so many mixed bloods around Iron County that one got accustomed to that slightly darker shade, at least I did. Maybe it was different for other people. Looking at his cheekbones, I knew LittleMan did have a little Indian in him. Hell, I did; a little bit of Cherokee from Great-Great Grandma Ma Duncan, Pa Duncan's old lady. They had lived in Kentucky. Ma Duncan was marching west down the Trail of Tears because she was being pushed from her home and got sick of it after a while and Pa Duncan took her in and married her. Our family tree had always been uprooted.

My Indian friends would always laugh at that story because they said whites were always bullshitting about Cherokee blood, and if my family was from Kentucky, that was even worse because that meant they were trailer trash. I didn't know what that was yet. Anyways, it was cool to have a little masked warrior blood, but if it was overtly apparent in your actions around town—getting thrown out of TJT's Nirvana Bar; open love affairs; taking off clothes in public; showing up drunk to Sunday brunch at Happy Italians; sending your kid to school with no socks; bragging about ancient descendants that could shape-shift into animals, shape-shifting yourself into an animal; driving a truck into Ice Lake, Sunset Lake, Smokey Lake, Bass Lake, Camp Lake, Brule Lake; talking too much about family curses and really meaning it; shitting in public; calling everybody your relatives, and sleeping with them; curling up at the Indian burial grounds at Chicaguan Lake under a spirit house—then it wasn't cool. You were just too reckless, too much "Injun."

If all of these things they said about Indians were true, then my family was definitely a tribe. Gramma always had the characteristics. I guess when I do the math she should be a quarter. You can see a quarter in her for sure. She tans really well and has cheekbones cut with a draftsman's precision. When she drank, she'd draw attention to herself on purpose by screaming really loud and wiggling her tongue up and down against her lips to make a wild goose sound, all the while exhaling smoke she had drawn from her ivory cigarette holder. She called it her U.P. mating call and made it whether she wanted to have a man or not.

I had a better idea about mating, making love, having sex, screwing, humping, fucking, and all of those things now. Making love was still about pressing bodies together until they stuck from the perspiration, but it also had something to do with an important part of the puzzle fitting into the other piece. I learned this from watching an Indian. I knew the location but didn't know where that pee-pee disappeared to. I just thought it was some Indian magic, or "good medicine" is what Jensen—the Indian Mother brought home—used to say, just like Gramma. I don't think he knew shit about being Indian; as a matter of fact I think his source of knowledge was the same as mine, Disney's *Hiawatha*. It wasn't his fault, though. I don't think he could find a teacher for being Indian, so he just read books, the wrong books—Louie Lamoure, dime rags, and Time Life books—if even those. He was the Indian that Mother dated when the moon was full just before Christmas came into my life. I didn't have the right adjectives to answer LittleMan's question, so I just told him a story.

"It's like this," I said, and started telling him this story....

* * *

Mother had Jensen when she got back to Iron River, the first after Eddy. They had two moons together and I was the sole audience for those days, watching from an aisle seat. Aunt Hope and Cousin Jason had gone to Lansing to live with Bruno. Bruno was one of the few people in the family who knew the right books to read. He was going to college in order to forget about what he called "Nam," pronounced just like "Damn." Gramma, Grampa Duke, Molly, and Ally were vacationing back in Battle Creek and Mom didn't want to have anything to do with that, so she took it upon herself to create her own vacation, right in Stambaugh on top of the hill with a smooth brown man who had a magnificent chest, racehorse hair, and a nervous shake in his hands and eyes.

As I sat in my aisle seat, a tub full of bubbles faded in. At first glance they were misty mountains, or lemon cream. I panned out and saw the figures:

Jenson lying in the tub with a cigarette in one hand and a beer in the other, and Mother in front of him with her back to his chest, tucked between his legs. It was like a Wild West movie; only the tub was ceramic and not galvanized steel. I saw it all through a keyhole on a closed door, which is always the case. It's easier to focus that way and not get drawn into all the static of each moment when things are trying to work themselves out, but failing miserably. If you're looking through a keyhole, no one else can share your view and give you some other interpretation. There is no right or wrong, everything is empirical: Jensen and Mother loved smoking, drinking, and fucking, and listening to Led Zeppelin on a cheaply made mix-tape blaring from the bedroom.

Some one told me that there's a girl out there
with love in her eyes
and flowers in her hair.

Jensen was hoping for feathers in her hair, but flowers did just fine.

The sea was red and the sky was gray,
I wondered how tomorrow
could ever follow today.

He took a swig of beer and poured the rest into the tub. He threw the bottle on the ground and ran his fingers lightly all over Mother's body. Her goose pimples popped the bubbles and the bursts misted the whole bathroom with smells of beer and lilac soap. She wiggled her tongue in her mouth and made Gramma's mating call under her breath.

"How I love you little girl. I'm gonna take you to Paris," Jensen said and ran his fingers all over her face as she sank deeper into the water and rested the back of her head between his chest and flat stomach. He closed his eyes, blind drunk, and smoothed her eyebrows and kept going past her temples, to her ears, and then wisped the tips with the breath of his fingers. Both of their eyes were closed, and I wondered why because the scene was so vibrant. They didn't know what they were missing. I had often fondled my silk the same way, and I did it now—I ran my free hand along my silk sling where my hurt arm slept. I went past my tricep to my shoulder and traced my clavicle.

The only feeling we really have is touch and wave. The waves of scent that tickle the nose with tatty compliments; the waves of light and sound that strike our eyes and drums; our heart deep inside that beats against a cage of bone; and our skin, the skin that Jensen and Mother drown in bathtub waves they created with their squirming ecstasy and closed-eye keyhole dreams. Zeppelin's "Rain Song" was playing now.

It is the springtime of my loving...

It was amazing how a bathroom could be transformed into a natural ecosystem by the simple friction of bodies sliding against each other. It was the same when I drew my silk across my lips. There was always a sunset and trees.

And so Mother had taken to loving again, and dragging me along because she couldn't find the time in between kisses to find a babysitter and it didn't matter much to me because at four-and-a-half I was already a voyeur.

After their bath they migrated to the bed. By this time I was in her bedroom closet peering through a little crack in the door to get a better idea about making love, but it didn't work—since their eyes were closed, lights weren't necessary so they didn't bother to turn them on. I rested on a pile of old shoes and closed my eyes while listening to the sounds they made, trying to get a vision that was supposedly better than the actual moment.

After an hour they wrapped themselves in swaddling blankets. Mother opened up the closet door and grabbed me by the arm like she knew I was there the whole time. She must have smelled me. I could smell her for sure—the two of them smelled like a brewery. They didn't bother to change into clothes, just dragged me out to the Ford Galaxy Mother had bought for a $100 and a quarter ounce of weed, swerved off to Cannon Mine for a joy-ride, and followed an old dirt road into the woods until it dead-ended.

Mother had made a bed in the backseat for me with an old blanket. I didn't have a pillow so I pulled a stack of maps out from under the seat and wrapped them in an old rag. There was something else under there; it was stiff and pointy, yet smooth like the hairless belly of a puppy. I pulled it out and had a naked Barbie by the leg. I cuddled her between the little pectorals I had and the silk of my sling to keep her warm. In the darkness, her hair was black. Mother and Jensen turned on the parking lights to illuminate the trees for a little atmosphere. They clicked on the AM radio and found a Canadian rock station that played rock ballads every Friday from midnight to sunrise. The music dictated the touch.

Oh my tears they felt like rain,
don't you hear them pour?

And Robert Plant was screaming. It was all about lament and people leaving each other, but people liked to listen to this when they are in love. I could never figure it out. Still can't. I guess it's because you're glad that it's not happening to you—but that's too easy. Maybe it is because people do want it to happen to them so they can simmer in emotion and feel what it is like to be devoid of thought. Mother was really good at that; she was a professional mourner. I'd like to say I thought more, but when I get real honest, like when I admitted I tried to read Aunt Ally's diary (even though I didn't understand a thing) I have to say that I'm often crushed, smashed really, as if run over by a big mother fucking truck, by emotions. It's as if there're birds in my stomach, but they're really mean and want to get out. They're too big to escape because they've grown plump feeding off heartworms and blue blood that beats harder than ever before. Then they get even angrier and start pecking their way out. It doesn't really hurt, but it tickles. It tickles like when you don't want to be tickled. The big birds in your body know this and don't give a shit so they keep it up until you almost break, and sometimes you do. At some point—days or years later—you get used to it and think that they have stopped. I guess birds don't hibernate, so maybe they just let up a little and hide in some secret cavity starving for another emotional crisis. The strange thing is, if we had the option to open our mouths really wide and let them out, we wouldn't. We would pretend we couldn't do it because their pathetic screeching is our favorite music. I held Barbie tigher. And the myth of a dark-haired girl I could have one day as my own.

Since I've been loving you,
I'm about to lose my worried mind.

This was the soundtrack to Mother and Jensen's movie as they stared out the windshield at the yellow light lit woods, bobbing their heads in a slight drunken stupor. Even with their eyes open they were still missing the scene. For me, I was watching a movie within a movie. I saw out the windshield, plus I saw Jensen and Mother framed in the opening between the front and back seats. That scene was really something beautiful: their profiles were lit with dashboard light and when they moved their heads back and forth trying to find each other's lips, their eyes lit up just like a deer's, and I knew for sure because a doe and two fawns were showing at the other movie within my movie—their eyes lit with parking light.

Jensen started the car and revved it up real good to warm up the engine so he could turn on the heat and remove Mother's blankets. She was already unraveling his blanket with her teeth, and she started at his bare feet. The blower whirled Mother's long-thin hair. The bleached strands lit with a red "check engine" light looked like the nebula from a supernova. Underneath us the ground was hollow and held the sound of the engine for a couple of seconds before it fed it back to us, only much deeper and frightening. That sound was even louder than the blower. Now sound overpowered light and I closed my eyes to get a better touch from it.

Mother and Jensen were puzzling together, faster and faster. Their waves were all over me. I didn't have to open my eyes to see it. I could even smell it, beer and fresh soil with a tinge of lilac soap and onion. Things were really moving now and I was a heart inside the cage of the Galaxy rocking over hallowed ground the night before Christmas, and all through the mine everything was stirring. I had been holding Barbie so tightly that her breasts left an imprint in my chest. I peeled her off, tucked her in my back pocket with my good arm, and crawled up on the seat and looked out the back window that was fogged with really hot breath from Mother and Jensen. That world was quite different since it was illuminated with red taillights. There were small spruce trees with thick needles everywhere watching me. Actually, it occurred to me that they had been watching a movie within a movie within a movie, and I giggled and I remembered Christmas. Lulled by the declining rock of Jensen and Mother, I made my own present-future.

* * *

Mother and I had our eyes on one of the spruces. She caught a glimpse of it out the side mirror as she tilted her head and held a breast in her hand, feeding it to Jensen. The tree was haloed behind an old rusty barrel like a fat angel in a faded church painting. There was a spaceship too, helping out with a spotlight, and some planets. The snow began to fall, but it wasn't cold a bit. Mother peeked her head in the back seat.

"Would you rather watch this movie or get the hell out of here and snap the trunk of that tree so we can bring it home with us?"

"Snap that tree trunk!" I said and she smiled, O.K. with the idea. At that point Jensen just dissipated into the fog he had created and Mother and I were suddenly standing at the back of the car, our bodies warm, heated solely by the red embers of taillights. Mother was in swaddling blankets. It was enough in that present-future. She kicked the barrel out of the way and pushed the spruce over with all her might. When the tip was close enough for me to grasp I jumped on it and tottered until it couldn't take my momentum anymore and snapped.

"Do you want to take it in the car or drag it through the woods?" she asked.

"Through the woods!" I commanded and off we marched in step past the frozen water pits.

"But how is that shoulder?"

"Really good." I assured her.

"We'll figure a way to drag this thing so you don't hurt your arm."

There was a different soundtrack playing, but it had no words. It was piano with a French horn accompaniment. We listened and crunched through the snow, dragging the spruce by the nape of its neck with our teeth like a cat does its kittens.

Mother paused in the middle of Cannon Mine woods and we released the tree from our jaws.

"Are you tired?" she asked.

"Nope, not at all." She smiled without showing her teeth, turned her head, opened wide, and bent down to pick up the tree. Since we couldn't talk with our mouths full, we just followed the notes of the piano once again while the French horn helped us endure the hike and pressed the cold into diamonds that we threw into the sky for extra light since the snow clouds were grazing in front of the cosmos. The light illuminated the red winterberries that weren't any good for eating. They looked so good that I still picked them since my arm was free. If I hadn't had the tree in mouth I probably would have eaten some of them, but poison couldn't hurt anyway in this reality. I stuffed a bunch in my front pockets in case I wanted to try them a little later.

After a while we came to the main road and crossed over into the Serbinski's yard to take a short cut. All of their lights were out so it must have been really late. There was only the light of the flames from the fireplace licking the inside walls. Half buried in a snow bank was an old Radio Flyer wagon. We borrowed it in order to free up our jaws for a little conversation. With a swift yank of our necks, we tossed the tree and it landed dead center. The spruce was so big that it disguised the wagon. When we pulled it up Roosevelt, it looked like it was levitating.

"Really something," is all I could think at four-and-a-half. Almost there, we pulled it up the steady incline of Roosevelt Street. The soundtrack was dominated by an acoustic guitar now, something melancholic like when you are in love with a little girl named Lisa on a Sunday afternoon with ice cream and stars are out in the day—then you realize that it will melt, everything will, just like that. I still liked the sound of it. It was best to start talking and think of something else now.

"Are we gonna give that wagon back?" I asked Mother.

"Sure," she said, "as soon as the snow melts in the spring," but there was no way she could remember. She couldn't even remember where she stashed the money she made from selling joints and dime bags. I always remembered those things, if I wanted to. Just last week she was bitching about being broke and I said, "What about the money in the black coffee cup on the top shelf of the kitchen cabinet?" She looked at me confused for a brief second, then ran into the kitchen and jumped up on the counter to reach the black cup. She jumped down and hugged me—bought me a Spider-Man coloring book a little later, too. We were almost to the house.

"What are we gonna do with this thing when we get home?" I asked.

"Well, we're gonna decorate it."

"With what?"

"With magic!" she said, but that was just too easy for me.

"Think, Mom," I commanded, "I know you have the answer."

"Yes, I have an answer, but it's better to just show you. I'm not too good at telling things. We can make it up as we go along, you know—improvise," whatever that was, but she seemed impressed with that word, like it was magic.

All the women in the family were magicians. Molly used to make the moon disappear and I didn't like that. Ally could make my Charlie McCarthy puppet talk without pulling the string, and I didn't like that. Gramma could wilt a flower with meanness if she wanted and I didn't like that. She lullabied Cousin Jason to sleep by singing "Chad, if you don't shut up I will break your neck." That magic was dark and scared the shit out of me.

I noticed Mother had a spruce needle in her lip and when she talked it looked like a nasty hair. "Bend down here," I said, and she did. I pulled it from her muzzle and wiped away the blood with a corner of my silk sling. She probably meowed. "Fat Cat," I called her and she kind of laughed. It was fun creating a story on a small town street in the middle of winter, at the cusp of dawn. It was as if someone was pumping purple into the black heart of night, and we were superheroes busting out of a frame. I was fearless and didn't want the moment to end, so I looked at my finger, the one with the invisible ring that the now invisible Eddy had given me. I punched the sky with my fist and willed it to stop changing colors so our pre-morning would last long enough for us to decorate the tree.

There was 711 Roosevelt. We tried to bring the tree in through the front door but it wouldn't fit. I went in and opened the den windows and popped out the storms. Mother pushed in the tree ass-end first from outside. "Wait!" I ran to the kitchen to fill up a bowl with some water and then ran back and guided the trunk into the bowl with my good arm. The tree flexed through the window until Mother managed to get the tip in and then it snapped upright. I balanced it from the base, holding on as tight as I could with one arm until Mother ran into the house to help me prop it up. We didn't have a proper stand so Mother grabbed an old wooden chair and smashed it on the floor in order to break the legs off. She placed the legs in a star pattern around the trunk and pot like a tee-pee. That seemed to brace it up.

Since my ring had stopped the colors in the sky, we had all the time in the world to decorate our tree. The first thing we did was pop enough popcorn to fill up a paper bag. I took some thread and an old resin coated needle that Mother used as a pot-pipe cleaner from the roll-top desk. I emptied my pockets and Mother and I threaded the popcorn and red winter berries until we had about 30 feet of what she called "cloud and heart" garland.

For ornaments, we sifted flour and salt together right in the middle of the kitchen floor, poured in a little water, and stomped on it until it was like clay. Mother rolled it out with one of the leftover legs from the broken chair. "Wait!" I ran to the closet and got a bunch of old hangers and pliers out of the junk drawer. After the dough was flattened across the kitchen floor we straightened out the hangers, then bent them again into the shapes of bells, Santas, trees, angels, bunnies, and whatever else we wanted. They were our homemade cookie cutters, which didn't cut so good. Most of the patterns fell apart. We managed to stick them back together, but sometimes we would confuse a branch with an arm, or a Santa's head with an angel. So we had a lot of Santas with wings and fat angels sprouting tree limbs.

The ornaments baked in the oven for ten minutes until they were like rocks. "Wait!" I ran up the stairs, paused at the bathroom, and went on to my bedroom to get my finger-paints. Mother and I used them to color the ornaments. For detail, we dipped cotton swabs in the paint. A newspaper was unfolded in front of the heating vent so we could spread out our creations so they'd dry faster, and they did—five minutes maybe. We also melted down a bunch of the plastic welfare coins on a cookie sheet. When they cooled we cut out letters with a pair of scissors so we could hang a little language on the tree. The letters spelled "London," "Paris," "Bangkok," "Budapest," "Tegucigalpa," and other foreign capitals that we might one day escape to.

While the ornaments dried, Mother ran down to the basement and got an old mildewed wedding dress that the previous family had left. We cut it up into long strips of fabric. The mildew had given the cream fabric a slightly green and brown hue that matched the tree perfectly. This was what the dress was really made for. Mother tied the strips into bows around the tips of the branches. After we dressed up the tree in the wedding gown, we threw colored plates at the walls. We collected the larger triangular broken pieces and glued them together like a star. Mother stood on the chair she hadn't smashed and tied the star to the top with a strip of the wedding dress fabric. We realized the only thing missing was the bride's glow. We needed lights.

We couldn't rig up anything for Christmas lights. The most creative thing we could think of was "borrowing" some, just like we had done with the wagon. We would surely return them in the spring. So I went to Old Lady Stojchov's house. I offered to go alone because Mother was still wrapped in a blanket and I didn't want her to have to go out in the snow again.

The Old Lady had a hedge on either side of her porch with white blinking lights and I unraveled them as fast as I could and unplugged the cords from her house. I ran back through the purple twilight and gave them to Mother. She swung the cord around her head like a lasso and then roped the bride. It was as easy as that and the tree was complete once we plugged it in. It flashed on and off just like love.

I punched the sky again with my fist to turn it back on, hugged mother with my good arm, and went to bed. It had been a busy night, but good. Lying there in bed, for the first time I dreamed of being in an airplane, but it wasn't very nice. I think it stood for something because I was alone and trapped over the ocean when the New Year came. I was older in the dream too, and that was weird. I mean, I felt almost five and everything, but I was hairier and taller. It was really loud and the pressure in my chest was really uncomfortable and I couldn't breathe very well. Above the clouds the light was blinding and shone right through your eyelids so that all you could see were little pin pricks of textured color that bounced around really fast.

* * *

I opened my eyes suddenly and found myself staring at the white vented vinyl of the car ceiling with Barbie on my chest. I was cold. I had pissed myself. Mother turned to me in the back seat and rubbed my temple. With her other arm she shook Jensen awake violently. She could split one half of her body into love and the other into violence at the drop of a hat. She smiled at me and I noticed she had a little pin prick wound on her lip. She licked the blood away as if she liked the taste. That's what memory does to you sometimes. Jensen shook his whole body like a dog does after a long sleep and stretched before opening the car door and puking. It took a couple of cranks to get the Galaxy going back into proper orbit with all the chaos of the rest of the universe, and then it was ready for revolution. We lifted off in search of some old clothes and breakfast.

We went to Happy Italians for breakfast and Jensen was pale and shaking from the night before. He was having hot flashes and Mother kept taking his clammy hands and wiping them dry with her paper napkins. After she used up all of the napkins she tore the paper placemats full of mazes meant to keep children occupied in half and used them. She had a whole pile of trash in front of her plate with crumpled paths that led to Hiawatha National Forest. We left the restaurant, and Jensen followed the paths into the forest and I never saw him again.

* * *

"That's an Indian story," I told LittleMan.

"What a story!" he said as if he had just watched a really cool cartoon. "When did all of that happen?"

"Yesterday," I told him. It was good to be back in the U.P. I took off my silk sling and gave it to LittleMan.

"Take this. It's good for stories if you ever want to tell one. Just rub it on your lips and the words will come." I shook his hand and he looked at my finger.

"And how about that invisible ring? How do I get one of those?" he asked.

"A Green Lantern has to give you one, and then you are in the corps. I am gonna put one on your finger." I raised his hand toward nothing and the ring slid down the tiny pole of his finger and spiraled down slowly over his knuckle. I smiled, turned around, and headed home to light the Christmas tree.

"Hey! What do I do now?"

I looked over my shoulder and kept walking, "Be honest and have no fear."

"And what's that in your back pocket?" he yelled.

"Just a little love, but that's another story." It was getting dark. Barbie needed to be put to bed.

And then we moved.

The Sharecropper's House. Wachula, Florida

I was lying in the burned out basement
with the full moon in my eyes
I was hoping for replacement
when the sun burst through the sky.
from "After the Goldrush"
– *Neil Young*

I rode in the belly of a dated Ford Falcon station wagon all the way to Florida, sleeping on 12 cases of beer and Barbie. I slept deep. The only time I shuddered is when John, Mother's new boyfriend of convenience, stretched his arm back to get a beer and was feeling all over the place until his lost hand grabbed Barbie and he stole her. "What the fuck?" he questioned, rolled down the window, and threw her into a ditch in Kentucky. He reached back again and poked me in the eye before tearing open a case and grabbing a beer by the neck and dragging it, just like Barbie, to the front. "What the fuck is a Barbie doing in the back?"

"It's Chad's girlfriend, or 'was' I should say, fucker," Mother said. I respected that she acknowledged our relationship. John finished his beer, rolled down the window, and threw the bottle into a ditch in Kentucky. I pulled a spare Barbie out of my pants. Why have only one when you could have two?

John was friends with Liz and Rock. They were following us in an old Buick that was filled with motorcycle parts. We were all going to Florida to experience a winter without snow supposedly, but everyone was really trying to escape their reputations in Iron River. Liz and Rock were wild, like multiple grasses blowing in a field and spreading their wild pollen everywhere. I guess Liz was mostly Indian, and Rock was mostly Biker. John was pretty insignificant because I don't remember shit about that Barbie killer. He had blue eyes and fish spine cheekbones. He looked like a dark-haired Fin and that's the end of him.

The car fell into our hands after Mother's party in the house behind City Market. Arnie, the old guy from across the street, sold it to us for $25 after he pissed green all over our toilet. Mother didn't even complain about the crazy monkey he had on his back that threw shit and semen all over the party. She was just mad about the white fake fur toilet cover being stained with green piss. I thought he might have been a member of the Green Lantern Corps. So Arnie was pretty sweet and cut her a deal on the car. The license plates read "Winter Wonder Land," exactly what we were trying to escape, yet that text was stuck to the car and never left it because when that Falcon hit the Florida heat and crossed over the Peace River into Wauchula, it conceded to victory and died before we could change the plates.

Around that time, back in the U.P., Arnie died too. I saw the clouds part when we pulled into the old sharecroppers house. The car coughed twice and stopped. Liz and Rock pulled in behind us and we all got out. I watched the car lift off into the clouds. They parted a little more, revealing Arnie. To see Arnie I had to stare into the sun, meaning I had to squint a lot, which made me look like I was smiling. The car kept ascending right toward Arnie with me on the ground smiling the whole time, at least that's what he seemed to think. And I let him think I was happy standing there staring at the sun shining through a crack in the clouds. It made repossession of the car easier for him. He was always trying to please everyone, and pleased most to death until the only person left to please was himself and he got bored with that and started drinking sweet liquors which, in turn, pleased him to death. No one even asked about the monkey. Mother didn't dare stare at the sun because she was afraid she wouldn't be able to stop since she was tripping on magic mushrooms.

For Mother and her friends, Florida was one continuous journey to the field next to the house where they would plunge their fingers into semi-hard cow patties and pick the psilocybin mushrooms that grew on them. I never was allowed to walk in that field, so I always thought they were growing something they didn't want me to spoil. The little money we had must have come from whatever we were growing there. Rock would return from the fields with a plastic baggy full of something that he threw in the kitchen sink, washed, placed on a cookie sheet, and popped into the preheated gas oven to dry it out. I had figured their shift in behavior was a climatic change.

In my developing years, my main role models were seeing objects and colors that no one else saw. Oddly enough, I was the only one that saw Arnie in the clouds and the car's ascension. Everyone else thought it had been towed because they were too busy giggling at the creases in the tie-dye curtains that hung over the windows. Mom was staring at them too because she saw the sun radiating from inside the house and was drawn to it. For six months, she mostly basked in an interior sun while sitting on an old wooden chair in the dark kitchen and I continued to stare into the exterior sun, looking for people I had known. I took to living a life of psychedelic tripping through osmosis and things were a bit clearer, like when you add a little milk to black cowboy coffee—it was tense and exciting, but you never got to see what was at the bottom no matter how much milk light and sugar you poured into a cup, and after a while all you could do was shake and fight for a breath.

Various fields owned by a schizophrenic farmer who couldn't decide what crop to grow surrounded the farmhouse we rented in Wachula. To the north, corn; to the south, something with a bushy green stalk; in the east were onions; and in the west there were only grasses which the cows fed on to make their magic shit which sprouted mushrooms. An old barn was situated out back of the house. I prayed for companionship and it came in the form of 24 dogs that emerged one by one out of the vaginal opening of the cracked barn door.

Everything in Florida that had any life came from a crack, whether it was cracks in the sidewalks, cracks in windows, or the rotting barn. The dogs were all the colors of a sick rainbow—dirty blue, burnt orange, piss yellow, blood red, a washed out green, bruised violet, and pure indigo. Guard was that indigo. He was a German shepherd. In his sprouting in the barn, something happened because he came out with only three legs. I always blamed myself for being too impatient because I was calling and calling for more animals to emerge from the barn and Guard, being so obedient and all, ran for the door before he was finished being assembled. He never cared much and loved me anyways and I figured he was crazy for it, just like Liz was crazy for staying with Rock who beat her at least once a month.

I had no toys so Mother ripped off some green felt from the old broken pool table in the basement and cut it into strips that she pinned around my wrists like the Green Lantern's superhero power-bands. I found a shiny green pebble in the field and embedded it into a crumpled piece of aluminum foil I found in the garbage and made a real Green Lantern ring. With a black permanent marker I drew the Green Lantern symbol. He was my mentor, or I was his. In Wauchula, people shifted characters constantly and it may have been more desirable for the Green Lantern to be a blond boy with crooked teeth than it was for the boy to have the burden of fighting evil and trying to restore peace in the universe. Green Lantern and I made some sort of compromise and shared our roles, which were really never that different anyways. Both of us had one-syllable first names and similar powers of memory, in addition to an emotionally and morally ambiguous existence.

You see, Green Lantern was originally Hal, a regular man with no fear, so a special alien who had crashed into the earth and was dying gave him the most powerful weapon in the universe, a Green Lantern ring. With this ring, Hal, now the Green Lantern, was to restore peace to a chaotic universe. The ring received its power from a battery on the planet of Oa. Similarly, my battery was charged from the minerals that lay dormant in the Upper Peninsula. If the Green Lantern ever wanted anything, like a weapon or some fast food, he would just picture it in his mind, and the ring would make it real. This is what draws a little boy to the Green Lantern. This is what draws someone to write down a history as he sits with sleep in his eyes, sipping instant coffee in a land where the language is completely unique, some say even passed on by a race of aliens. This is what draws someone to revise history as he sits with sleep in his eyes, sipping tea 33 years later at a great ape sanctuary five miles from the sharecropper's house that was destroyed and replaced with a yellow mobile home.

The Green Lantern's only weakness was the color yellow, which possibly foretold his noble fate. His downfall was when he wanted to change destiny. A Mongu with yellow skin had destroyed his hometown and he decided to recreate it with the power of the ring and his imagination, which, unfortunately, was against the rules of the Superhero Corps.

Creating a new home with imagination required an incredible amount of poetry/power, so in order to recharge his ring he killed other minor heroes who had rings and stole their power. Eventually the Green Lantern was so seduced by the ritual of acquiring power that he went into the actual battery and absorbed all the power, making its power source himself. This is when the Green Lantern became Parallax, a rouge superhero who beat up the others and stole their time stream powers to create Zero Hour, his attempt to erase reality from the end of time to the beginning of time and re-create reality in his image. He wanted to play God. He wanted to be God. This failed.

Eventually he realized he had gone bad and couldn't do anything about it. One day his old superhero friends approached him. It was the final night on earth. The sun had been destroyed and everything was going to die. The superheroes, except for Batman and a couple of others, wanted him to help. So Parallax used his power of light and dark, and summoned his old Green Lantern powers and recited, "In brightest day, in darkest night . . . no evil shall escape my sight . . . . Let those who worship Evil's power, beware my mightiest, Green Lantern's Light!" and he was changed to the new sun for Earth. Parallax sacrificed himself to be the new sun, which means that he died a hero, not a villain, and the people were happy to see that and now they miss him.

* * *

I didn't wear clothes much in Florida and ran around with only the power bands and the ring. My ring enabled me to round up the dogs with a simple raise of the hand. I ate with the them, feeding on my hands and knees, while Mother and the others were inside eating mushrooms. I was growing up. A mean dog named Eggroll had eaten my Barbie after he won a duel where we each put one of her legs in our mouths and shook our heads violently in order to get the other to relent. I had lost all my Barbies, but not the desire of women and libations. Barbie, whether identified as such or not, would forever be my weakness. I continued to seek out her gaze in the wondrous eyes of girls, and am still cursed. Without her, and now mostly without Mother, I had to rely even more on the powers of superheroes and the love of animals.

This was the scene in Florida. And I can't help but use "grown-up" language to make sense of it. "Make sense." The phrase itself is entirely devoid of sense. We were all sparring with radical escapism which often led, in our psychedelic delirium, to epic stories reconstructed from the light of dogs circling the farmhouse so fast that sparks shot from their heels. I guess I don't qualify these events as stories. Rather, I will call them "Happenings" because I knew that had something to do with performance art, and Liz screaming at Rock; and him in turn beating her ass was classic drama. Happenings reject traditions and don't assume anybody sees the same "picture" in a performance. I'd never want someone to accept my picture without thinking a little for him or herself what it was all about. Why did I color the Green Lantern red in my coloring book?

* * *

Civilization was a single orange water pipe coming up out of the ground and running alongside the house to a single tap in the kitchen. From this tap we brushed our teeth, washed our asses, drowned tarantulas, and cooled our foreheads after a hard day's work, if we ever had one. We did work in Florida. I see it now. Everything was orange and I was in a tree shaking a branch. I straddled that fucker like I was really meaning it, staring off into the blue eye of Florida sky with oranges falling on my head and bouncing down through the crotches and branches of the tree into big green "hoppers"—a big wooden box as big as a car, full of orange blood and dried orange flesh. The air smelled like juice and the warm water we drank from a suede bota-bag tasted like sulfur.

We were picking oranges with the migrant workers in groves at the heart of Florida. Payment was based on how many hoppers we could fill. If we had a family system in Florida, it worked best among these trees. I was small enough to crawl to the top of the trees where the large oranges grew from the smallest branches so they were easy to knock down. Rock would be near the center of the tree getting the oranges that held on harder. Mom, Liz, and John were on the ground frantically picking them up and throwing them into the hopper before our neighbors at the next tree scarfed up the ones that rolled onto their turf. Our system worked well, and at the end of the day we would gather around the tap and praise our orange civilization, with the adults rejoicing with magic mushrooms and me slipping on my ring and pinning on my superhero bands to go and run with the dogs until sundown.

* * *

Eventually I started Kindergarten. A bus just magically stopped in front of the house one morning and I got on and ended up in a classroom with people my own age. We watched Captain Kangaroo in the morning on a television mounted in the corner and took naps on red athletic mats. There was a lot of show and tell too, although I never showed or told. The heat and the psychedelic osmosis followed me everywhere and the intensity of mundane experience never left me. Within feet of wherever I was there was a precipice that taunted me to cross over. Sometimes it was simply the dark space behind a couch or the frown and flutter of Snoopy's sidekick, Woodstock. At the playground it was very real. It was the place where alligators resided just beyond the shrub fence at the edge of the playground. Near the shrubs is where I would meet girls with pigtails and jump ropes, and try to get them to go a bit further with me. Travel with me.

My meanness was disguised in Florida because I was terrified of the emotional barometer that rose up to the back of my throat. It pushed a tremendous pressure into my head and stifled any ability I had to make speech. So I stopped talking to people after a while. Speechless, I did my class exercises with a pencil stub; I climbed the delicate orange trees; I closed my eyes while holding Mother's hand and hallucinated with her. Naked men in silk cocoons hung from trees instead of oranges. They had aromas of scented pipe tobaccos so strong they traveled on the breeze like crests of waves crashing toward the shores of Mother's tiny nostril pools. On the cocoons men had written different advertising slogans, intent on getting picked. Some were descriptive and blunt like "Well hung," and "Multiple climaxes," while others were somewhat more complex, "Hands like sterling silverware, will feed," or "Jeweled."

I did everything I was supposed to and no one minded if I was silent. I was amazed at the possibility of going an entire day among others silently without them realizing a thing. I began to think that their body's weather instruments had been damaged by the thick Florida heat. Bodies began to break down and people started forgetting how to act and react accordingly. Even the dogs knew their places better in Wauchula than the humans, so I began talking only to them and they talked back. At first the conversations were mostly simple, like "I am hungry," or "Pet me," or "I am afraid of it" (dogs didn't use gendered pronouns). After a while we could have whole conversations and talk not only about the present, but tell stories to each other about the past and how we saw the future.

La Grange, an old terrier, was a friend of Guard, and they, along with me, had formed a coalition against Eggroll, who had recently been screwed by another rogue dog named Lex. Eggroll was being overly protective and assumed that all males wanted a piece of her, so she took it upon herself to act rather than waiting to someday react. After she had bitten all of us, we started to talk about what we would do to her puppies and it wasn't good. It was easy to talk shit about the future, about lining them up in the road like bowling pins and waiting for the school bus to come and knock them over, or fill them so full of magic mushrooms that they'd simply be transported into another dimension.

Or there were reveries about Mother Nature on the run in the 1970s.

There was a band playing in my head
and I felt like getting high.
I was thinking about what a friend had said,
hoping it was a lie.

At night the moons would be full, all of them. One was over a village in a land I made up so I had a future to think about. In that village was a dark-haired girl that I could play with. We would have an old bunny I'd name Tirpala, the kind with short nappy hair and limited stuffing, wire ears that I could shape any which way to hear a church bell rung by hand, or a bird perched on an old butter churner eating seeds. There was a moon to Disco dance under, too, in a city on a river that flooded every spring.

This talk was good. But talking about the past, about fur on the highway, and relatives lying stinking and bloated in the ditch was a bit harder. Guard would often break into a howl recounting his police dog experiences. He had seen babies dangling from the grip of angry fathers who didn't want to give up their seed. His job had been to go for the ankles and distract the assailant long enough for the police to move in. He often watched Liz and Rock and howled. There were so many moons everywhere that I assumed he was just howling at Liz and Rock and that's what he let me believe most of the time until I was really persistent and then he'd give in and tell me about it, the memory—what it did, what it looked like, who shot it, but never a word about him or her in his non-gendered speak. We could also have a laugh at Eggroll getting it from Lex, and his look of pure determination. One thing dogs could get away with was screwing in public. Liz and Rock tried to do it but it was strange. When Rock got frustrated working on his Harley that he had brought in a basket, he would either beat Liz, or bend her over the handlebars and take her from behind, "doggystyle," and she whimpered much the same. Rock was frustrated a lot and it could only result in something permanent for Liz, perhaps a scar, or a child. And she received both in Wauchula.

* * *

Rocky was always too small for me to play with so I watched him from across the room and tried to make him think by summoning the power from my ring and transferred it across the room towards the red birthmark on his forehead. I knew his history of Florida would forever be a thick cataract over his eye. He would always feel Florida, but he'd never remember it. It would be a phantom limb reaching out from the red spot and waving its invisible fingers, trying to get his attention, but only managing to irritate his eyes to the point of tears, at which time his mother would yell and yell, begging him to stop crying and he'd always blame himself when it was actually the fucked up Wauchula weather that really did it. Liz was overprotective of him because he was the only thing in her life that worked properly.

I liked Rocky, and since I couldn't play with him, I chose the next best thing, which was a tiny puppy that Eggroll and Lex had made. I simply called him

Puppy. Puppy was black I think, at least that is how I pictured him. Skinny. This is something I want to stop remembering now. It got sick. I nursed it best I could, feeding it cake, trying to make it run with me. "Come on Puppy! Come on Puppy!" I said. It lunged a little. It had happy eyes. That is the only way I can say it; but the grass was too high, too green, and it stumbled, it stumbles—small, fat, weak, and bloated. It seemed unfathomable that in the morning with the sun like a big orange balloon that no needle could penetrate, it would be stiff, so cold.

"Come quick mom! Blow on him! Blow on him!" I said, pulling speech from my back pocket, "Get some blankets! He's cold, please Mother, blow on him!"

He died. Rock and I took Puppy out into one of the fields and buried him in a shallow grave. Rock brought his bow and shot an arrow straight up to salute him. That was a time when I liked Rock and loved a puppy and mourning seemed completely normal and justified.

Rock went back to the house and lifted Rocky from his crib where he lay asleep. He stood near a window and cradled Rocky in his arms and rocked him. I watched the whole thing with Puppy's family from outside as I stood on all fours and lifted my leg to take a piss and mark my territory. I shoved my words back in my pocket.

* * *

When the school bus dropped me off at home the birds weren't singing. I knew that no one was home when the bus rolled away and the smell of the diesel washed up on my shore, more like brown scum and fish skeletons than the crest of a wave. And my house was full of wait. No one was there and the dogs were gone somewhere in the fields. They had left me. I was sure of it. And I decided to speak again because it was all I had left—something I had saved for a time like this. I emptied all the words from my back pocket.

I walked a half-mile down the gravel road through the dust the bus had created to the nearest house. There was a garden with a sprinkler spraying over the stalks of a small row of corn and some onion bulbs. The sound of the water falling on the stalks pacified me enough to build up my courage to go to the door of the house and use my speech to let someone know that I was now on my own and I needed help, just like Mother had done most of her single-Mother life. I pushed the tears away from my eyes toward the back of my neck to cool myself in the Florida heat that made people forget how to act accordingly. I didn't ever want to do that, forget that is, so I cooled myself and walked to the door of the freshly painted wooden house, so distant from our house. I ran my fingers up and down the screen door.

"I guess I'm alone now," I said when a boy a couple years older than me came to the door.

"What do you want us to do about it?"

"I guess you should feed me first, if you wouldn't mind, and then I'll need some sleep. Tomorrow I will have to try to move on back up north."

"Well, let me ask my mom." He turned his head backward toward a wonderful smell. "Mom! There's a little boy here claiming he's hungry. Can we keep him for a day?" A woman came to the door with flour on her hands.

"Let him in, let him in," she said as she brushed her hands on her apron so she could put them on me to see what I was made off. She bent down to my level and created a lilac breeze with her sudden movement, which pushed away the harsh diesel air that had followed me to her house.

"Come in," she said plainly, as if she knew exactly what to do, "we have been waiting for you." It was really impressive for someone to make a decision like that. She seemed like the kind of woman who would never have to smell milk to see if it was good. She just knew. She knew when meat was bad and little boys were good. I fell in love with her immediately. She placed her flour-dusted hands on my cheek and rubbed them like little cakes. No questions were asked. She invited me in.

I sat at the table with her and the boy and ate batter-fried meat and vegetables. All of the plates were matching hues of blue and the silverware was heavy and thick enough that it wouldn't bend if you stuck a spoon in ice cream, or used the butter knife as a screwdriver, or the fork as a radio antenna. It was a good set. This silverware demanded perfect posture and no elbows on the table to be used properly. I rested my elbows on a bubble of air and brought a fork to my mouth. The mother and her son did the same, and we all smiled. We all smiled, not because of happiness, rather because this is what the unwritten manual of "how to take care of a child that wanders into your home" would have said. Right in the preface: "Under no circumstances do you let the subject sense that he is in danger, or that you may feel in danger. You must assume, for the safety of the family, that the subject is emotionally reckless and has the capacity to do violence and disrupt the family system. Keep the subject pacified enough until the proper authorities can be contacted. Feed it if you have to. Avoid direct intimacy, such as bathing; subject may be cunning and work its way into your life through long, pathetic narratives, which generate a primal mammalian sense of empathy and responsibility, making detachment extremely difficult. This is exactly what the subject wants."

I knew this preface well, albeit with a vocabulary adjusted for Kindergarten comprehension. I guess the Kindergarten translation would be "act as if." So we all did until a solution presented itself. I went with the feeling that I had been primordially, unconditionally accepted into another family system. I eyed the mother, who was, like most mothers, older than mine. Her auburn hair was done up in a bun with two sanded, finished, and painted twigs, full as a bird's nest mounted in the soffit of a silk factory and built from tailings left by seamstresses. Her eyes were like a couple of number two polished billiard balls in TJT's Nirvana Bar in Iron River, and the skin they were embedded in, although a different color, was as soft as the green felt that owner Toivo Takala had replaced every six months whether the table needed it or not.

This was the first thought I had of my old family, and the Upper Peninsula for that matter. It had been a whole hour since I had been abandoned and already I was associating things with the past. I guess it's quite normal, and it would take me some time to forget. In a day or two, after I moved on to the next family system, I would be better at forgetting and would associate things with the previous experience of this family rather than Mother, Liz and Rock, and all the others.

It all seemed, looking at this mother's breasts now, that it would be so easy to forget. Underneath her freshly pressed deep black linen dress, they were like the front tires of a Matchbox car held vertically, ready to launch straight up into the clouds. Perfect half circles with no treads, simply soft and smooth, with a little give to make the suspension just right. This is the origin of objectivity. It starts innocently and sincere before you have any idea about the difference between organic and inorganic objects. I really liked Matchbox cars, and I liked shooting pool. Both activities pacified me as much as sucking hard on the breasts of Mother those first couple of weeks in Battle Creek, until I sucked so hard that she had to wear bandages on her nipples. I wanted to place this mother face down on the floor and gently push her around by her buttocks, making engine noises like "vrrrrrrrroooom" all afternoon, running her up the backs of chairs, down my arms, and jumping her over furniture. This is how you treat someone you love.

"Would you like some dessert?" she asked, and her voice this time was like mint pudding, refreshing and thick enough to get stuck on the roof of your mouth so that you have to tongue at it for hours, savoring the minty taste the whole time.

"Yes." And at this point the little boy disappeared, thoughts of the manual disappeared, all associations with shapes and forms disappeared, and all I sensed was green. This was the color of Wauchula, the color of my slice of rainbow spectrum I was confined to where I'd walk the green hallways totally content and imagine whatever I wished. Green. How I love you, green. Green wind, green branches. Green Lantern.

"Why don't you take Chad to the garden," she poured thickly from her lips, and I was back. I went with the boy to the garden. He had questions to ask, and in our boyish ways we talked frankly.

"Did your parents really leave you?" he questioned.

"I guess."

"Well, how do you know?"

"I think I could smell it."

"Smell it?"

"Yeah, you know, just like when cookies are burning in the oven, and you smell it and know it's past time to take them out—well, I smelled a house full of wait and knew it was time to leave."

"But what if the cookies weren't really burning? What if a piece of another cookie from a different batch that had already been baked was stuck to the cookie sheet and was burning, even though all the other cookies were good? Maybe you smelled something from before and thought something was wrong when really everything was just like it was supposed to be."

"But this all feels so comfortable, like it is what is supposed to be happening: Your mother, her wheels, the silverware, this garden and the sound of the water splashing all over the ground. I am sure I smelled a whole batch of cookies burning."

"Well, I'm just saying…" and then I cut him off.

"Yeah, I know. You're older and all that too. Maybe you know a little more. Have you ever lived anywhere else besides this place? Like in a different state, or somewhere where it snows?"

"No. I've had the same room all my life. And the same weather. We thought about leaving after my Dad died, but we still stayed. Mom liked the garden. She was all into smells just like you, saying something like she loved the smell of the soil when it was wet. That's why that sprinkler never stops running…so she can smell the wet soil and know she made the right decision to stay."

"Well, I don't know if I could stay in one place that long. We've been moving all over the place and it's pretty cool sometimes. The weather's always changing. And faces, I can read faces just like if they had short words all over them—wrinkles, the eye size. I'm more like an adult, you know. I can take care of myself and swear really good if I have to, you know what I mean?"

"I guess I get the picture," he said, and I wondered what picture that was. Whatever it was, I knew it couldn't be wrong because it was his and I didn't want to give him too much direction or he just might leave.

"Hey you guys!" his mother called from the house, "Come in here. It's time."

And what time was this? Anything would have been cool as hell for me. Maybe it was tea time. I had heard something about that. Or maybe these people streaked too and we'd get naked. I took my ring out of my pocket and slipped it on my finger to summon some power to make something generically good. This left a certain amount of mystery, which was always better than specificity. We went to the house.

"Hey, Chad!" Mother said. What power had I summoned from the ring? Was this indeed good? Mother was in the black-linen-dress-lady's house. I didn't say anything. She was puzzled at my silence. It was the first time in a while that she had taken the time to notice it. "What's the matter? Didn't you read the note on the door? I wrote it with a big green crayon so you wouldn't miss it. I talked to Ms. Williams earlier and asked her if she'd keep an eye on you because we'd be working late in order to meet the month's quota of oranges. I got her number from the "fresh vegetables" sign by the road. I had arranged everything. I was being responsible!" she exclaimed. She looked deep into me like she was trying to figure out a math problem. She was looking for the logic in the situation. "You didn't read that note? You just came by chance? Well whata ya know! You just came all by yourself!" She kept talking to me with an inflection that begged for a response from me but I just started being silent again because I was trying to figure things out too.

"Come on!" Rock yelled from the car, "I'm fucking tired."

"Shhhhhhhh!" I could hear Liz begging, "don't embarrass Kate. This lady really helped us out. And you're gonna wake up Rocky."

"We gotta shrooooom!" he said under his breath.

"Well O.K. then." Mother sighed, smiled, and took my hand to break the awkward pause. No streaking, I thought. "Thank you so much, Ms. Williams." Mother fumbled in her dirty pocket full of soil and leaves and pulled out a five dollar bill and passed it to the lady with the black linen dress—I guess her name was Ms. Williams, but I liked it better when I hadn't known. I hoped no one would reveal the boy's name. She wouldn't accept the bill.

"Just drop me some oranges sometime. And let Chad come back, Billy doesn't get a lot of visitors out here." Damn! She said his name—but she said my name first! It was really something to be desired and I would never forget that. I'd plant an orange tree, grow them good, and bring them to her myself.

I stared at Ms. Williams' black linen dress and wanted to race her all over Wauchula. I blinked, but only one eyelid shut. Ms. Williams liked it, and she did it back to me and I was happy that I could leave the house with a certain amount of mystery. I trusted that the ring had brought some good and put it safely back in my pocket.

"Let's go Chad. I guess he's being shy." Mother and I turned to walk out past the smell of wet soil, but before I had the chance to turn completely—turn, that is, back into being with my other family—Ms. Williams put both of her exquisite hands with fingernails painted lilac onto my shoulders and stooped down to my level and kissed the eyelid I'd shut. She did it rather quickly because Rock was getting louder again and the horn beeped twice. I mouthed "thank you" to her, bowed, and continued my turning with Mother.

* * *

We all drove in a shitty Buick to Daytona Bike Week. I saw some 50,000 Harleys racing up and down the street, some dragging Hondas and Kawasakis with thick linked tow chains until a spark sprouting from metal and asphalt friction would ignite the gas fumes pouring out of the Jap bike and explode like a miniature sun being thrust out of the road, dissipating among a larger sun's light. I never knew which motorcycle won; the brute overpowering force of the Harley, or the restrained pacifism of the Jap bikes, which turned to suns and descended to a heavenly kingdom while the Harleys continued to wreak havoc in an earthly kingdom. Empirically, the Harleys won. Theoretically, with an emotional cherry and shot of spirituality, the Jap bikes won. Much later, my first motorcycle would be a Jap bike, until I succumbed to a Harley. Then I would abandon both for motorcycle neutrality and buy a Triumph. Both sign and symbol would come together, allowing me to contemplate the past kingdoms of motorcycles in Daytona where I couldn't hear for seven days, except once, and relied solely on engine vibrations and eyesight to orient me toward maturity.

The night I heard was after Rock shouted for three hours in the grandstands while naked bikers raced super-Harleys up and down the strip. His mouth was stretched as wide open as it could, sucking in the carbon monoxide and blowing it out his nostrils. When his throat got dry he wet it with cheap, flat beer from a plastic cup that had been dipped in a beer trough because the tapper was worn out and refused to work. The veins in his neck were like gas lines where fuel traveled to his brain up and down the strip. His hair was generic brown, thin and too greasy to blow properly in the sea breeze. When I looked up at him I knew he was a failure because his Harley still sat in pieces in the farmhouse because he never did find the bolt, even after blaming four dogs and Mother and Liz. He didn't blame John because he had simply left and that's all I have to say about that. The past is like that sometimes—pure with nothing to analyze, no symbolism. So, I didn't really hear Rock shouting in the day, I just saw his mouth opening slowly and it remained that way for a while so I knew what the gesture was. I didn't actually start listening and comprehending until later that night when the whole Florida family was walking across an old parking lot and somebody yelled out in the darkness "cute kid," at which time I remembered desire.

"You can have him," Mother replied, and Liz and Rock giggled. I wasn't sure if the giggle meant that it was obviously a joke because she would never feel that way, or if it was because the thought of not having me around made them genuinely happy. It was hard to figure out on this night with the noise and the heat, the tattoos and body odor. This night was particularly extraordinary for everyone because no longer did my Florida family simply have to settle for mushrooms. In Daytona, everything grew wild, right out of the streets. Rock had pockets full of what looked like ju-ju beans but I wasn't allowed to have any. He became increasingly more impatient.

"No! You can't fucking have any. Don't you get it?" His personal weather system was about to turn into something really mean, something that could wreck houses. It occurred to me that the labor behind every orange Rock had picked was for this moment here in Daytona.

Eventually we all settled into a cheap motel. I woke up in the middle of the night and everyone was gone again. This time I looked for a note. There was nothing, except for Rocky in his portable wooden crib set up in the corner. They had left both of us this time. They had even taken our clothes because both Rocky and I were completely naked. I knew I was older than him and decided to take charge, thinking the whole time of how Ms. Williams had taken control of the situation before. But she had the benefit of expecting me, although I didn't know it at the time. I kind of expected that it would be up to me to break down and touch Rocky, nurture him a little, but I didn't know it would be tonight. The pressure was unbearable. I didn't know if I could take it and figured I'd need some help so I took my nudeness with me out into the hall to find some. I sound brave now, and I'd like to portray myself as such, but I was bathing in melancholy. I lay back into the emotion and felt its warmth. Somehow I needed this time in a utility-carpeted hallway completely naked with tears running down my chest and off the tip of my pee-pee. I started to run, hoping for the breeze to dry my tears. I ran to the end of the hall and took a sharp right and slammed right into the knees of a large police officer.

In 1976, with a family like mine, I was taught that police were not your friends so I was in a predicament. I wish I could have run into some softer knees, like those of Ms. Williams.

"Where's your room, boy?" he said firmly.

"Where's your clothes, boy?" another one chimed.

"Where's your Mommy?"

"Where's your sense?"

"Where's the moon?"

"Where's Iran?"

"Where's the ketchup?"

It just wasn't sinking in so I pointed to the direction from which I had come. I led them like the dogs had led me, but with less love. I thought of the dogs back home in Wauchula fending for themselves among the fields, tearing up vegetables and devouring magic mushrooms. They were probably mounting each other left and right, eating shit and pissing all over festively. Jupiter and Venus would be on the horizon. The moon was black and new and the dogs sucked on the teats of the Milky Way and howled when their bellies were full. I would give up written language for that life.

We entered the hotel room and the police saw Rocky. One reached for his walkie-talkie, but before he could press the black talk button, Rock showed up in the doorway with a paper sack full of beer.

"What's going on?" he said startled and buzzed.

"The boy was naked in the hallway."

"What?"

"He didn't talk much. Just pointed and led us here. We figure he thought he was abandoned."

"Well I'm right here!"

"You are now, but you weren't. Where is the mother?"

"I just ran out for a minute to grab something to drink, man. Honest. The baby in the crib is mine, but the boy isn't. His mother and my wife are out on the town I guess. No problem here really. Honest man, really." Rock started pleading unnecessarily as if he was facing a different reality than the reality at hand, which made things worse. "Do you hear what I'm saying man? No problem. Just a lot of Harleys and noise and chicks but no problem if you know what I mean."

"Where's your wife sir?"

"Where's your sense sir?"

"Where's the moon?"

"Where's Iran?"

"Where's the ketchup?"

Liz and mother showed up at the door just in time to prevent Rock from going into convulsions.

"What's going on?" Liz exclaimed.

"The boy here was naked in the hallway, Ma'am," a policeman said.

"What?"

"He didn't talk much. Just pointed and led us here. We figure he thought he was abandoned."

"Well, we're right here!"

"You are now, but you weren't. Are you the mother?" he asked Liz.

"We were just out on the town. The baby in the crib is mine, but the boy isn't. I guess Rock ran out for a minute to grab something to drink."

"Yes Ma'am, that seems to be what happened. How can we resolve the situation?"

Finally Mother spoke, "The boy is mine. We never had any intention to leave the children alone, not now or ever, and we will stay with them for the rest of the night."

"Well, good," both policemen chimed, "you may want to take special care of him," and simultaneously they lifted their right arms and pointed at Rock which caused him to hit the floor for cover. He stayed down.

"Everything will be O.K.," Mother assured again. The assurance carried across Florida retroactively and I realized I never had anything to worry about. The police left. After they were around the corner, Mother and Liz lifted Rock from the floor by his shoulders, all the while shouting at him.

"You fucking asshole!"

"Idiot! What's the matter with you? The room's full of mushrooms, grass, and pills!"

"Wake up, you fucker. Listen to me!" Liz started yelling with the force and history of almost a year in Florida. Rock's head was bobbing back and forth as if it was attached to the rest of his body by a spring. Mother and Liz seized the opportunity to smack him. Liz was first—a slap hard on the cheek with her free hand while holding him up by the hair with her other. Then Mother reflected the motion. It went back and forth like this for a couple of minutes, Rock's head tethering and Mother and Liz competing to see who could knock it all the way around. After a while his head sprung a leak and blood trickled from his mouth like juice from an over-ripe orange fallen to the ground from the highest branch. Liz had an inclination to squeeze the juice from his head into an empty can and pour it down her throat, gargle, and spit it back in his face. Mother had an inclination to go for his crotch with her knee and did. The only problem was that Rock probably wouldn't remember, and Liz didn't want him to forget so she filled a pitcher full of ice while Mother braced him against the wall and continued to knee him in the crotch. Liz poured the ice over his head which indeed caused Rock to come to. Not only did he regain consciousness, he regained his strength and coherence, which didn't work to anyone's advantage because now he was really pissed and threw Mother across the room, knocked the empty pitcher from Liz's hand and grabbed her by throat. That is when I really learned how to swear. He called her things like "dirty filthy cunt," "greasy Indian pussy," "two-faced bitch-whore...." And then there were the imperatives.

"Suck my fucking cock you bitches. I'm gonna jam my fists down your throats until they come out your fucking asses. Come here." He grabbed Liz first and I realized his threats were real. He grabbed her by the back of the hair and yanked her head back so that her mouth was opened wide as if she was screaming up through the ceiling at the black moon. With his free hand he made a tight fist and tried to screw it into her mouth. His fist was too big and Liz's lips crushed into her teeth like strawberries. I put my ring on and thought of something quick so I could make it real. I thought simply, "stop beating Liz" and pictured an aerosol can flying across the room and it happened—Mother hurled one. It was heading right for Rock's head, but he ducked and it bounced off the wall into Rocky's crib—who had managed up until this point to remain sleeping—and ricocheted off a wooden rail, making a loud noise near his ear which made him scream. Liz and Rock both looked over their shoulders at the crib and assumed the can had hit Rocky.

Rock stopped beating Liz and she lost the desire to punish Rock. Instead they both formed a coalition against Mother who had broadened the conflict by supposedly hitting Rocky who continued to scream louder. Now I was in a corner, Rock and Liz were shoulder to shoulder against the wall, and Mother was opposite. I had seen the same play before back at the farmhouse when Lex and Eggroll ganged up against a female who had tried to nuzzle Puppy to make sure he was O.K. Lex and Eggroll thought she was sniffing Puppy's ass in order to figure how close death was so she could plan some sort of incursion. The same sort of canine irrationality was at work in the hotel room. I knew that I was in another position as spectator about to witness a Happening, left to interpret the situation on my own. But Mother had just affirmed her willingness to keep me and I wanted to participate. I summoned the powers again, "In brightest day, in darkest night, no evil shall escape…." Before I could think of how to word the command properly to ensure the desired outcome, Liz and Rock lunged at Mother. She ducked and rolled toward me, knocking me backwards and my hands flew up and slammed against the wall. My ring flew off. Liz and Rock joined hands and squatted. They jumped up on the bed to get a better perspective of Mother's position. Rock spread his right arm like an eagle and Liz spread her left so that the span stretched across the entire room. Mother and I were both near the window and the door was to our right. They took flight and were gliding across the room at us. The arrow that Rock had shot up to salute the dead Puppy was coming down and anything that he may have felt for me then was being made null by his downward ascension. Liz's flat, fat red lips were stretched open wide and blood still trickled from Rock's mouth. They were coming down on us fast. I felt a breeze on my neck. It was cold. Incredibly cold. I grabbed Mother's hand and sprung up with all my canine energy and we somersaulted backwards out the open window. Liz and Rock crashed to the floor and fumbled for the door but gave up. All the aggression was contained in the theatrical space of the room and we had managed to escape past the curtains where we were distanced from the performance.

As spectators we were free to flee the situation and ran like hell with our tails between our legs in a weather that had changed drastically and become freezing. Mother took the Indian scarf she was using as a belt and wrapped me up in it to cover my nudeness. We ran to the front desk where she explained the spectacle to a balding middle-aged guy not much bigger than me. He didn't seem surprised. He said he had heard of that same performance last year.

"I might be able to arrange something for you. I bet that little boy is tired," he said as if he was figuring out an equation on the blackboard of an 8th grade classroom. "You should put him to bed. I can maybe help you, ummm, watch him, you know, protect him or something."

"Listen, are you going to help me or not? What can you expect from me now? You want this?" she said, taking her left breast in her right hand pointing it right as his chest. "Because right about now it is shooting bullets, and it sure isn't a love-gun. Do you think I could enjoy anything with anybody? You like it like that? I don't think so. You'll feel better if you simply give me some fucking keys to a fucking room where those fuckers can't find me and my son. Do you understand that? Do you understand that I don't want any more beating or fucking or drinking tonight? Is your head in your ass? Can you help me with that? It will be your one good thing for the whole fucking year. Please, man. You'll be rewarded, but just not by me right now, understand? Please. And don't tell anyone where we are. We'll be gone by sunrise."

And that was that with him. He called our room a little later claiming he wanted to see how we were doing, and that's all he asked, and Mother said "Fine," firmly and "Thanks," a little softer, then asked him for a wakeup call—strictly by phone—at 5 a.m., two hours away. She hung up and called Gramma, taking the phone with her into the bathroom. She emerged about 10 minutes later.

"We are going home in the morning," she said confidently as if she had finally gained control of the situation.

"Back to Wauchula?"

"Back to Michigan."

At 5 a.m. the rumble of Harleys was subtler and matched the mood of the sun coming up through the smog. The black moon was silhouetted in earthshine. Luckily, Mother had the keys to the Buick. Our plan was to drive the car to a Western Union place where Gramma had wired some money to Mother. The car wouldn't start. Mom popped open the hood. Rock had pulled out wires everywhere and Mother simply yelled "Fuck!" once and we flagged down a biker who put us both on the back of his Harley and drove us to Western Union. We were almost blue with cold when we picked up the money. We walked across the street to the bus station and purchased two Greyhound tickets to Iron River. Layers of clouds drifted in, some moving faster than others, and in their shifting shapes I saw some dark clouds that looked like a puppy and a station wagon eclipse a whiter and slower cloud that was shaped like a smile. A green ray shot from my naked finger. For the first time in thirty years, snow fell in Florida. Billy got his change in the weather. The trip would last fifty hours.

Well, I dreamed I saw the silver
space ships flying
in the yellow haze of the sun,
there were children crying
and colors flying
all around the chosen ones.
All in a dream, all in a dream
the loading had begun.
They were flying Mother Nature's
silver seed to a new home in the sun.
Flying Mother Nature's
silver seed to a new home.

And then we moved.

Sometime Before 1975

Lost Chapter for Euridike, Stambaugh Hill House. Stambaugh, Michigan

When you wish upon a star
your dream will take you very far, yeah.
When you wish upon a dream
life ain't always what it seems, oh yeah.
What you see you're not so clear, hey
in the sky so very dear, yeah.
from "Shining Star"
– Earth, Wind, and Fire

"You're tired, Huh?" says the Man-Worth-Mentioning.

"No, I'm just thinking about this house," and I really am. Adult-like. I've written over this house. I realized that after writing ten chapters on ten different houses that Mother forgot to mention this one, but we were here. The evidence is everywhere, Euridike, and I want to tell you about it right now, tonight, in this sitting before the sun blinds it all and my melancholy for you sets in. Sometimes emotion succeeds in pushing all the intellect away and all you can do is burrow in it, trying to find a place that's not too warm and not too cold.

The-Man-Worth-Mentioning has been my father figure for over 25 years now and it's a whole new millennium. He bought this house five years ago, not remembering that I had lived here the year he first dated Mother, a process that would end and begin numerous times until they figured they couldn't fit together like that anymore and disassembled their romantic love and left it littered throughout the Midwest in broken down houses. The whole thing started right here, Euridike. You will see it in less than three weeks when you come from your own alien land in a larger city on a larger river. I have a modest room with a few antiques prepared for you. Tomorrow I will cut a piece of plywood for a wrought iron antique bed we will sleep in. There is a tiny dresser with a mirror. I will look into it with you so you won't be afraid that you'll get disoriented. I know you are frightened by such things. We can get lost in that reflection together. I will make it good for you.

Tomorrow I am fixing the rotted stairs off the front. In the basement is a decayed window I have to take care of. Around the bathtub I will put a new plastic surround. Everything will be in place for our few nights here and we will sleep in the room I have fixed for you, the room where I was woken up at age four because the police came in the middle of the night to search the house for marijuana, and Mother, Lisa, and Ed who were all living here flushed everything they could down the toilet. I woke up from all the noise and looked out the window to the river where I saw the blue and red reflections of the police sirens on the water. They were exquisite and I thought finally the U.F.O.'s had traveled from Oa, the power center of my invisible ring. I pretended to sleep so they could lift me out of my bed and take me. Instead, the police came and searched under my bed. Everything was O.K. and it was all just another day in the end and I continued to look through cheap binoculars every night at the phases of Venus and the moons of Jupiter.

The walls have been painted, but the siding is the same. Ugly brown and flaking. It is a humble summerhouse we keep for reserve. There is still the coat cabinet in the front entryway where I was trapped for two hours. I had heard Mother talking on the phone to some friends she had invited over. I was bored and alone so I wanted to surprise them. They would never come. Mother was inside doing her nails. It was one of those moments that define childhood, the creative downtime when we forget about consequences. I crawled in and the latch clicked and I was trapped in complete darkness. It was on the porch that has a rotting floor I will also replace in the morning. The door to the kitchen was closed so she couldn't hear my screams. I pounded on the wood as if I was all heart and screamed. I screamed really fucking loud for my love and hate of Iron River and its romantic ignorance of the world spinning 1000 miles an hour. I felt for the lock and fingered it until I had little cuts on my fingertips. I just couldn't get out. Finally I stood up, grabbed the dowel, and kicked as if I were Spider-Man jumping through a window. I ran into the living room, where I am lying now, all frantic and crying and Mother just couldn't understand what had happened.

"How could you not know?" I asked, "I was screaming for 20 minutes. Couldn't you hear my beating?"

"I'm sorry, honey," she said still confused, "I just couldn't hear you. I didn't know. I am sorry."

That is when I learned no matter how close you were to someone, there was always doubt that they could make everything better and I've never been able to reconcile that. I hope it doesn't hurt us, Euridike, Euridike with the Greek name just like the stars and stories I turned to.

Euridike, the stars are absolutely beautiful here, even in the center of the city. There are so few buildings that the Milky Way still glows like the exhaust from Apollo's chariot. I realize why I wanted to be an astronomer for all those years. I remember all the constellations. There sits Cassiopeia on her throne with Cepheus near. Daughter Andromeda, Perseus with his sword and the head of Medusa. There is Taurus, Orion, even Venus is at the horizon like a good eye staring into me. In the yard are tiny wildflowers, Indian Paintbrushes and Buttercups lit by starlight. I will gather them in a bouquet and rub them all over your body so you'll glow brilliant orange and yellow (which will likely seal my doom), then I'll paste you to heaven with all the others. It will be here, in this recycled house that you'll help to rewrite.

Tomorrow the Man-Worth-Mentioning will make me pancakes and fried tofu sandwiches while I work all day. I will sand these floors and erase more evidence of my childhood existence here. The only thing left is the oil smell from the furnace that has been leaking for over 25 years now. I can hardly keep my eyes open. I will play something on the radio and type with one hand while I cradle my head with the other as I lay on the floor where Oh-My-God-Margaret, a frantic puppy, bit me. I remember that too, and all of Mother and Lisa's lovemaking with men with wild hair and beards, tie-dye shirts, and bandanas around their heads. I will rub the melancholy in my stomach in tight circles to bind it up until morning. I won't sleep in our room just yet. My eyes are heavy and I haven't forgotten that I am to think of your cat that I also love. Have you received something from me? They came across an ocean and are white with a smell like the small of your back. You should have received them today. I am drifting, Euridike. I will always turn my head back to see if you are following. It's not simply my pride. Will I dream? Oh-My-God-Margaret wagged her tail as I sat bleeding.

And then we moved.

Near City Market.
Iron River, Michigan

We sweat laugh and scream here
'cause life is just a dream here.
You know inside you feel right at home here.
Welcome to my nightmare,
welcome to my breakdown,
yeah.
from "Welcome to My Nightmare"
– Alice Cooper

We were back within 100 feet of the house behind City Market. The big white house, where a kid named Billy James used to live, became ours. The basement had been full of oats that we would stuff into our pockets in preparation for a long day of exploring down by the river. I wouldn't bring Billy James up if it weren't for his absence. I started thinking that this moving was a kind of bug that was going around. I asked Mother if Billy James had gone to Florida and she said she thought he went back to Texas. Back to Texas? I bet there were minerals in Texas too that drew people back. Iron River was for Billy James as Wauchula had been for me. I bet his sister got beat up bad one night by a Yooper and her family took off the next night. That was the last conversation

I had with Mother for sometime because she had taken to working a real job. She was tending bar in much the same way she had tended to me in Florida—she'd get a good buzz going and ask "What do you want?" and if you were lucky, you'd get it.

Positioned the way it was across the street from the other house, this house served as a constant reminder to Mother that she could have made a different decision, so that's why she stayed there as little as possible. She preferred the beds of *Diablo Lobo* bikers and needy veterans returning from a fucked up war they didn't choose to fight in. And the Man-Worth-Mentioning wasn't around so she couldn't really start much with him. He was away at college studying Opium, LSD, and Special Education. I was glad she stuck with her original plan. Florida warmed my bones, though to the point where they could have turned to ash. Sometimes it would have been better to be swept into a dust pan and thrown out the window so I could travel in a hundred directions at once and have a hundred possibilities to actually meet the right family and stay somewhere.

I was convinced I could live without Mother and didn't need shit from adults anymore. Staring at the other house across the street, I remembered that the adults weren't any different than boys and girls. They wanted to strip down Barbie dolls, or scrape the paint off of action figures and crawl into bed with them. They wanted to push brightly colored matchbox cars down Main Street making screeching sounds the whole while as if they were burning rubber. The only difference is that the adults had better toys. They had real cars and real bodies. With these things they could cause a lot of pain, but I could smash my cars and abuse action figures over and over and there were no consequences. I was even better than adults because I knew that within my toys, and within dogs and cats and red birds in the trees, was an integral part of living that everyone was overlooking. It was this whimsical perspective that people started pushing away with their height and mass as they grew bigger and closer to adulthood. I was going to start being an adult early so I could do it right, and maybe Mother would learn by example before "all her boozing turns her in to a pickle and some man eats her," is what Gramma would say. She said this from a barstool at Pike's Bar across the street and over the fence of Harleys, where Mother was working. "Duke, get me another Bloody Mary," she said on exhale. Her smoke fled to a sign across the bar that read "Ashes to ashes, dust to dust, if it wasn't for women, your ding-dong would rust."

"Bang!" Grampa Duke yelled, and everyone hit the bar while he just sat in his stool smiling like a happy Buddha. "I wonder how that Chadillac is doing," he said under his breath.

* * *

Aunt Ally was about fourteen now and was one of my new babysitters while Mother worked days and nights at TJT's Nirvana Bar, looking for freedom from craving, anger, and other afflictive states. The few times I went there on a day shift it might as well have been night because there were no windows, only black-lights. It smelled like bleach and cigarettes and there was an incessant echo of coolers opening and closing. This was the perfect atmosphere for a spook house for sure and at night, biker ghouls with chains and knives would come in and terrorize the locals and even stab Toiva Takala, the owner. Aunt Hope was there that night, pregnant again, and hid in the corner under a barstool, "Pleaseohpleaseohplease," she chanted as her cheeks pushed up into her eyebrows from squeezing her eyelids shut so hard, seeking enlightenment.

I had entered into the new world of babysitters. It was a new type of virtual nurturing where I entered families for a day. I was pretty good at that and remained pliable so I could mold myself into any situation and fake it if I had to until I could see Mother again. It was an opportunity to practice living on my own and take some responsibility for my new found desire to be the ultimate adult. I used the time to paint a landscape for my dreams, or found others to help me.

Since I had been away Aunt Ally and Aunt Molly had discovered they were real artists, and in addition to sculptures of bongs, marijuana pipes, and ashtrays, they were painting real landscapes and sketching their boyfriends shirtless, modeling over-sized dark sunglasses and homemade tattoos of Rolling Stones tongues, initials, and pot leaves. They were cool and I knew they hadn't lost that ability to jive with the souls of toys and animals. They inherited the genes from Jack Hartley, and a small trust fund that they spent mostly on marijuana and record albums. Ally would bring a stack over every time she babysat. With her I discovered how to live vicariously through song lyrics. The Eagles' *Hotel California* album was my favorite, "*Johnny come lately/ The new kid in town/Everybody loves you/So don't let them down.*" After being away for a year I had to re-introduce myself to the kids in the neighborhood, and first impressions were really important.

I used to shop at what was called "The Clothing Store," a free second-hand shop run by the county. What I was looking for was something silky and tight. Ally said that was cool, so I went with polyester. The bigger the collar, the better. A big belt was cool too. And jeans, low cut and flared with the knees ripped out. This was the look Ally had for me. At age six, the wide collars and bellbottoms and bright colors looked something like a bird costume. It made perfect sense to me that everyone simply wanted to fly. Whether it was into hell or out of hell, to heaven, like an eagle, to the moon, the desire was everywhere. The one desire that most didn't have was stability. I found a brown shirt with orange spirals and antique cars that were racing off in a thousand directions. The collar was long enough that I could rub it on my lips when I got lonely, nervous, and too lost. Ally said I was ready for the neighborhood and I walked around looking in yards and down alleys for kids playing. There was no playground to speak of, only those empty parking lots. And LittleMan was two miles away up the hill in Stambaugh.

In my unsuccessful attempts to find friends, Ally decided to put her artistry to use and put together a spook house in the shed adjacent to our house in order to attract some kids. It was full of abandoned rakes and gardening tools because the area in front of the house had been paved over and made into another parking lot where no one parked. We cleaned it out good and piled everything on the curb. We had transformed the shed into a dirt-floored void. I wasn't sure what the theme of the spook house would be so we talked it over a bit.

"So what do we do? We don't even have masks. Whose gonna come to see a bunch of nothing?"

"Well, no one has to see anything," she said, "It will be all dark."

"People can see dark anywhere," I said, "All they have to do is close their eyes. That will never work."

"But at our spook house people will feel the darkness," she said shaking her head up and down slowly as if there was a mutual understanding. But I still didn't get it.

"What does that mean?"

"We'll just have a bunch of stuff that people will have to touch, but they won't know what it is. We'll tell them it's brains, or intestines. Stuff like that. You remember that game we played with the wet rag and the egg? Remember when I blindfolded you and told you to put the egg in your hand and I never let you see the rag then took the egg from your hand and slapped the wet rag on your head and you screamed because you thought the dirty dishwater running down the side of your head was egg-whites? Do you remember?"

"Yes, I remember that, but that wasn't very cool," I said.

"But you thought it was an egg, right?"

"Yes."

"Well, it'll be the same thing."

"What if their parents come over and whip us like Gramma whipped you?"

"Goddamn it! Listen to me! Don't start that whipping and victim stuff again," she screamed, completely transformed in tone, volume, and vocabulary. "They will be too afraid to tell their parents because then they'd know that their little fuckers were hanging out over here with the witches. So now is our chance to make them afraid of something for real, not just B.J. and her wild girls stealing their men. Now let's build this fucking thing you pansy bed-wetter."

I didn't have those words, so I struck back the best I could, "Well your boobs still haven't grown in a year." Yet I didn't even care about her itty-bitty-titties. She socked me in the mouth and then I started to help her create a bunch of nothing.

We gathered coins from Mother's pockets in the dirty clothes, stuck our hands and arms deep into the old plaid sofa Mother had covered with an Indian tapestry, and searched her collection of small pillboxes, ending up with a couple of dollars. We went over to Ben Franklin's dime store and purchased what we could: Barbasol shaving cream, wood putty, three packets of chocolate pudding, and stole some ketchup, mayonnaise, and oats from City Market next door. Butch the Butcher gave us some pig's blood and goose livers and the carcass from an animal, probably a rabbit.

On the way back the clouds began to block out the sun, which was heavy and burdensome. We passed an old mangy mutt and I stooped down to pet it. Ally took her pink comb from her back pocket and ran it through its hair. She pulled the gray and brown hairs from her comb and stuffed them in her pockets.

"Should we take the dog too? Cut him up?" I said half-jokingly.

"No, I think we have enough stuff," she responded plainly as she strutted down the street shaking her new hips past the abandoned red-brick buildings situated between the parking lots, running her fingers through her hair while she lifted off the sidewalk slightly as a breeze stirred her bell bottoms and we levitated the whole way home.

Back at the house, we emptied all of our horror supplies in the center of the living room, which was decorated solely with furniture that either had no legs or hung from the ceiling. We got a bunch of old canning jars and plastic containers from the kitchen cupboards. Ally put on the Eagles' *Hotel California* and the title track started playing. She was grooving to the music, but I was listening to the lyrics as the clouds descended and my anxiety kicked in. My breath was turning in on itself and taking language with it. What we had set out before us didn't look fun for me and I wasn't sure how it would get me any friends in the neighborhood.

On a dark desert highway
cool wind in my hair

"Close your eyes now," she said, "What does that feel like?" I stuck my fingers into something.

"It feels like the stomach of a dead puppy. It's cold." I quickly took my fingers out of my pocket and wiped them on my pants, then blew on them to warm them up.

"Great! Now put your fingers into this." I put my fingers into the bottom of a coffee can and felt something really thick and sticky at the center and wet on top.

"How about that?" she asked.

"Feels like wood putty and spit."

"How did you know?" I took my hands out quickly and rubbed them all over the carpet, which just made the dirt stick to my hands. "You're supposed to think it's brains or something like that." Ally pushed herself up off the floor and tossed her long auburn braid over her back and walked back over to the record player. She took a cigarette from the pack that was stashed in her crotch and put on Alice Cooper's *Welcome To My Nightmare.* She stood with her legs a shoulder width and a half apart, tilted her head to the left slightly and brought her lighter to her cigarette and inhaled deeply while scrunching up her brow like she was really thinking. "Hey, we can put a speaker out there too! And make a sign. Yeah, we can mix up some wood glue and hay, make an outline on the shed, and stick the hay right to the side of the shed and it will stay up forever! Pick up some hay next time you're at the Aimes house; they've got that horse living right in town in their garage you know! Or grab some handfuls from the front yard of the Big Eagle's house. We'll get it done in a couple of days."

"O.K. As long as I get some friends," I said.

* * *

The Indians in Iron River always stuck together and dwelled in three-story, rotted wood siding houses that were usually white and displayed the natural rot proudly. It was as if they let the paint chip off so the wood exposed itself openly to the elements of a hot sun and humid dripping moon. The smell was fabulous and things were alive in Big Eagle's house.

Every Friday night I went to the Big Eagle's to spend the night with Clint, Kerry, and their numerous cousins, sisters, mothers, and grandmothers. They lived on the backside of town where miners had built cheap houses in a day back in the 50s. There were never any older men around so we boys chewed tobacco and smoked cigarettes, trying to fill their shoes by stuffing everything we knew of what it was to be a man in the toes of boots that were always too big, no matter what.

At night we would play house upstairs. Even though we were in a house, we created another house-within-a-house out of blankets and sheets that we draped over old broken chairs and tucked the ends into dresser drawers to make the roof taut. It was more of a tent than a house. After we had the roof, we gathered lamps, paper plates, and a handful of cousins to make the living situation complete. It was at this time I fell in love with dark-haired girls, maybe because my hair was so light. Or maybe it was because of my love of staring off into the dark and imagining an exotic future filled with a dark-haired girl with high cheekbones and the smell of cream rinse in her hair, and a path for my finger to run up that cheek and to the ear where I would whisper stuff I heard in the songs Ally played for me.

You look in her eyes
The music begins to play
Hopeless romantics
Here we go again.

This Friday, Clint and Kerry had the Littledove cousins over. There were Rachel, Roberta, and Ruby—the darkest of all in both speech and looks. It was a good darkness, filled with the waves of northern lights and comet tails. She had an orange tabby cat that she stroked in her lap, starting at the nose and running her long finger all the way over its head, down the spine, and to the tip of the tail, which the cat would curl into an ecstatic circle like the spiral arm of a galaxy. And the kitten did meow. A cosmic deep bass meow that split the siding outside the house a little more so that the starlight and its stories sneaked into the house and gave us a chill that could be mistaken for cold when it was really the history of something deeper, beyond toys and animals, that made the wild Indians more mature than anybody knew. I knew the Indians were cool because I had seen *Billy Jack* on TV. We had a purpose inside that house. I had a purpose inside that house, and the potential of a friend that I could keep forever.

We all huddled under the house we had created in Kerry's bedroom while the adult women drank obliviously downstairs, smoking so many cigarettes that the air had turned into amber and we pretended it was the smoke from our fireplace that Kerry had fashioned out of an old shoe box. We decided to pair off into married couples. Kerry was the oldest and had the longest hair. He told us all to pull a hair from our heads. We would draw hairs from his fist and the closest length matches would be husband and wife. Rachel, Roberta, and Ruby all had long braids, and Ruby's was the longest. Clint had dark hair down past his shoulders. My hair, by contrast, went to the nape of my neck. I ran my fingers through my hair looking for something long and settled on the very top of my part. It was still pitifully short and glowed in Kerry's hand next to the dark hairs.

Ruby drew first and pulled out a really long one, which appeared to be her own. I had to draw a long one too so I knew not to pick my own. I glared at Kerry's hair trying to match his color with the strand in his hand. I pulled it out slowly and it kept coming and coming, royally, like a carpet being rolled out toward my future with Ruby.

"Come on, just take it!" Clint yelled. And I pulled for what seemed like an hour, fantasizing about my future with Ruby and her cat, how our hands would follow the galactic tail of the orange tabby to something deep, where animals shifted into humans and humans barked and meowed and licked each other silly.

"Hey! Looks like Chad gets Ruby!" Clint said. She had no reaction, as if she didn't even want to play. But this wasn't playing. I was pliable and molded this into my reality. Kerry had Roberta who was about eleven and was already budding breasts, which left Clint with Rachel. They didn't care one way or the other who their partners were.

We didn't know much about what "house" meant. Most of us already cooked for ourselves, dressed ourselves in the morning, took baths when we wanted to, and even cleaned and decorated our rooms. "House" was really about practicing screwing with our clothes on—or "humping" is what we called it—and everybody knew it. For me it was about escaping Iron River and being privileged. It was about sipping tea and speaking good grammar like they did on the *The Young and the Restless*.

"Stoke the fireplace," Clint said, and Kerry pulled out a pack of Swisher Sweet cigars from under the mattress. The boys/men lit them up until our house-within-a-house was completely blurred in the smoky amberness of pre-adolescent matrimony and we all said, "I do" and did.

The blankets covered the whole bedroom so the bed and dresser acted as partitions to the different rooms. Ruby put the cat on her back and we crawled around the edge of the bed toward the half-exposed window. Clint went behind the dresser with Rachel, and Kerry stayed by the shoebox/fireplace with Roberta. We were far enough away and quiet enough that we had a certain amount of privacy. Ruby still wasn't talking much and took the cat from her back and put it in her arms once again, stroking its nose to tail-tip. If I really wanted to make this work, I needed to treat her like the Indian princess she didn't even know she was.

"Would you like some tea?" I asked her, pinching my thumb and index finger together as if I were holding a teapot.

"Yeah," she said. But she said it like she was just regular eight year-old Ruby, and not my wife. If you wanted to be really like "married" you had to use good grammar.

"Do you mean 'yes, it would be quite nice'?"

"Sure," she said stroking her cat in her lap, "What's up with that shiny shirt? The collar is so big it looks like you are gonna fly away," she said with a glance and minimal interest.

"It's supposed to get me 'Tush' is what my Aunt Molly told me. Now, would you be so kind as to hold out your cup?" She stuck her arm out like a board and I poured my air into her palm. "Take a sip. Is it too hot? If it is, I can blow on it a little for you. I have some sugar and milk too, if you are interested."

"This is dumb," she said flatly, staring at her cat.

"But I love you," I said imitating myself imitating sincerity since I was, after all, sincere.

"No you don't. You just want to hump," Ruby responded. I looked out the window. It was mostly black except for the shadow cast off a tree caused by some light source in the distance.

"Listen Ruby, I just want to run my finger down your nose to your tail just like you do to that cat. If you like petting that cat so much it's gotta be because you want to be treated that way too, and I think I can." When I said this, I wasn't pretending and forgot to use good and formal grammar. "I mean, it would be wonderful to smooth that braided mane of yours," I said real polite-like. "Maybe some music will help. What would you like to hear, dear?" I pulled a radio from the air and sat the nothing down next to her and began tuning it.

"We can't hear anything."

"You are wrong! We can hear anything you have ever wanted to hear. It's easy. Just tell me. You'll see."

Sternly she commanded, "Play some Elvis then," while stroking the cat. That was good because I knew Elvis. Gramma used to play him on the jukebox all the time at Friday night fish fries at Pike's Bar on top of Stambaugh Hill.

"O.K., what song?"

"Make the World Go Away," she said, uninterested. I knew that one! It was a country song! Gramma used to sing it to Grampa after she had drunk about five Bloody Marys.

Make the world go away
get it off my shoulder.
Say the things we used to say
and make the world, make it go away.

Gramma would wave her arms in the air, spin around in what appeared aimless circles, and then, without any effort, hit her target, dropping her arms on Grampa Duke's shoulders and sang the last verse into his eyes.

I pretended to turn the knob on the radio that wasn't there until I found the song and sang the first verse to Ruby in the deepest voice I could.

She laughed and looked up at me. "You're crazy." And she smiled. She smiled and the shadow of the tree outside became more prominent and I knew where the light was coming from. It was like a real relationship. We were drinking tea and laughing, listening to music in our house-within-a-house and that incessant flatness had swelled into a bright balloon.

"How do you know that song?" she asked.

"What do you mean? That's Elvis on the radio," I assured her, trying to keep with the fantasy.

"You're crazy." And we both laughed, me a little and her a lot. I really saw her cheekbones this time carve into our near-dark where a lamp shined through the thick yellow blanket and smoke continued to obscure everything beautifully. I reached over and stroked her cat.

"How do you know that song?"

"My Grandfather use to sing it to me when I visited him at the reservation. He'd get drunk and then put on the record and start singing. He was pretty bad, but better than you! And then there was a part that skipped right when Elvis said 'Do you remember when you loved…' and then it skipped saying 'love-love-love-love-love' over and over again and grandfather pretended like he was hiccupping. He would do it until he cried and fell asleep."

"That is pretty funny." I really had her talking now. Clint mumbled something in the distance and Rachel said "Yuk!" really loud. I wanted to take the world off Ruby's shoulders, so I figured I'd start with her braid.

"Would you be so kind as to let me take your hair down?"

"What are you talking like that for?"

"Well, you know. I am trying to keep the house going. I want it to last."

"You're crazy. People don't talk like that around here and you never will. Just sing that song. Do you know the rest?"

"You mean you want me to play the radio again?"

"Listen, there's no radio, just sing. Sing that part that used to skip. I don't think I've ever heard it sung right." Her voice had changed. She was sure of what she wanted now, and it was more sincere than that good grammar stuff. I dropped the married bit and just let everything happen. The song had become the fantasy, and if I could sing it well, everything I had hoped for—Ruby and me in a little house with real tea, a real radio, and a real fireplace—would be real.

Do you remember when you loved me
before the world took you away?
Well if you do, then forgive me
and make the world, make it go away.

"Don't leave me, Ruby," I said when I was all done. I think I meant it; it sounded real good, even if it was grown-up.

"What do you mean?"

"I don't know, I guess I just want to take your hair down and see what it looks like when it's loose. Can I do that?

"Yes," she said, and she made the kitten a little bed with the corner of the blanket that hung down on the floor and placed the kitten gently. She turned her back to me and stared out the window. "Go ahead, take it down." I blew on my fingers to warm them up and she just stared at the tree's shadow, cast from her subtle smile. I took out the beaded multi-colored tie that had been wrapped around a bunch of times. I untwisted it slowly, slower than I had drawn the hair from Kerry's hand. Even in the dulled smoky-amber light the thread was brilliant and as I untwisted it the brightness made me melancholy because I was messing it up by thinking about how it would all be over before anything had really begun. After I had unwound the tie, her hair still maintained its thick braid. It was the texture of a newly sprouted Bass leaf. If I would have had my eyes closed and someone asked me what it was, that would have been my answer. "Bass leaf." Those big, deep green oblong moons that hung from trees. Even through the cigar smoke that still burned from Kerry's fire was the perfume of cream rinse. It smelled like a songbird call, if that makes any sense at all—a songbird calling from the thick grasses of a field beyond Cannon Mine, near Smoky Lake, but late at night when birds are supposed to be sleeping. I unraveled the braid and fanned her hair out across her entire back until her whole body seemed to be a mass of bird-calling, singing to me through the near-darkness. I ran my fingers through it, running across the field to find the bird, stumbling over and over until I was so full of melancholy that I stretched out my arms and squeezed all of the hair and Ruby-body that I could and stared out the window with her.

"I'm making a spook house, will you come?"

"You're crazy," she said laughing a little. "I like the way your shirt feels."

"Am I hurting you?"

"You're crazy," she whispered and I sang to her in our real house-within-a-house over Clint and Kerry's call asking me if I had gotten some, and the imitation wife love moans of Roberta and Rachel.

Now I'm sorry if I hurt you,
let me make it up to you day by day.
And if you will please forgive me
and make the world, make it go away.

The kitten gently purred.

* * *

The Aimes' house was in the middle of town and had a big barn in the backyard where they had kept a horse for two generations. This is where I met Sheila and kissed someone like I meant it for the first time in my life. I kissed her for all the girls I never had the chance to. She cornered me in the barn when I was collecting hay for my spook house sign. She put her hands on my chest. "Nice shirt," she whispered. "I wish we could drive away in one of those cars together." My pockets were overflowing with hay and she stepped closer into the darkness and slid her hands down into each of my pockets and fingered the hay. "What is this stuff?" she smiled. Our noses were almost touching.

"It's for my spook house. I am making it with Aunt Ally. We're gonna make a sign with glue and hay and it's gonna stay there forever like a 'monument' is what she said. It's gonna be full of darkness like the barn and…" and I just kept talking and talking until she caught my mouth when it was open and stuck her lips in the way so that I almost bit down on her. I just kept moving my lips like I was talking and it was as easy as that, kissing was. The hay in my pockets started overflowing. I kissed her for Lisa Lantini. I kissed her long—longingly—for Ruby, and little did I know I was already practicing for Euridike. I learned that you could make it spring anytime you wanted by pursing your lips together really tight and then releasing. Release. All the muscles limp and lifting off, expanding like a balloon pushing at the horizon into the Milky Way where the stars attached themselves to the body in little bursts grafting onto the outermost layer of skin.

At the Aimes' I learned about Jesus at the dinner table and he was thanked for providing them with their fridge full of food and wallets full of money. They really had Grampa Duke to thank because David, Sheila's dad, had "ripped off" Grampa is what Mother used to say. The Aimes patted my head a lot and said I was a good kid and that Jesus loved me. I smiled and that shut them up. If I wanted anyone to love me, it would be someone I could see right in front of me.

"Have hope," David said, "He loves you." That was that.

"I'm making a spook house with Aunt Ally," I told him.

"What happened to your lips?" he questioned, half-assed. I touched them and they were all puffy.

"Nothing."

"What were you talking about? A spook house? What the hell kind of demon work is that!"

"There's no demons there, just dog hair, mayonnaise, and a rabbit fur and stuff, but you won't know it in that house because everything is dark."

"Demons," he kept saying. "Your family is full of them."

"But you can't see anything in there," I pressed him.

"Well, there'll be demons in there." Then he just watched TV and told us to go play and we did like the heathens we were, kissing, fighting, swearing, and pissing in old 7 Up bottles and making Bobby Flannigan drink it.

My houses outside my house opened me up to systems of family I might never have experienced had Mother not been a barmaid. There were the Vogels and all their blond kids that smoked when they were coming out of the womb; the Nordics, whose kids spent the days with chainsaws in their hands swinging from trees in the forest; the Timbrooks, making music out of what they could; the Ayers; the Big Eagles; and all of them taught me things that conflicted. All that conflict works out over time and the creases get smoothed out, but you can still see where they were. I was still in a state of residual melancholy from Wauchula and over-inundation of pathetic rock ballads that became part of my 70s reality. I was kissing Sheila on the one hand, and on the other beating up high school girls while Aunts Molly and Ally looked on, warning them that if they tried to move they would personally beat their asses. I was doing everything except acting like a first grader. I had gotten frustrated at school because I was in the B reading group when I belonged in the A group, but the teacher was punishing me because I missed too much school. It was really because I belonged with the other poor kids. It had nothing to do with how good you could read and I knew it so I bit my lip, played tough, and hung with Molly and Ally, smoking cigarettes, listening to rock and roll, and longing for something different that had to do with staring out the window with Ruby. I "wasn't gonna find shit in this sorry ass town" is what Molly told me. "Forget it," she said, "You can't have a life in this town. People rip you off, stab you in the back, and leave you for the fucking dogs."

"Really?" I said.

"Yeah. Mom and Duke said we're leaving sometime soon. Gonna start a new life away from this sorry ass dead mining town full of hicks."

"Gramma and Grampa are leaving?

"Well, maybe. That's what they say. They said they want to get it all off their shoulders."

"Really?" I asked Ally.

"Yep," she said, letting Molly do all the talking like usual.

"I want to go too," I said. "This town isn't shit. I can't find any friends in my neighborhood. Everybody fucking left, and kissing Sheila isn't getting me anywhere except wanting Ruby," I said assuming the tone and stature of Molly.

"Holy Shit! What are you doing kissing and swearing? Mellow out! Kate's gonna beat your ass!"

"No way!" I said, really pissed off now, "She's never even around."

"Yeah, getting shit-faced after work and falling on her face," Molly said with a cynical giggle. I didn't know that part. All the babysitters began to make sense. It took a lot of time and energy to be "shit-faced." So much energy that eventually Mother just collapsed dead-drunk and the ambulance Ally and I would hear the night after our spook house opened and closed was on its way to pick her up and drive her straight out of town to Marquette, Michigan where she spent a month crying and "drying out" is what Gramma would later say. And I figured Mother had become a wet sponge soaked with tears and couldn't absorb anything else.

* * *

A couple days after the Indian house and the Aimes, Aunt Ally and I put up the sign by making a mixture of glue and hay in an ice cream pail, then dipping our cupped hands in and smacking the mix onto the side of the shed one splat at a time. When we were all done it read "Chad's Spook House" and would stay there through two tornadoes, 30 snowstorms and 325 rains until the house was torn down in the 80s. We were ready to pull everything out of the fridge and set it all up. We put the speaker out the window blasting Blue Oyster Cult's *Don't Fear the Reaper*. Ally brought a flashlight into the shed and I followed her with a bunch of old sheets and clothespins. We hung the sheets from the ceiling to make a little maze for people to feel their way through. We gathered all the tables we could from the house in order to set our monkey brains, human intestines, brains, veins, and werewolf shit on. Within hours our darkness was complete. Ally sat a chair outside and put a coffee can next to it with a sign that read "Spook House. 25 cents."

"Well, you want to try it out?" she asked.

"But I know what everything is."

"You just have to forget about everything that happened before and start fresh. Then it will be really scary. You'll see."

So I tried to forget everything we had done. Not only that, I tried to forget all experiences that had come before. I dropped a quarter into the coffee can and it pinged off the bottom. I drew back the insulated blanket hung over the doorway and walked back into a darkness I had descended from. I held my hands out to the sides feeling the sheets for direction until my feet kicked a table. I searched the table until I felt a container. I dipped my hands into a hot liquid foam: Werewolf froth! Yes. There was one near for sure, and I hoped to hell he would jump me. Scar me. I turned left and felt my way to another table, much lower. I had to stoop down. This was mostly thick with smooth balls and pieces of what felt like bone and fine hair. It was the crushed head of a stillborn baby. I knew it! That baby shouldn't have been born into this shit anyway. There was a pounding coming from the walls, as if I was trapped inside the heart of a goblin. I baby-stepped forward and to the left. I ran into a table that was eye level and had to reach up and over an old aluminum bucket. It was gritty and mud-like with pockets of cool liquid and nodules of velvet. It was some bitches brew and I decided to eat it, take in all the evil I could. I lifted the bucket with both hands and tilted my head back. The pounding at the wall was louder and matched the sound of my throat as it flexed to swallow the different textures overflowing from my mouth and drizzling down my cheeks. I swallowed as much as I could and ripped down one of the sheets to take a short cut. Pound. Pound. I kicked something else and felt for a table that wasn't there. I got on my knees and felt the ground. There was a little circle of twigs. I felt toward the center and found a bird's song singing into the darkness and I couldn't forget anything anymore. I realized my hands were full of goose liver and shaving cream and that I had drank pig's blood mixed with sand and cottage cheese. I started tearing down all the sheets. I realized that maturity meant you would be forever alone in your head, so I tried to fight it—tried to fight the demons.

"Ruby! Ruby!" I yearned. Ally burst in laughing, pointing a flashlight at her face.

"It worked, didn't it!"

My chest expanded and I held my breath. Exhaled slowly. I regained my composure.

"No," I said flatly.

"What's the matter? How come you wrecked all this stuff? Whose gonna come now?"

"No one," I said, uninterested, and went back into the house. A cat crossed my path. I drew the shades and put my silk collar to my lips. I slept. I even slept through the sound of the ambulance, but the light of the siren pricked permanently into my skin and I sang its song in short anxious breaths.

But after a while,
you're lookin' the other way
It's those restless hearts
that never mend.

* * *

I drove to Marquette with Gramma to pick Mother up at the treatment center. When Mother saw me she held me in her arms.

"Say the things you used to say," she whispered.

And then we moved.

Further Down Lincoln Street.
Stambaugh, Michigan

So this ain't the end,
I saw you again today.
Had to turn my heart away
smile like the sun,
kisses for everyone
and tales.
It never fails.
from "Barracuda"
– Heart

The house was mustard yellow, and the wood smelled of it. From the front porch I could look up the hill and see the Lincoln Street house on top where we used to live, the house where I dreamed I put Lisa Lantini on the back of my big wheel and we coasted down until we stopped about right here in front of the stinking mustard house that I would live in.

I was spending most of my weekends at The Roller Rink in Caspian where I regularly won candy bars during the pee-wee speed skate. It was the perfect opportunity to practice flying and close my eyes while getting lost in a music I wasn't accustomed to, the BeeGees and Disco. The music was good for flying because it was full of heavy string orchestras and regular beats. It made everything fold into each other and told simple stories of people surviving and getting the person of their dreams. The mirror ball in the center of the rink threw stars and lights that rocketed off my polyester clothing and I was a solar system on wheels racing around a galaxy I had created every weekend night, while Mother's world was still revolving around not being alone, and trying to keep her mind of off drugs and drinking—

Back at home the Man-Worth-Mentioning had returned from college and was coming over a little more often and the sound of a mantis rubbing its legs together behind the bedroom door was back again. This time I wasn't as worried about Mother as I was The-Man-Worth-Mentioning. When Mother was riding him, full and heaving, he was poised to suffer the same fate as Grampa Boyd had recently encountered—death by drowning in two inches of water after being thrown from a car wreck as he lay unconscious in a puddle contemplating, but not doing. Just simply passive and noetic with his head placed silently in dream fluid, red and emergency flavored—

I was taking diggers at The Roller Rink and "Staying Alive" for hours during the Jerry Lewis Skate-A-Thon. I had to skate 30 hours without stopping. This coupled with the pledges Mother had gotten in her month of sober bartending at TJT's would get me the Raleigh ten-speed Budzack's Bikeshop had donated. I was dodging boys twice my size during the speed skate because I had a purpose. The trick was to zone in on a mirror ball reflection on the rink floor and just skate your ass off trying to catch it—

Mother had been out of treatment a couple of months when she received the notice about Boyd. I met Grampa Boyd twice and was named after him, at least my middle and last name. That's all I can say about that. There was no father's name on my birth certificate because Mother couldn't figure out if it was the short and stocky biker turned preacher, Dale, or the one night fling with the tall and slender photographer/global playboy, Earl. She settled for Alan Faries, but couldn't resist "Chad" as a first name since it was really Chad Everett, the new apostle of drama TV, who kept her alive while she was in labor at the hospital. He was a real life saint healing with his sexual eyes and the orbic flex of his mouth. Boyd had a build like Chad. Both Chads: a little too slender, but fit. In a couple of years it would be obvious who my real father was, but no one really cared about seeking him out. There was always The-Man-Worth-Mentioning who occupied his place.

Molly and Ally skated out into the circle and gave me half-filled cups of Mr. Pibb so I wouldn't sleep. After a while I just closed my eyes and had Molly and Ally pull me while I slept on my feet. They pulled and pulled until my body went completely limp and I collapsed in the center of the floor and sneaked a sleep while the masses of people skated around me at the perimeter.

"Get your ass up! You gotta get that fucking ten-speed you little fucker!" Molly was shaking me, "Your Mom's gonna beat our asses if she thinks she wasted all that time and money getting all those pledges. 100 bucks of it was her money she got from her dad getting killed! Come on, just a couple of more hours!" Mom and Aunt Hope—Boyd's daughters—and their half-brother Tim who lived down in Texas, had apparently each received a couple of thousand dollars.

After 30 hours, a reporter came and took my picture. In a Texas newspaper there was a picture of a car accident and a photo of Grampa Boyd. In the Iron River *Reporter* there was a picture of me with my eyes closed, resting my chin on the seat of a ten-speed while I held a certificate that said I had raised $500 and skated 30 hours. Small spots of light were all over me. I won the ten-speed, but never received it. It went up in flames with the rink the night after the skate-a-thon. Mother bought me a record player and a new girlfriend as consolation.

* * *

Mother didn't like being alone anymore, especially in her newfound sobriety which would last a couple of months. She needed a sounding board so took in a roommate, Linda from Alcoholics Anonymous, who had a daughter a couple of years younger than me. Shelly was her name, and her mother let her swear all the time. The easiest way for our mothers to take care of us was by letting us live a pseudo-adult existence so that we were responsible for ourselves. Shelly and I sat around listening to music and swearing about friends that we didn't have while we ate burnt macaroni and cheese that we cooked over the gas stove. We roasted hot dogs over the flames and chopped them up with a rusty butter knife.

I heard Mother telling stories about the Man-Worth-Mentioning—how he visited her in treatment and how she was thinking she might really try something with him—because Mother's new habit was drinking coffee 24 hours a day and she never stopped talking. She said he had a nice dick and that she saw it in the woods because that was where he brought her to screw since they only had two visiting hours and he was a student so he was poor and didn't have money for a hotel room. He drove up there in a 1968 white Thunderbird that got five miles to the gallon with white leather seats that gave light to all his brown earth tones. He had a bottle of cheap wine and a dime bag of weed. She went on and on and on and I knew where I had gotten the endurance to finish the skate-a-thon:

"I mean, can you believe it? I'm in fucking treatment and he shows up with booze, pot, and a hard-on telling me that I'm a naturally spiritual woman and he thinks he loves me. Three hours earlier I had been in a group session getting railed for being addicted to sex, on top of drugs, and that I was a no-good parent being raised by my child. I was fucking crying so bad my eyes were swollen like the bellies of these dead fish I won at the fair and forgot to feed. I couldn't even take care of fish. Fucking goldfish. Fucking Eddy. Damn summer heat up here. I left those fish on the windowsill and at the end of the day they were almost boiling. All I could see was the scales peeling off their white bellies that poked out of the grayish murk that was their water. There was no more gold left in them. And there was no more gold in my eyes anymore either. So I just kept saying 'yes' to everything those counselors were dishing out, 'yes I'm a bad mother, I'm an alcoholic, a whore, manipulative, selfish,' and so on. And after all my admissions to being the devil's personal bitch, my fellow addicts in the circle started hugging me and saying 'We love you Kate, keep coming back.' And the counselors, after getting me to admit all those things about myself said that I really wasn't those things—that was the booze and such. Then I was so fucking confused I cried more and then my eyes were like bloated bellies of road kill—porcupines, skunks, and white rabbits. And the whole time all I wanted to do was hug Chad and be some mother that I had seen on TV. I wanted to make him a nice square sandwich with square slices and not that commodity welfare shit with the big black letters on the white packaging that said 'government issue.' I wanted a bright yellow package with smiling kids on it that said 'Velveeta.' I wanted to be that image because I couldn't figure out on my own what a good mother should be. 'Fake it till you make it' is what they would tell us. So then everybody gets in a circle and hugs. For the first time I think maybe I can at least go without the alcohol. I'm not so sure about smoking pot, but I'm thinking maybe that will come next week. We're there in that circle and I've got both arms braided with someone else's on either side of me and I feel that same warmth from the bodies as I do when I'm making love riding on the top, and blood and friction is so great I feel it all over down there, hot, you know. I am a big girl and can really make some heat! I figure this circle is what I'm after, not coming and coming all the time with my feet stuck into the ass-cheeks of clouds. I want this warmth. I'm all dizzy and it's like, you know, 'ecstasy,' but with a different kind of penetration. It's not like smoke in the lungs or White Russians going down your throat—I'm gonna miss those—it's more like a ray of sun shining on your back as you're sitting near a window doing something and the sun is the last thing you're thinking of until its heat seeps into your shoulder and you feel better but you haven't figured out yet that it's the light that's calmed you. It's subtle, you know, you gotta be a little patient. So I'm having all these 'epiphanies' I guess you call them and forget about Greg coming to visit...."

For the first time I had a name for The-Man-Worth-Mentioning.

"I leave group with my fish eyes and head to my room feeling the best and worst I have ever felt. So then I'm napping and have a wild dream that I'm flying, although it's not so incredible in the dream. It's just natural, all that flying. I'm way up over the city, but I must have some eagle-vision or something because I can see the color of people's eyes, and my hearing is perfect too because I hear all this talking. Some of the languages I don't even understand, but one language really comes to me, 'resonates' is what Greg would later say. I understood the language, though I couldn't speak it to you right now. It was a mixture of slogans, song lyrics, scientific texts, and children's stories all mixed together. It said something like 'I think I can, I think I can shake dreams from your hair my pretty child by symbioses through keeping it simple stupid.' You know, it's *The Little Train that Could* with The Doors, AA, and scientific shit I don't even get totally. It doesn't sound or mean much now, but you should have heard it in that dream language! It had some rhythm like a train that made a lot of stops and sped up and down. And get this, I'm looking toward this voice which is coming out from the middle of a park that has old castle buildings on one side, a desert on the other, and then some rivers and oceans and stuff on the backside, and I swear it was Chad, though he's a little older. Then he starts calling me Kate. 'Kate! Kate!' he says, 'You have visitors,' and I'm looking around to see if anyone is flying next to me and there's nobody so I start gliding a little toward Chad to get a closer look to see if I'm really right. I decide at that moment, if it is Chad, I'm gonna grab him in my talons and pick him up and never let him go. When I think this, I have an eagle head because I can see the shadow of the smirk of my face and beak reflecting off the clouds. He's still calling me "Kate" and I want him to stop because I want to be Mom again. I'm almost close enough to make out the exact details of his nose and small ears—because he's a little older you know, about 30— and then he yells 'Kate' one more time and I open my eyes to Mary, my roommate standing over me saying I have a visitor. 'No Shit,' I said, 'I was flying.'

"'Relapse dream,' she said convinced.

"'No, not that kind of flying. This was natural I guess. I turned into an eagle.'

"'Me too, after taking a sheet of acid at a Supertramp concert in Tiger Stadium under the grandstands. I jumped off what I thought to be the top of the grandstands and fell on my face. It must have looked fucking stupid, jumping into the air and diving on your face. Nobody saw it happen, thank God.'

"I go to see the visitor. I don't put makeup on or anything, just a pair of jeans and a tank top with no bra. On my way to the visiting room one of the care workers tells me it's not appropriate attire so I go back and throw a dark t-shirt over it so you can't see my nipples because I didn't want to lose my daily points and be short of cigarette money at the end of the week. Greg's in the waiting room. His hair is all frazzled and you'd swear he was part black with that afro, and that bulge in his brown hip-hugger corduroys. His glasses are tinted purple, but everything else on him is brown. He's smiling really big like he's already stoned and says 'Hello Goddess.' And that's about better than the group telling me that they loved me. We hop into his car and we just sit there for a minute looking out the front windshield. I guess we are both thinking.

I'm thinking that goddesses must be able to fly, and if they are always good, but I knew they were bad sometimes. They had been preaching to us in treatment about finding some 'higher power' and I didn't give it much thought until I found this book called *The Masks of God* which was really hip and covered all times and all places in the whole world, not just Jesus and a bunch of guys—this was about women and stuff. But the thing was, nothing was really clear. I mean I couldn't tell what was good and what was bad. All these ceremonies and sacrifices seemed to cancel themselves out. It was about killing a bad chicken to have good eggs. Then there was this part about earth goddesses, which Greg said I was. Goddesses were almost always mothers and usually had some child at their breast which was supposed to be an enduring force, and the goddess and child together were like one thing, one unit inseparable. Both the mother and child felt the same things through 'symbioses,' you know, both physical and psychic. I always knew I was psychic. A gypsy woman told me that once. So this unit of goddess and child was like a universe trying to be good and bliss, which is like ecstasy, you know, orgasm. So that's the good part. But the bad part, like always, is that not even goddesses can anticipate everything and there are times when the universe doesn't correspond with what is really needed. This happens when that little child starts remembering how we was pushed out of a big black vaginal hole, a pussy, all bloody and screaming. At this point, the child forgets everything—his mother, the universe, the bliss of sucking on mother's boob and then the mother is identified with the kid's destruction. I was reading it under the covers in the middle of the night with a Zippo and started crying because I'm thinking Chad realized this a long time ago and I was never gonna have him back at my breast again so I realize that's why I'm sticking my tit in everybody else's mouth and that's why the counselors are on my ass about being promiscuous and stuff like that. So the goddess is beatitude on the one hand, and terrible destruction on the other. Damn. And if that's not heavy enough, the book starts getting really specific and talking about a Hindu goddess named 'Kali' which looks a little like 'Kate' when it's written out, and she has a long tongue, which licks up the lives and blood of children just like a pig sometimes eats her little piggies. And yet this goddess is not bad, she's often portrayed with a child at her breast. So you've got heaven and hell and what's in between is this fucking treatment center so I start thinking that I am a goddess, good and bad, and I tell Greg to start the car because I'm waiting for something at my breast and bliss. I'm ready to be a cannibal too, if you know what I mean girl! Next thing you know we're at the end of Forestville Road surrounded by woods and a little house where a chainsaw sculptor lives and he's got huge carvings of eagles and bear and old men smoking pipes, and the Madonna. We park and get out. There's a big slam because the door is so heavy and I shudder a little because I'm still sensitive to loud sounds. Reminds me of fists and all that stuff, you know what I mean.

"'Cool,' I say as I stop and really take a good look at the art. Greg takes my hand and pulls a little, but then he stops too and we have another moment where we are just staring together and that's when it felt like we were talking the most. Then he pulls again after a couple minutes and we go off into the wilderness and strip down buck-naked, but it's fun. It's not really just about sex. Things were always a little different with Greg. He had some kind of special wits, though they weren't always there. He's completely naked except for a backpack and I ask him what's in it. He says a good bottle of wine and some weed. Then I question his wits.

"'What the hell is that for?' I say, 'You know where I am? I am in treatment. I could lose everything. I could lose my Chadillac.'

"'Kate, you are with our Mother,' he says.

"'What?'

"'With our Mother. You know, the goddess Mother Earth,' and then he starts quoting the Bible for justification, 'Genesis 1:29. And god said behold, I have given you every plant bearing seed and tree bearing fruit which is upon the face of the whole earth. To you it shall be meat.' It sounded good to me, but I just didn't think it was right. I could tell he wasn't so sure either so he didn't pressure me much after that, but he did take some for himself and rejoiced with Mother Earth. Next thing you know, he's got the open bottle in one hand, a joint in the other, and I'm bent over a tree getting it full throttle. I'm flying again, thinking about Chad, and thinking that Greg's got some downfalls, but he's getting educated and loves Chad so I give in and let myself really go and the ecstasy come, and come if you know what I mean, girl! We get dressed and time has really passed so he speeds me back to the treatment center.

"So I get this idea that I'm a goddess and tell everybody at treatment that

I'm a goddess and that's my spirituality and then they say that won't work because you can't be your own higher power, you need to have a power greater than yourself and then you can be restored to sanity. Well Jesus fucking Christ. I had never thought that hard before about anything, and it was all for nothing. 'But I feel good about myself now,' I said. 'I've got a man who calls me a goddess, I've got these huge life-giving breasts full of bliss, child-bearing hips…what the hell?'

"'Right on Kate!' Johnny W. says, 'I'm with you baby! You're my Higher Power!' The counselors just shake their heads and tell me to keep coming back which means I'm supposed to stick with the program and these twelve steps that tell me I'm powerless and pretty soon things will be revealed. Ain't that a bitch? And here I am, blabbering and strung out on coffee and cigarettes."

The conversation was long and I was taking notes the whole time by assigning stories to various toys as mnemonic devices. The bionic man was the dream. My Charlie McCarthy puppet was Greg. My Legos were the treatment center, and the weeble-wobble people filled in the rest of the gaps. I built the story right in the middle of the bedroom and then asked Shelly if she wanted to really play. "I mean really play," I said emphatically. I stripped Shelly down to her panties and went over to my new Fischer Price record player in the corner. I swung the purple plastic arm around and dug the needle into a 45 of Heart's "Barracuda" and turned it up until the cheap speakers were distorting. "Fuck yeah" I said at six. I floated over to Shelly in my birthday suit, bent her over and jammed to "Barracuda" as I faked adult ecstasy the best I could while gyrating all over her emulating Greg and Mother's story. I reached around to grab her breasts that wouldn't be there for another ten years. I just couldn't fly like Mother. My wings were clipped. I had become The-Boy-Worth-Mentioning in Shelly's private mythology, full of knowledge and lacking sense. That's what ecstasy does to you. I bent her all over the bedroom.

Greg came over and filled Mother full of compliments and weed in the next room. Her complexion flushed and the familiar warmth that drugs brought heaved in her breasts. She forgot she was supposed to be powerless and let the goddess run wild. She poured wine into her mouth and let it run down her chin into her cleavage. It was beatitude and it was devastating. We all dug each other.

And then we moved.

Pittsville and Stevens Point, Wisconsin

Though nothing
will keep us together
we could steal time
just for one day.
We can be heroes
for ever and ever
what d'you say?
from "Heroes"
– David Bowie

Greg was really my dad now, and this is the story of how. Although I would never call him "dad" because his frizzy brown hair that poked the air was too much of a contrast to my spider silk straight hair, he was just as much a good father. He never could manage that "Greg" was just "dad" in a different language. "Dad" in English had too many traditional adages and was loaded down with baggage like a sad traveler you may have passed here or there, hitchhiking, or dragging ass up the stair; a traveler with too many carry-ons perpetually harassed for exceeding the weight limit and retreating into lament. "Greg" was a first class name and traveled lightly off the tip of my tongue. I could say, "this is Greg" to friends and teachers and it sounded sung and he retained his individuality, and I the same. It wasn't bad. There was never an occupying force hijacking Chad. He bought me books. I read in bed, legs spread and relaxing, and I would kick them and fly. And I would take my book and shake that thing until I had wings. I flew right out of bed toward the sun, and no dad could stop me, not even the Greg one.

Greg had just gotten his degree and certification in elementary and special education. Now, with his long hair "hanging out like a dick" is what his father would say, he faced about 15 years of upper Midwest prejudices associated with dope smoking, protesting hippies. Indeed Greg embodied most of their counter-culture anxieties. He had taken a year off of college and traveled out to Colorado where he went to live off the land on a sheep rancher's property and had a brief stint with opium too. He described his vision to Mother as including a bunch of horses and cars promenading down the highway. The cars were jacked up and the horses had foot high metal platform shoes. Greg ran with them down the Rockies and over the plains, through cornfields and woods until he was back in the safety of his parents double-wide home, the only one of its kind in town, right on a huge square of property in Stambaugh, First Street to be exact. The house was delivered on semi flatbeds in two halves that were fit together over a pre-dug basement. Greg would often complain about it, but I loved it for its cleanliness and newness, which was really foreign to me. Mother was always clean, but she didn't mind little messes. She wasn't much different than Gramma. Greg's mother on the other hand didn't really fit him and he didn't really fit her. She was a petite church-going Catholic. Her tablecloths were ironed, as were her rag rugs, faded from weekly washes. She cleaned the kitchen linoleum on her hands and knees with a whole bottle of Mr. Clean, undiluted, and three rolls of paper towels.

I was the closest thing she ever had to a pet. I'm not talking about the kind of pet that I envision, something made for petting and companionship. I'm talking about a dirty, shedding, shitting and pissing beast. She would always feed me good, though. Microwaved stuff or cake mixes, this or that. But I'm not sure she ever chopped up a vegetable or kneaded dough. I liked that nuclear food. To me it represented affluence. Not just anybody could afford such waste.

One night after she fed and watered me I pissed all over her couch. I always had a problem with that and it never ceased to embarrass me. People think of you differently after they find that stuff out. It's like you're an accused felon or maybe worse, like a kleptomaniac or schizophrenic, or any other number of long complicated words that I learned at too young of an age by watching public TV whenever I could. Greg and his family were just as safe and familiar to me as Mother's, though maybe this isn't saying much.

* * *

The first time Greg fell in love with me is a perfectly framed print, not to be confused with the original, which is lost. It was dusk at Planet's Resort, Greg's father's small recreational area on Sunset Lake. He and Mother were on one of their first dates. There was an elevated porch jutting off the front of one of the three A-frames on the property. They were on it, Mother folded into Greg's arms. I was in the purple evening grass with a plastic lawn mower filled with multi-colored balls that would pop up as the wheels turned. All I could hear was the popping, and the scene was full of it. It disturbed everything—the fish, the deer in the woods, the night crawlers, bees, gray squirrels, martins, neighbors, the leaves sturdy on the trees in a hearty Upper Michigan summer. But nothing ran or fell. Instead they all watched. And in the watching, light was receding and purpling as time continued to progress no matter how hard love tried to stop it. I could have stopped it with my invisible ring, but I didn't. It would not have been true and would have violated the power of the ring. Right before the total darkness, when being fuses with shadow, Greg looked at me and I looked back into him past Mother. Nothing scattered, just faded into the darkness and the crisp evening air lurching up from the shore had lost its edge. There was always something sentimental hovering on a current of dark lake air.

* * *

Mother made the decision to try a neo-responsible life and we hopped over the border and gave Wisconsin a try since distance had made it possible for Greg to do phone interviews and hide his beehive beard and long hair. And

Mother had convinced Greg that her Goddess life was one not polluted with alcohol and he agreed to lay off pushing wine on her, and he did—just like that and stuck with it forever, even when she "fell off the wagon." It took me a while to figure out the wagon was not the Radio Flyer Mother and I stole in my Christmas tale. And it wasn't a Pontiac either.

Northern Wisconsin was no different than Upper Michigan. In fact, Yoopers felt closer ties with Wisconsin than we did with Lower Michigan. We shared a natural and significant border with Wisconsin, the Brule River, named after the first European to visit the region. Brule was just a trapper, not a colonist. He hung out with the Natives and even took one as his wife. Lower Michigan only had the artificial bridge that forced us together. The U.P. was Michigan's recompense for ceding Toledo to Ohio. Had it not been for this the Yoopers could have chosen their own path, perhaps breaking with a state system altogether and chose a kingdom.

* * *

Greg was a special education teacher and landed his first job in Pittsville, Wisconsin. Population 3,254. For the first leg of the Wisconsin journey we lived outside Pittsville in the country for about a month and a half until our apartment in Stevens Point was ready. It was summer. Greg was gone most days preparing his classroom and Mother was alone all day which she could never really handle so Aunt Ally came down for a while to take a break from smoking dope and screwing. She wanted to see what it was like to just be 15.

Mother took a job as a waitress in Stevens Point at an old boxcar that had been converted to a restaurant. It was perfect for her nomadic style because it feigned travel and movement yet remained put and secure. So during the days when I wasn't reading rhymes, Ally and I would run around the woods adjacent to our house. No matter how adult she tried to be, she always had the need to play, be it with toys or sexual organs.

There were no old mines in Pittsville, just forests and fields. The ground was flatter and easier to navigate. Ally and I missed the disorientation of the hills of Iron County and would stop periodically to spin each other around a while until we couldn't walk straight. We were searching for something, a more fitting house. In our dizziness we stumbled upon a hunting shack in the center of the forest. It was locked, but we hadn't much sense about ownership. Ally picked up a big stick and smashed one of the windows. I climbed in and opened the door.

The shack was no bigger than a large closet. There was a bunk bed and a small dining set with Lucy chairs. A couple of old cupboards hung on the wall where the studs were exposed. Just like that, the house was ours. It was always just a matter of stepping over the threshold and assuming a stance. Then the house was yours, no matter what. The bunk bed was to the left of the inside of the door. It made sense to lie in that bed and stake the territory. I climbed to the top and Ally took the bottom.

We lay there for a while on our backs using our hands as pillows. I was staring at the plywood ceiling and Ally must have been staring at the springs under my bed. We were content with looking into nothing for a while. I guess that is what you do when you are more concerned about the other senses. I was interested in the smell of mildew and pine needles, Ally's fabric softener. I was interested in the hay poking through the mattress onto the small of my back which kept me awake so I could think more and more about my future in this state—about my hair getting blonder, and being in numbered grades—having real name-brand shoes maybe someday soon.

"Hey Ally," I said, "Draw any pictures lately?"

"I'm not drawing so much anymore, I am painting."

"Wow, cool. What are you painting?"

"Just pictures that I like."

"You mean things that you see in your head, you know, things you remember?"

"No, not really. I just collect pictures from books, usually real things, and turn them back into their original colors."

"What's original?" I asked.

"Like when you break something down," she said.

"I don't get it, you mean like when things are explained in books?" She didn't get it either.

"I don't know, everything in those pictures has a story of its own independently of the picture. And that story includes stuff about being born, moving, and all of that. So, when I paint a picture, I do it one object at a time so I can feel what it must have been like to create that."

"Don't you ever see squiggly lines, or things that don't make sense just floating around in your head? Don't you ever want to paint those?"

"Not really. I don't want to have to think too much. I feel safer making someone else's vision. No one can blame me if they don't like how the picture was set up. I guess I'm more interested in putting things back together than I am making it new." I wasn't sure about this. I think I liked putting things back together, like for instance coloring Spider-Man, but doing it wrong on purpose in order to make something that everybody was familiar with new.

"Why don't we rearrange this shack?" I suggested, and we did, breaking everything we could for no real reason other than maybe we wanted to be something else in another picture, but we didn't know what.

A couple of days later Aunt Molly showed up with Martin and Bud Shaver, Grampa Duke's boys. They said they came to help us move into town, but they came for the Hartley girls for sure. Greg said Mother was crazy for thinking anything different, but nevertheless they helped lift a couple of old recycled sofas we had pulled out of the trash and a bunch of decorative bricks Greg had used to make a cheap desk and bookshelves. Martin found an old metal box in a corner.

"Does this go?" he asked, "What the hell is in here? It's fucking heavy!"

"Don't open it! I mean it! Just put it on the front seat," Mother yelled nervously.

"O.K., O.K., O.K.," he echoed.

We were off to Stevens Point, a college town in North Central Wisconsin where things started looking a little different, and it didn't have much to do with geography.

* * *

Straight and then two lefts was the path to school. I see myself passing objects I found interesting but I can't seem to make them out. There were some nuns and a fire truck. A spotted dog. I took the walk alone. There were more people around, and fast food shops—shops that never made it to Iron River.

And there were girls, and magical playgrounds on each corner of the school that had artificial turf that was softer than moss. A shiny chain link fence encircled the whole thing too, which kept us away from the road.

My first grade teacher checked my reading level and put me in the top group and I dug her right away. There was fresh paint on the walls and the hallways were carpeted. Once a week we saw films that taught us how to get on the busses properly and how to shoot pool using geometry. The library was two stories and I could read all the Dr. Seuss and Berenstain Bears books I wanted. I reproduced these stories like Ally did paintings. Take for instance Roberta:

Roberta lived in a little house at the end of Kablunker Street and she had rabbitty feet. She would hop and hop and hop, sometimes she would not stop and once hopped her head right off! The superty-duperty doctors were able to put it back on, but one of her eyes was gone! They looked and looked, looked under trees right at the roots, under her knees and under her boots. No eye anywhere so they put a patch there. It was a black hole and little did anybody know that it was better than an eye—for instance it would never cry! It was so strong that it sucked in heavy thoughts and happy dreams and everything in between! Stars were in her head. She sucked them out of the sky while she lay in bed. And do you know why? Just to replace the twinkle that used to be in her eye and the sudden loss of friendly heat on Kablunker Street. In the end I became the only friend and no longer was she cold because in my arms I did hold her starry head, smoothed her comet hair, and wished I could just stick my lake eye there to lessen my own pain and give her ecstasy again.

Give me more than one caress. Satisfy this hungriness.

* * *

Greg started to make connections with people that were different than anyone I had met before. They were organized and had a strict lifestyle that included limited television, low meat diets, liberal talk radio, non-representational art works, and regular attendance at public events. I'm not talking about pig-roasts, street dances, or Friday night fish fries—I'm talking about lectures by César Chávez at the university, book signings by Garrison Keillor, and low-fat dinners at The Coffee Trader. Granola and yogurt every morning instead of milk-gravy and biscuits. Mother even started to cook whole foods and really tried hard to fit the mold of Midwest-college-town-U.S.A. She even started to go to A.A. meetings but was still doing the "marijuana maintenance program." She always managed to meet the others on the marijuana maintenance program at the meetings. It usually took about a week of subtle hints and prying before you were sure they were on the same level as you. Most people in the program proclaimed a drug is a drug is a drug, but Mother had Greg's "Genesis 1:29" on her mind (that thing about every herb bearing seed and how it was supposed to be meat for us or something like that), and her major in life was rationalizing and justification.

Actually the pot was about the only unifying factor between Greg's new connections and the old crowd of Iron River. Everybody, except for Greg's mother, smoked dope in the 70s. I guess she was the only conservative person I knew. Even though Greg's friends were educated, they were all neo-Marxists, even if they didn't know it, and readily accepted the working class. To them it was romantic to wield a hammer and dig ditches. They even volunteered to do this stuff on the weekends in addition to their intellectual activity. They would put on coveralls and help break ground for the new health food co-op or volunteer to frame a house for the influx of Hmong people who were arriving in Stevens Point due to an intelligence deal that had been negotiated after Vietnam. I guess Nam was another unifying factor. Greg's educated friends had been in college during the draft and protested the war. The poor working class from the U.P. on the other hand had fought the war. But the liberals had sympathy for the working class victims of the war—both the American soldiers and the Hmong people—so they did what they could sharing joints and breaking ground to help them accordingly. For example, when we visited Toivo "the Yooper" and "his old lady" on the weekends in Iron River, Greg was extra understanding and brought a lot of joints so they could really bond. Music helped too. Everyone liked Urijah Heep. One of the albums had a mirror on the front, but nobody ever wanted to look into it.

There was something different about Greg's liberal friends. They paid attention to me. And oddly, some of those male liberal friends paid special attention to Greg, and he would let his wrists go limp and strike poses not unlike all the women who raised me. I even heard Mother say once that she thought he was a fairy and I figured that meant they were going to get married and I would have a proper television family, or at least a public television family and we would be united as the Faries and live in the woods of the U.P.

Those liberals were always trying to show me books and get me interested in stuff, and when they saw I was truly interested they would give me the books to keep. I had books about space, books about Gnomes, and historical texts that I read as fantasy books.... They had me listening to radio shows on National Public Radio instead of plopping me in front of the TV. They included me in their conversations and instead of impressing them with my knowledge of "fuck," "piss," "shit," and other advanced vocabulary, they were interested in my knowledge of astronomy and rock and roll music.

So when Mother brought her boss home from the restaurant who was a working-class veteran who smoked dope, Greg had to be accepting. The guy was dark and hairy and had a cowboy hat with boots to match. Sideburns framed his face. Mother had told him I liked books so he brought me *This is Elvis* to score points. Basically he didn't want anybody to suspect anything, which made Greg and me suspicious anyway.

Mother and Greg always got along better with each other when they were separated but that would take them years to figure out. Greg was into behavior modification and was always trying to reward their good days together by making her dinner or having a romantic bed-time joint. He was always too suspicious though and had good reason to be with the Sideburned-Guy. That old boxcar he owned must have had a wagon attached to it because Mother fell off it one night. Since Greg had kept his promise and refused to be Mother's drinking partner, she needed the Sideburned-Guy.

Greg confronted Mother about the Sideburned-Guy. He was working on dealing with his suspicion so hadn't said anything for a couple of months, but driving home in his 1968 cream Saab he was putting the sentences together in a way that would allow him to communicate respectfully and effectively. When he walked into our lower-level brick duplex that he had chosen because of its proximity to the Stevens Point Health Food Co-op he had planned on saying "I'm really glad you are being responsible and working so that we all have a better life together, but I am concerned that your choice to have late nights after your shift is affecting our relationship in a negative way." It didn't quite come out like this. Instead he said, "Are you screwing your boss?" I was in the living room watching "ZOOM" on public television. "Come on and Zoom Zoom Zoom-a-Zoom," the kids were saying as they jumped around on geometrical figures playing non-competitive games. Mother and Greg were in the kitchen and the sound was all over the house again. Mother's voice was like a tree falling. There was a loud crack and then a rush of wind as branches and those leaves were propelled toward the ground before the final "Boom!" that shook the earth and all the stories and memories fled in every direction.

"What the hell are you talking about?" She had been waiting for this. Head-on confrontation had been diluted by Greg's behavior modification, but now he slipped and gave Mother the opportunity she had been looking for. She wanted to "rearrange the shack" like Aunt Ally and I had done back in Pittsville. She too wanted to be in a new picture, but I'm not sure if she even knew it.

"I'm just saying...." Greg tried to say something but Mother didn't give him a chance. It was too late. He wouldn't be able to say a thing for a while.

"Don't say a fucking word. You don't know what I need. You never have. I'm sick of this life and your tree-hugging activism. I don't fit in with your new crowd of liberal intellectuals. I can if I want to, and I don't even need a degree to do it. You don't know shit about making me happy. You can't even handle your wine when you drink with those elites. Last month you came home and pissed the bed. Be a man." She pushed him against the wall. He was small, about 5'9" and 135 lbs. Mother was about 5'5" and pushing 200 lbs. He was just a twig bending from her wrath. I was a leaf in the other room cycloning in a whirlwind. "Come on you fucker, why don't you hit me or something. Come on! Come on!" She grabbed both her breasts and fired them at him before she pushed him into the dining room and they were in clear sight.

"Stop!" he managed to say timidly, "Chad is...."

"Come on you fucker!" The Sideburned-Guy never did get to be part of the conversation. Nothing really mattered anymore except for Mother venting. And she really was. She started panning the room in between her sentences looking for something to throw. Greg and I started panning the room too to see what she was going to throw. We didn't have much, thank god. There was only big furniture and a coffee table. On the coffee table was a metal box that had no significant history. Now she was determined to give it one. In unison we all directed our attention at the box and paused for what seemed at least a minute. This was the contemplative space that reminded me what was unfolding was pure stage-drama. I ran around the perimeter of the room and hid in the kitchen. Greg fell back on his ass, placed his palms on the floor, and coiled up his spine so he could spring out of the scene. But he froze in another contemplative space. "This isn't really happening," I kept telling myself because I had heard someone else say that on *The Young and the Restless*, Mother's favorite soap opera. Her hands opened like a wicked breed of flowers and I thought that if I had a camera I could snap a picture and Ally would be able to paint them perfectly. Mother's face contorted. Everything was silent again and again. She bent from the waist and her breasts were heaving and firing over Greg as she reached for the metal box. She grabbed it and raised it above her head as if she was offering it to the gods before she sacrificed it. For a moment I thought the one benefit of the whole situation was that I would be able to see what the hell was in that box for once. Greg started to mumble "Kate." He got a little louder, and then Mother would inhale deeply as she strained to hold the box over her head. After each breath, Greg got louder and louder. Her breathing picked up and Greg started yelling "Kate! Kate! Kate!" in circular breaths.

"I'm gonna fucking kill you," she said with tight lips that exposed her teeth, "You fucking miserable limp dick!"

"Kate, I'm gonna call the police!"

"You won't be able to."

And suddenly in my contemplative space I remembered reading the story of Pandora who was made out of clay by Hephestus. She was very beautiful. All the gods and goddesses gave her a gift and Athene, the goddess of wisdom, gave her life. Hermes did not give her a very good gift. He gave her too much curiosity. She went to earth, got married, and received a beautiful box from Hephestus. Everyone told her she better never open that box. But she was curious of course. Mother was about to unleash on the world like Pandora. But there was a good thing in that box too—hope, the idea that everything would get better. That wasn't enough for me. It wasn't worth it and since the box was still closed up, I didn't have any hope that things would get better. I left the house and ran across the street to Roberta who had the rabbitty feet. She swung on her swing.

"Roberta, you have to help me! Mother is gonna kill Greg and unleash a bunch of bad things on the world!" I looked into her good eye and could see the stars she had sucked out of the sky.

"Don't be afraid," she said, "The mess your mother has made will be better soon, and you'll dance to a different tune. Let the song of the tree be; it wants to grow, you know! Gather your books and find your hat because you'll have to leave here and that's that! Now come here so I can hold you one last time and for a change I'll pretend you're mine."

She held me in her girly arms and filled me full of her patched-eye charms. She swam in my lake eyes and I rode on the tails of her comet hair high. My fear she did soothe.

And then we moved.

15

The Last Time at 711 Roosevelt Street. Stambaugh, Michigan

I could'a swore her hair was made of rayon,
she wore a Milton-Bradley crayon
but she was something I could lay on.
Can't remember what became of me,
Carolina hard-core ecstasy.
from "Carolina Hard-core Ecstasy"
– *Frank Zappa*

LittleMan, Ragsy, and I lay panting on top of a 100-foot high ore hill at Cannon Mine with our exhausted bikes at our sides. "I'm glad you're back, man," LittleMan gasped as he lay there doing nuthing.

"Me too." His dog Ragsy tongued my ear and I fluffed his wiry hair. "That was a hell of a hill we made it up. I feel like I really did something, know what I mean?" It was good to feel like I finally did something because again Mother and I had failed. At least that's how she saw it. We were back at 711 Roosevelt, but this time the house was empty. Gramma and Grampa Duke had taken Molly and Ally with them down to Texas where Grampa Duke was working as a right-of-way agent for the gas company. Greg stayed in Wisconsin after Mother left him. He was alive, but not well. He missed me. Pretty simple. He drove himself crazy trying to think how he could show how much he loved me from another state. The solution came to him one night while listening to Mott the Hoople. After hearing "All the Young Dudes" two things came to his mind: firstly, this song would be played at his funeral; and secondly, that while he was indeed alive he could be my father by simply calling it into being. He called all his family and told them that he had adopted me as his son.

"What?" his mother said. "Is it all legal?"

"No, it doesn't have to be." He told her that it was a spiritual adoption, and that counted more than anything. He wasn't shitting. Even though Greg was prone to forgetting things, even if he wrote them down on his daily lists he kept folded up in his back pocket with his brown comb, he never forgot this and stuck to the commitment, just like he had stuck to not being Mother's drinking partner. Nothing really changed for me. I guess he was like my dad, but it was hard to figure out when the models that were presented to me on TV, and what we learned in school about "family values," were so different. He was supposed to play baseball with me. And what about hunting? He never taught me how to shoot or anything like that. And he "kind of acted like a girl" is what LittleMan said. So I must admit that I was always looking for these things in the men Mother continued to screw. But the men she was bringing home got worse and worse. It was summertime and living was easy.

Mom started tending bar at TJT's Nirvana Bar again. One night she brought home a Diablo Lobo—a real biker/TV repairman visiting from Chicago with a patched jacket and all—and he was tossing her all over the house. I guess it was a weird combo of love and hate that brought them both the release they needed. In the morning I made them breakfast. Fried braunschwager and eggs. He was confused. I wanted to see what kind of man he really was—if he was that TV dad sort of a guy under all that denim and hair. Well he fixed our TV and didn't eat the food. But Mother ate it and she smiled and then secretively cried and mounted him after I left the room.

Her real love, though, was Silvio Badamanti. He was a pocked-face Italian from down the road in Caspian. With him Mother danced late into the evening to multitudes of what would become known as classic rock, because she and Silvio made it so. I could never figure out what it was about that guy. Maybe it was the way he rested his hand on her hip with a joint pinched between his fingers and held the neck of a beer bottle with the other. Maybe it was his rhythm and the shifting of weight from leg to leg as he spun her in circles until she fell to the ground and he slid into her like a love letter into a mail slot that you've been watching from a distance for weeks. Just when you've almost given up and the sun is sinking, it slips through the slot in the door and falls onto the carpet, and then it goes into your hands. You bring it to your chest before reading it because this is what you saw in the movies. She really wanted things to work with him. The problem was she never read the letter. It was probably blank, or full of deceit. She wanted a real relationship and he kept acting as if that was what he was gonna give her and then he would go missing for a couple of weeks. Apparently he worked on the boats that sailed around the Great Lakes and up the St. Lawrence Seaway.

* * *

Maybe there is a better way to talk about Silvio. What I need is a tool that fixes tools.

Every time Silvio left, Mother went running to her new best friend, Caroline Friend. If Caroline didn't have that last name I don't think she would have ever been able to forgive Mother for sleeping with her husband, Stan. That's how they met I guess. They worked things out somehow and Caroline started to help us by letting Mother use her car, and lending her ten bucks here and there to get her through the week. They were big dope-smoking partners too. Caroline was a little different because she was able to secure a decent job. She was a special education teacher, just like Greg. And she was hip to me right away. She was always telling me she liked my drawings and asking me about school and stuff. That was cool, because I never got that from Mother too much.

Caroline had a daughter who was a couple of years older than me. Suzanne. We were pretty close, close enough to rip each other's hair out and spit in each other's face. Suzanne had the right shoes, a record player, tons of Barry Gibb albums, and all kinds of pop-star posters. She had long hair and dark skin, kind of like Silvio, and it helped me understand Mother's attraction a little more. Even though I would never tell, her skin was exquisite and I idolized her. She got this skin and hair from somewhere else. It wasn't Italian, Scandinavian, Eastern European, Western European—it wasn't from Stan. It was from someplace exotic I wanted to travel to but didn't know the name. As much as she tried to mask it, she wasn't perfect either and spent many nights wondering about her real dad who she never met, just like me.

I was good for Suzanne because she was old enough to babysit me which contributed to her savings and the opportunity to exercise her dominance over me in front of her pubescent friends that she surrounded herself with to mask her own history which, after all, wasn't that different from mine. I got to thinking that there was no one in Iron River that had a life that would qualify as anything we were watching on TV in the late 70s. I know it had something to do with that ore LittleMan and I were lying in. Take him for instance. He didn't have a Dad around either. He did have two sisters, three brothers, and a mother who never left her couch. She was like a pillow won at a fair and he knew she would do for a mother.

Her mother, LittleMan's gramma, would wander over sometimes because she had jumped out her ground-level room at the Senior Citizen's Center looking for Drummond Island. She'd always go to LittleMan's trying to convince someone to get her to that island somewhere in Lake Michigan where battles were fought and Indians had revolted.

"How are you, Gramma?" LittleMan asked.

"Gooood," she moaned, "I need to go back to Drummond Island." She said it as if she was reciting a sermon to a congregation, but the speed had been turned down. Like a 78 record being played at 33. Her voice was a little shaky and she would emphasize her consonants and trill her R's. The stresses were always on the first syllable in every word. Maybe it was the Finnish influence. That's where they all were from I guess, at least a long time ago. I asked Mother once what nationality I was and she said, "Dutch, Nigger, and Dog," which didn't mean a thing to me. She was full of shit too, but she didn't realize that words were loaded with shrapnel and when you said them out loud fragments would scatter in all directions and hit those you never intended.

For example, LittleMan tossed the word "cunt" around all the time. To him, his younger sisters were both "cunts." I tried it out on Aunt Molly once when she was babysitting me. She was teaching me how to draw and I simply said, "Nice picture, cunt." She socked me in the mouth without even thinking.

I told her I was leaving and packed a paper bag full of clothes and walked out back and climbed the apple tree in the backyard that I breast-fed from when I was a baby. I waited a while and tried to get back in but she locked me out.

"Let me in you cunt! You're gonna be in trouble!" I shouted as I beat on the door window with my fist. "Gramma's gonna whip you; you're not too big yet; you always think you're big and you're not. It doesn't matter if you kiss and stuff. I do it too. Just let me in. I want some food!" I pounded more and more because I got to thinking that even though I was screaming at Molly now, I really wanted her around. I wanted as many people around me as I could, even though I mostly played alone. I didn't want to be alone in that tree anymore so I had come down expecting to open that door and go into my house and be with Molly. But it was locked. And I was still pounding until the fat of my hand broke the window. My knuckles followed the blow and slid along a broken piece that sliced through to the bone and I really started screaming. Then she let me in and later Gramma socked her in the mouth. Only then was I sorry.

I never was in to calling LittleMan's sisters cunts after that. I was pretty respectful. When we played house upstairs and stripped bare-naked I would take them into the closets because they were shy in the light. We would assume the personalities of older family. Today I was with Tracy playing "Marky and Nancy." I was her older brother, Marky, and she was his girlfriend, Nancy. In the closet I put my hand on her hip gently.

"You're not doing it right," she whispered so we wouldn't disturb the pillow on the couch. "We have to kiss longer, that's how they do it. And put some music on." I sneaked out and held my pee-pee in my hands as I ran across the bedroom to get the push button mini-recorder beside Marky's bed. I sneaked back into the closet. In the darkness I fumbled around for a place to set it down. We were standing on top of a bunch of dirty clothes. I ended up sliding my wrist through the handle and wore the recorder like a bracelet.

"Press play, I can't reach it." She pressed play and it was Neil Young.

* * *

When Mother left, I went running to Caroline as Mother had when Silvio left. The Great Northern Bluegrass Festival always took her away. It always took me across the cemetery to Thirteenth Street where Caroline lived. I knew better than to go to LittleMan's because I was never sure about getting food there. There were too many mouths to feed most of the time, unless the boys were gone. All of them, LittleMan, Pete, Marky, and Jimmy, were in and out of what they called "Juvi" which meant that they had "fucked up" as Mother put it and they had to go to a kid's jail. Jimmy was the cockiest of all and I remember him running from the police right past me when I was down the road at the Johnson's place. He jumped over a hedge and made eye contact with me when he was airborne and then landed, skipped once, and ducked into a tent they had set up in their front yard. He looked at me through the mosquito net and put his finger to his lips. I walked home and heard the sirens.

"Jimmy's gonna be the first one to go and it's too bad because he's the sweetest," Mother said. And she was right, maybe not about the sweetness, but he was the first to go. Later he would be running from a siren down a riverbed, and fell on some rocks. And his eyes became agate, tumbled in silt, staring up from the Iron Riverbed. Jimmy Biggins.

And what did Mother know about sweetness? I was sick of running across the cemetery from my own siren and remembering shitty things by association—still am, but without the blame and bite.

Caroline was a little better at being a traditional mother than most of the women in my family. She took good care of me and I loved her for that. She was another mother. And Suzanne, pent up in her palace of pop, was my sister, even if she didn't want to be. She made herself my sister on a Wednesday when we were coming over the crest of a hill about to enter the cemetery with a bright yellow sun squinting our eyes.

* * *

Suzanne and I met LittleMan and his friend Todd who was about twelve, like Suzanne. I looked at their dirty hands and ripped jeans and Suzanne's long hair and white chinos. At that moment I realized I didn't know what world I belonged to.

"What are you doing, Faries?" They were checking my allegiance.

"Nothing. Just walking and stuff."

"What the hell is this?" Todd said disgustedly. I had a flower in my hair that Suzanne had stuck in there when we were goofing around. I pawed at it and knocked it to the ground. Suzanne laughed.

"What are you laughing at?" Todd said wrinkling up his face as if he had been sniffing shit. Todd was mean because his Dad used to beat him publicly in the front yard. He lived on the opposite corner of the cemetery near Lincoln Street, right down the road from where I had lived and rocked on my horse on the front porch. I can remember Todd screaming the usual stuff, "Stop Daddy! No! I'm sorry Daddy!" and all that other stuff you can see on TV meant to turn on the tap and get the tears flowing. Those movies are for people who don't see this stuff every day. Once you get used to it you just have to chuckle:

"There's old man Clug beating Todd again (chuckle)."

"Oh boy! He's really getting a good whippin' now (chuckle)!"

"There's that Biggins boy."

"The one who died in the river running from the police (chuckle)?"

"No, that's the one they call LittleMan. It looks like him and Todd are trying to pin down that young girl and rape her right in front of that church (surprised and chuckle)!"

"Geez, those boys are something else!"

These were the voices that didn't save us. These were the voices that perpetuated our back-hills myths and rotten stories of ignorance and neglect. But it wasn't all like that. There was something else behind it that kept people coming back to Iron River.

"She isn't laughing at nothing guys." I said in my pitiful effort to stop them.

"Is she babysitting you?" Todd asked.

"No, we're just friends."

"Yeah? Are you doing her?"

"No, stop it. We're just friends." And the truth is I never messed around with Suzanne like that. Never even asked, because maybe I thought I belonged more with those other guys. But what was "other" about them? There was no way around it. It was money and education. At least money. I know Suzanne never had to use food stamps. She had Barry Gibb records and I had Kiss.

Now we were all at an intersection. Nelson Field to the West, the church to the south, cemetery to the east, and someone's house to the north.

"Well if you're not doing her, who is?"

"Nobody, she's not like that," I said. But maybe she wanted to be. You see, I stole her journal once. She had a secret love and it wasn't me. It was a different poor kid. He had bad teeth too. But he was a real Yooper kid, and based on her music and room, I had thought she wanted something she could never find in Iron River. Something that represented TV and class. Anyway, she had written that she wanted to kiss this guy on the trellis behind the cemetery. She described everything, how there was a little log near where they dumped all the plastic flowers at the southeast corner. Nobody could see them there, she wrote. She would hold his hands for seven minutes and kiss him on the lips for two and stick her tongue in for one. She even bought a digital pocket watch with a calculator and everything so she could plan it all out. Planning took her mind off of things. Measuring quantitatively was better than feeling bad qualitatively.

"What would she think of ten inches?" Todd said.

"You mean three," I said, and he popped me in the mouth.

"Keep your trap shut fairy boy."

LittleMan looked on uncomfortably but still said reluctantly, "Yeah."

Suzanne said, "Let's go," and grabbed my hand, maybe for the first time ever.

"You're not going nowhere. What do you got under there?" Todd said as he stepped in front of her blocking her southern entry into the graveyard. I was on her right with the church at my side and all the memories of Nelson Field and sledding and running and kissing behind me. And I thought about using my invisible ring, but the truth is, I had fear, and it wouldn't work like that. And I remembered that LittleMan had one of those rings too. But standing there looking into his eyes, I could see he and Todd were far from the Justice League of America. LittleMan was using the ring to instill fear. His up was down. LittleMan, standing there complicit, had become my nemesis, Sinestro.

"Cup her!" Todd said and LittleMan stood next to Todd facing me. He looked me in the eye and then took his right hand and cupped it as if he were getting ready to fill it with water from the tap after a hard day of playing at Cannon Mine. But he didn't bring the cupped hand to his lips. Instead he shoved it between Suzanne's knees and then dragged it quickly up her things and filled his empty cupped hand with Suzanne's "cunt." I had scars on my ring-finger knuckle because of that word. Though I had no power over the situation because of fear, I was still part of the Green Lantern Corps and I was now banishing Todd and LittleMan to the anti-matter universe, a counterpart to the "real" universe made up of "negative matter."

Suzanne screamed for the first time. She stopped holding my hand and ran in place while LittleMan held her. Todd pushed her off balance and they fell against a small hill adjacent to the sidewalk. Suzanne now had a perfect view of the steeple, which would shortly be replaced with Todd's three-inch hairless dick.

"Take this," he grunted as he threaded it easily through the unzipped crotch of his greasy jeans. "LittleMan, get her pants! I'm gonna butter that muffin," he said, along with a whole string of other words and phrases that we had picked up from our homes. It was surprising that it didn't take long for LittleMan to get caught up in the scene, and any reservations he had in the name of me being his friend were gone.

Sinestro was condemned to death for going against The Corps, and he even cheated that by hiding his evil essence in the ring's Central Power Battery and shut it down.

Todd's dick dangling in Suzanne's face placed his ass in LittleMan's face, who was trying to get her pants undone. They were so clumsy. I thought that I could have done it much better. I did think it. And I could have done something to stop the whole scene because I was the only one still standing while those three wrestled on the ground and I watched. I managed to say that it wasn't funny and they should stop. I even pleaded, but I never once tried to physically stop it. LittleMan managed to get her pants undone and stuck his hand inside her polyester panties, damp with sweat and struggle.

While in that battery, LittleMan had made a discovery—he found the ancient weakness of yellow.

It was Todd's turn to look me in the eye, "What are you gonna do you fucking fairy?" he said as I just stood watching.

"Why don't you piss your pants you fucking bed-wetter," I heard LittleMan yell from behind Todd's ass. "She's got peach fuzz!" he chuckled in discovery.

Todd looked back over his shoulder and turned his attention back to

LittleMan, "So Faries is a little piss-pot! You watching this, fairy-boy?" he said while staring at LittleMan's hand fumbling under her panties. "Get a finger in there!"

"I'm trying! It's too tight!" Todd had her shoulders pinned and continued to wave his limp dick in her face trying to wipe her lips with it. LittleMan was lying on her legs.

"She won't stop squirming, I can't get it in. It's too tight!"

"Happiness is a tight pussy!" Todd said. His Dad had a shirt that pictured a strangled cat with its head sticking out of a beer bottle with the same phrase written underneath it. I started thinking about how Suzanne might like Billy, the boy in her journal, to touch her. I closed my eyes and imagined it. It was more of a petting that she was interested in, like someone petting a cat, or a mother stroking the fuzz on a baby's head. She wanted to cradle Billy much the same way, and this is how I had wanted her to cradle me, but she never did. And then I started getting angry thinking that she maybe deserved this. She had actually beaten me much worse, though she hadn't grabbed my pee-pee. She's the reason my hair is still thin to this day. And the damage she had done to my pride was unforgettable, but it was forgivable. I didn't think Todd and LittleMan wanted to really "grease their poles." For one, they only had little sticks, and they were limp for that matter. And I started getting mad too because not once did Suzanne call out my name to help. She really didn't care about me.

It was so easy to get caught up in this war. I was in love with Suzanne, and witnessing the images of her fall from innocence for a couple of minutes was enough to snag me into supporting a battle against a weak enemy that really hadn't done a thing to deserve this. Well, maybe she was hiding some things in her journal, but it didn't have much to do with me. I guess she didn't deserve this. I summoned my superhero strength and forgot fear just long enough to enter the battery, restore the power of the ring, and defeat Sinestro, whose essence would remain trapped and impure in that battery.

"Stop!" I screamed. It didn't make them stop, but it did get the attention of the homeowner whose lawn we were in. He stuck his head out the window and told Todd to put that thing away and get the hell out of his yard.

"What the hell's a matter with you? Church is starting soon!" he yelled.

That was enough to break the boys' concentration and they stopped, laughed, and jumped up while Suzanne remained lying on the grassy hill trying to catch her breath. Laughing and drooling, trying to catch their own breath, they looked down at her on the ground. My breath had been completely depleted from the scream and the struggle to restore power.

Todd nudged Suzanne with the tip of his boot for fear of touching her as if she were an animal that had been hit by a car. "You can get up now bitch. And we're gonna kick your ass after, Faries." Suzanne kept staring at the church, but it didn't seem so significant. It only meant something if you had seen the whole thing played out on television. Then zoom lenses and different perspectives could have been used to make the church seem like it was really something, otherwise it was just a big new wood-sided church where she occasionally prayed to meet Billy in the cemetery and kiss quantitatively. Suzanne might as well have prayed for alcoholic Yoopers, because that is what she ended up getting most of her adult life, and only then did I realize that maybe she had liked me. Still laying on her back, she turned her head in the grass 180 degrees away from the church and saw the flower she had put in my hair, smushed into the ground from Todd's boot. She did not know what to think about that.

"Don't worry, I won't tell," is the first thing she said when she got up.

"I'm sorry," I said, "They didn't mean it." She didn't even ask why I didn't really help. We limped through the cemetery together and rested when we crossed it and came to the corner of the discarded plastic flowers beyond the "dead end" sign. We collapsed right into the dirt and sat Indian legged.

"Don't get your pants any dirtier," I said. "I can fix your hair a little."

"Go ahead." It had gotten all matted. I ran my fingers through it smelling cream rinse and Todd's grease-monkey hands. The sun was low and the yellow was turning a brilliant red.

"What time is it?" I asked. She looked at her watch and punched in some numbers on the calculator.

"It doesn't matter," she said. She punched in some more numbers and then took it off and presented it to me. "Do you want it?"

"No. I don't think I should." The sun fell below the horizon but leftover light was still dripping from us. "Do you think you could hold my hand again and I could walk you home?" I said. "You know, I don't want to bring him up, but LittleMan's got this gramma who is different than him, and she is always talking about some island. She talks about it so much that I think it is a good place. Maybe we could go there sometime. We could go together, to Drummond Island."

"Maybe," she said, "but just take me home now. We've done enough." She didn't hold my hand. "Your mom might be back."

"Maybe it is better if she doesn't come back this time." I didn't want to talk about that so I drew out my vowels really long and tried to sound scary, "I waaaaant to gooooooooo to Drummond IIIIIIIIIIIsland," I said to her again. She laughed.

"Maybe." She stood up and brushed her hand against mine as if she were going to take it, but didn't. "Drummond IIIIIIIsland," she said.

The plastic flowers disappeared into the darkness, as did any hint of yellow and we crested the trellis where locomotives full of steel once ran. Now the tracks were uprooted, but the paths were still obvious. Drummond Island.

And then we moved.

A Trailer Park.
Karnes City, Texas

There were seven Spanish Angels,
at the altar of the Sun.
They were prayin' for the lovers,
in the valley of the gun.
When the battle stopped,
and the smoke cleared,
there was thunder from the throne.
And seven Spanish angels,
took another angel home.
from "Seven Spanish Angels"
–*Willie Nelson*

Abel slapped the flanks of his Huffy bike as he took off down the dirt road to his two-roomed house where his grandmother slept in one corner, and his brother who was screwing my aunt Molly slept in the other. In the other room were parents, cousins, and cockroaches with antennae the length of bridges that could span from Karnes City, Texas all the way back to the U.P., or a sentence transcribed from the ramblings of a big kid who was little once forty miles south of San Antonio, Texas and rode bicycles to death, got beat up by Mexican boys for falling in love with their sisters and made friends so good they'd turn on their only family in order to protect his blond locks, small frame, and his desire to hold on to a friend for once and not have to bring him/her back to life on a page ridden with deceit, anxiety, and some sort of ecstasy that could be anything hidden behind a breath and a gasp for air in a steady aura of panic that never left him after Texas.

Abel was the friend I was gonna keep for sure. He practiced his English with me outside La Hacienda, a neon taco stand set in an empty parking lot across from our bourgeois trailer park where Mother and I lived with Gramma and Grampa, and Molly and Ally. I met Abel at Karnes City Elementary in the principal's office after we had been sent there for causing trouble on the playground. The events weren't connected. He had been slugging someone over by the swing set, and I had made a girl's fingers bleed by grabbing her hand on the merry-go-round and squeezing her cuticles until red appeared under her nails.

"Why y'all making troubles like that? That ain't the proper way to behave on these grounds boys," is what the principal said.

Abel said "*No se*." I thought it was some Southernism so I too said "*No se*." And then we each got whipped three times with a big paddle that had a rubber handle and holes to cut wind resistance. For each paddle we received a pink note that had to be taken home and signed by our parents so they knew why we were whipped. I stuck the pink slips in my Wranglers. Abel shoved his right into the front of his pants.

"Now you boys go on and get. Play good." We strutted back out to the playground, straining every cool step as our ass cheeks burned.

"Hey, what are you gonna do with those slips?" I asked him.

"Nada," he said, "my family can't read them anyway."

"Well my family can."

He grabbed my shoulders, spun me around backwards, stole the slips from my back pocket, and ripped them up.

"Now they can't *Blancito*. I'm gonna go beat that *bendeco* that snitched on me and then *vamo*. Coming? I got a box of cigars in the woods."

"Yeah." I said, and I did. And that was a day in Karnes City, similar to all the others when I was sent home for wearing a "Toad Suck, Arkansas" shirt Gramma got me on her vacation ("Here is a story and I am sticking it to you," she told me, and pulled it down herself right over my head before school); sent home for making fun of the English teacher's grammar; sent home for licking Heidi's ear; sent home for accidentally stabbing my palm with a pencil (I wasn't carrying it right across the classroom like we had been instructed in the safety video). So, I just didn't go to school so much. Mrs. Masuga had taught us most of the stuff we were talking about back in Iron River in second grade so it didn't matter. Abel taught me something though. I learned "brotherly love" for the first time because I never had a male friend like that. I thought LittleMan was it, but he had become Sinestro, Green Lantern's nemesis. I had decided to retire that ring for a while until I understood its powers a little more, but it was still there, seared invisibly to my finger. At night we watched the sun set over Mexico together and then I went home, relieved the yellow had subsided, and listened to his brother bang Aunt Molly and his uncle bang Aunt Ally in their black-lit room where furry posters were stick-pinned to the plastic walls. The ache of the metal trailer frame could be heard around the whole trailer park and the other trailers chimed in until the whole red-necked Karnes City was nervous with excitement and I knew things could only get more intense in a place where I didn't have the power to bring snow, and heat prevailed. In the distance there was the massive deep and breathy blowing of Foghat singing "I Just Want to Make Love to You." It echoed off the metal for months, down the alleys and through the loins of all animals.

* * *

Now that I visualize the "house" I realize that Mother and I slept in some virtual space because I can picture every room of the trailer, yet can't picture a bedroom where we slept. We must have rolled the room out of the closet, or took it out of a box and filled it full of air. Or maybe we just never slept. Mother never slept for sure and I think she had taken to doing speed in order to stay up while she waitressed and tended bar at the Hanging Tree restaurant. She had traded the exoticism of Silvio Badamanti for the southern wits of Junior. He was some sort of a worker and "didn't have no education" because he said he made more money digging ditches and laying pipe than he would sniffing the dirty cracks of books. He said he really liked laying pipe and looked at Mother and sort-of blinked but it was hard to tell because thick glasses distorted his eyes.

Junior was lean with greasy curls that moisturized his sun burnt shoulders. His glasses were as thick as the glass on the bottom of a bottle of St. Pauli Girl beer. He fell in love with Mother one night because he thought she looked like the St. Pauli Girl, plump and ample and goddess-like. But Mother was still simply fat, and a little bloated now too. There was nothing wrong with that. She carried it well. It sounds like a half-assed excuse, but it was true. She draped beautiful fabrics over her body as if her build was fine oak furniture that she was upholstering. I didn't cuddle up to her much anymore, but I still wondered at her body, which was a receptacle of comfort.

Education was everywhere, except in school. School was more of a social commitment. Ally and Molly were going to school, but never quite made it into the building. They spent most of their time getting educated in vans full of dope smoke with tinted glass windows traveling through the dark to stadium shows, the stench of wet animals rising up from the wetlands everywhere. Molly was dating Danny Soliz, Abel's brother, and Ally was dating Danny's cousin, Hector. This is how they learned culture. And a lot of this culture, though separated from the U.P. by some 2,000 miles, wasn't that different, just a little darker and uncircumcised.

Mother was getting educated at the Hanging Tree. She discovered that cockroaches could carry ten times their weight when she observed one carrying a potato chip out of the salad bar. Indeed the tree out back was a big splayed hand and the trunk was a big middle finger to civility. Bodies once dangled from that tree like discarded puppets in the hand of a demonic puppet master. I went for lunch once and looked out back long enough to see the second-hand Charlie McCarthy puppet Molly and Ally took from me swaying in the wind chomping his wooden jaws together as if he was gasping for breath. Someone had removed his monocle so I didn't recognize him at first. I thought that maybe he didn't recognize me either so I walked over to him. The shadows cast Bengal stripes on my body and I moved closer with my head and shoulders hunched. Charlie squinted and focused in on me. His jaw started chomping faster and faster and his eyes got really big and then he just stopped and his eyes closed as if he had been laid to rest in his box.

When Mother had to work at the Hanging Tree and nobody was around the house, Ally was glad to baby-sit so she could rock the trailer with Hector. Hector was a total Mestizo with lead eyelids and a fat bottom lip. He was solid and wide as he was tall. Ally was cool about having Abel over too since he was family, but then again, everybody in Karnes City was, except for us. We were the exotic people that had strange accents. The Mexicans said we sounded like rubber stretched over a guitar body. The whites asked us, "Why y'all talk so fast?" We talked fast because we thought we had a lot to live. And we did. Still do. We are all still alive, even with the years of damaging relationships and drug treatment behind us—years of cheap Wonder Bread full of mold, and sour milk. No one has died, at least none of the women. They have centuries left I am sure. That's why I love them so. All of them. I was willing to fight wars over them and move again and again if I had to, even though I dreamed of a single house I could call home. A whole family would defend a good woman if they had to and there were four in my family who would be defended by at least three families if need be. That is, if those women didn't kill me first.

* * *

Abel and I were crossing streams in the bathroom at the back of the trailer off Gramma and Grampa's bedroom. He pissed a little on the floor between the toilet bowl and sink. I pissed on the seat and wiped it off with my left hand and then shook Abel's hand with my right. That's when we heard the revving of the engine and the Mariachi music that was closer than usual. Hector started shouting in Spanish and I knew he wasn't speaking to Ally. We ran to the other end of the trailer and saw Ally and Hector peeking through the front bay windows. I thought they were wondering at a low-rider driving by with the hydraulics raised high. Abel knew from Hector's language that the "shit was hitting the fan." That's how Mother used to put it. The shit was always hitting the fan. All I had was a visual and I figured it meant that things were gonna get messy.

"Puta Madre! Mire el camino!" Hector said under his breath. Abel and I jumped on the bed to look over their heads. There was an old truck with a speaker on the roof blaring the mariachi music. In the truck-bed was a

200-pound Mexican man in a multi-colored poncho sitting on a recliner with a shotgun in his right hand. He rested the butt on his knee and pointed the barrel at the same sky the Hanging Tree protruded into. He was so big that the 20 relatives scattered in the bed around his feet seemed like miniature disciples. Maybe there were even 40 of them, all in the back of a Ford 4X4. They were motionless as if posing for a portrait. They wanted Hector and Ally to see the picture clearly. There was no need for explanation beyond the Mariachi music. The festivity of the music was undermined by the stoicism of a truck bed full of families—and that was the idea.

"Make them go away, Hector!" Ally whined. She pushed us aside and ran out of the room with Hector tailing her. She was the most pitiful thing and I resented her whining and weakness. What I was drawn to was the awesome spectacle of such a family portrait. I had seen these portraits before in old Time-Life books about the Wild West—scarred men in ponchos and wide women with flat butts and braids as thick as the trunks of hanging trees. Not having any idea as to why they would be in front of Gramma's house added to the absurdity of the scene.

"Don't even tell me what's going on, Abel. I don't want to know," I said smiling.

"I won't," he said, "I do say nobody's gonna get shot. Not *ahora*. So you smile *Blancito*."

"I am."

"What you looking into?" Abel said when I started to stare in a single direction.

"I'm into her," and I pointed to the passenger seat where a Mexican girl about the age of Aunt Ally sat with a nasty scowl and teary eyes. Her braids were hanging out the window and her breasts were pressed to the glass as she stretched as far as she could to get a good look at Ally.

"*Si. Este es la chaquita.*" And she scowled more.

"Wow, who is she?" I asked Abel. "Now you can tell me."

"I think she's my cousin, and your aunt Ally made her really mad somehow. She insulted her," Abel said trying to use the word correctly in English. "It's just a show, you know. A warning. They only hurt somebody later if it happen again."

"How come my family doesn't do that?" I asked.

"*Blancito*, they do!" he said. "I am your family now."

"How is that?"

"Hector and Ally are gonna get married."

"No shit!" I said.

"*Verdad*! Yeah, *mi abuela* told me. She read it in a tortilla she was cooking over the *estufa*."

A door slammed in the distance and seconds later Aunt Ally appeared in the scene outside the bay windows. Pushing the whining and weakness away, she made me proud. "Get the fuck out of here, *Puta*! I whipped your ass once, I'll whip it again." Hector approached her from behind, took off his shirt, threw it over her head, and dragged her back into the house, kicking and screaming.

* * *

So Abel and I lived as brothers for the next six months. And there was a myriad of more babysitters, but these ones spoke Spanish and let us have even more freedom than the Indians in Iron River. We went to see R-rated Mexican movies that advertised X-rated movies beforehand and we all giggled at the boobs and sighs because they were familiar to us and made us think of good times spying and getting educated. We ate sunflower seeds and littered all over the floor. The images on the screen reflected on the faces of mostly children who had come to see Mexicans fight Texans and win. They held on to Mexican catch phrases and recited them and waved their hands in the air. All I saw was bodies of different shades bouncing off of each other. I understood the movies more by watching the reflections on dirty white shirts and lips smeared with sunflower shells. Once in a while kids would look over at my blond head and wonder at the brilliant reflection and its resemblance of a globe, rotating at full speed.

For once, I was the one from a "good family" where everyone worked and went to school. We had a nice trailer in a nice part of town and had almost enough space for all of us. Abel had two families living in two rooms at his house, not to mention the cockroaches that stole half their food while they slept. Never mind any of that filth because it was all magic, just like Abel's

Gramma's tortillas. And they had a whole other language. I loved to be dipped in it, wet with rolling r's and Latin vowels. I didn't have to speak, all I had to do was smile. I had wished that Mother had found a Mexican. I am sure she did find one for a night, but why she settled with someone even whiter than us, I would never know. Mom even had it in her to take Junior away from this place. Actually Ally and Molly had it in them too to rescue their Mexican boyfriends from Karnes City and take them up north. I just didn't get it because I would have rather stayed and gotten educated real good from movie previews and family feuds, from watching cockroaches carry ten times their weight and learning the steps to Mariachi toward my own Mexican sweetheart.

Regardless of my desire to give up the cold and sacrifice a white Christmas for a new family and education, my family was itching for another move. Gramma and Grampa Duke were the first ones to leave. They were hardly around anyway since Grampa was traveling a lot trying to convince people to let the pipeline travel through their land. He was getting tired, and it wasn't physical.

He was relocated again and they left us the old trailer and took off for a new one. With Grampa gone I had no one to take me out of the city into the country where I could run down the center line behind the Mercury Grand Marquis screaming "How fast am I going?" while Grampa gently leaned out the window and yelled back to me, "Keep going, you're gonna hit 20!"

I wanted to stay. I saw Brahma bulls and barking pigs, horned toads and water moccasin snakes. I saw shotguns and low-riders, and sunshine that melted everyone's stories into one massive plastic gem. I saw enough to pry me away from any mythic magnetism the iron of Upper Michigan had.

* * *

Abel and I were smoking cigars next to the jungle gym. We were bruised and dirty from playing hard and making a moped out of lawnmower engines. Meanwhile less significant things were going on: Jimmy Carter was president now; The Shah of Iran was flown to San Antonio and it was all over the local news. Everytime I saw a limo I thought it might be him. I didn't know if he was good or bad, but he had a turban and a big beard and looked important. I also knew the long rides that Abel and I took with Hector and Ally on babysitting nights brought us across the border into Mexico where we would put things into the trunk that shifted around even when the roads were smooth. And I knew I wasn't afraid of attaching an engine to a bicycle and trying to fly.

Greg—alive and longing for a return after Pandora's box had given him hope—had wired the money for an orange huffy at Christmas. By summer it was a synthesis of abandoned parts that littered the alleys of Karnes City. Abel, Jose, Jesus, and I stole a slide from the neighbor's swing set and kicked over their birdbath while fleeing just for good measure. There were mean reflections in the grackles' stares. Mother was packing at home while Junior was going up her shirt and pressing his whiskers into the side of her neck as he looked for her ear with his tongue because he couldn't see shit. Abel and I stacked five tires in the outback. Forever that summer, events were "outback"—that place where angle ruled—the never-ending system of rain gutters tracing the perimeters of garages, stray trash can lids, and the 1,000 tiny blue square windows of the blue milk crates and 1,000 wires intersecting a horse-blue sky. Molly was convincing Danny to go with her. She was off to live with Aunt Hope in Northern Wisconsin, which would prove to be disastrous because Danny panicked after he saw a tornado and then got news once the phones came back that his grandmother had died during a heat wave. He would go back. Ally and Hector were preparing to leave with us, even though Junior and Hector hated each other. The power of the women prevailed. Abel rested the slide on the tires.

Hector was somewhere rolling Ally's panties down to her ankles. The four of us pulled hairs from our heads and Jesus held them in his fist. I picked last, a blond hair that was my own and the shortest—I began to hate this game. I got on the makeshift moped. Junior brought Mother to the floor. Hector lined up his angle with Ally's. Abel pulled the coil. Junior tickled Mother's "little switch." Hector had his hooded dick in his hand. My head jerked back in unison with Mother and Ally's. There was no throttle, just a speed and some alley dust. I gripped the bars, tightened my shoulders, and aimed the front tire best I could. Sky seeped. The tires left the ramp, I shot ten feet straight up, straddled that banana seat. Ally and Mother screamed. Junior and Hector were rooting for me, and they didn't even know it. The rear wheel came off, and I saw the grackles, the moon in the daytime, and it was good. They put their wings together, caught me in a feather-woven cradle and laid me down in the grass. After that, Jose, Jesus, and Abel stood over my body and threw their arms down to me like rescue ropes and pulled me up. We picked our scabs, stood in a circle, and put our bloody elbows together, and were all brothers for a time.

* * *

"I'm old enough to say I don't want to go now, so, I don't want to go back to the U.P. again." I told Mother firmly.

"But we're not going to the U.P., we're going to Montana," Mother said. I didn't know what to say to that because I didn't really know where it was so I said, "O.K." I was too proud to be ignorant after being educated in Karnes City.

And then we moved.

Lost Chapter for the Shamrock Bar.
Gaastra, Michigan

Well I'm standing next to a mountain
I chop it down with the edge of my hand
I pick up the pieces and make an island
and raise it from the sand.
from "Voodoo Chile"
– Jimi Hendrix

It's too much to remember sometimes, or re-collect the paint and fixtures, furniture, and rock albums from the different houses and put a wooden frame and plaster around everything. Things are lost in the clutter. I know we ended up living in that bar where Mother first met the Man-Worth-Mentioning who we now know as Greg. Maybe it was right after Florida. It came to me while driving in a place where the sirens speak a foreign tongue. And I saw black cracking against the wall—something like music. I had found a box of old 78 records upstairs above the Shamrock Bar where we lived transiently for a couple of months in a time of exceptional blur when the sounds couldn't have been any louder and I added to the noise by smashing the records.

My room sat above the bowling alley where the setting machine tumbled the pins until they fell into their proper slots, at least that's how I heard it.

The tumbling never left and manifested itself in later years at the center of my anxious heart which would often beat mercilessly, fearing the pins. To me, the setting machine was a torturing machine that took nice people, tumbled them around and passed them through its steel intestines and waste came out in the form of mean drunks and chronic smokers set on barstools waiting to be struck. Of course everybody forgot this place. We had to.

Mother was about 23 and I have no memory of school so it was either summer or before Florida. I'd tell a real specific story now but the only thing that comes to me is those 78's, brittle, heavy, and jet black, smashing against the wall. I was competing for sound. My pants were full of piss. Maybe it was before Florida. Mother had always managed to make everything look livable by turning trash into furniture and pop-art. She would take milk crates and stack them on their sides to create a modern open shelving system for my clothes. The same crates could be a bed frame complete with storage units. Dried weeds hid the cracks in corners. An old rag tied around the fluorescent light was a priceless hand-made shade. But at the Shamrock I don't recall any of this. Only filth. Literally wading through it. Dirty jeans, torn sheets that had been used for shades to keep the atmosphere dark, old bottles shoved in a corner waiting to be redeemed for cigarette money, a can of tuna, and some Wonder Bread. Maybe I even lived in this apartment alone. Mother must have lived downstairs where she worked until she was too drunk and then simply sat on the other side of the bar until she drank herself to sleep and awoke to sober, at which time she'd return behind the bar and start the process all over again; while the pins were set and struck the whole while in the wrath of mid-1970-something when there was so much pity and so little thinking that I almost drowned in my own pissy pants that were so saturated they dripped from the cuffs all over the floor.

I am questioning this memory now. I never wanted this. My idea was to let recollection be and whatever fact or fiction stuck would be pure phenomena, at least that is what my mind leads itself to believe in its cloaked intellectualism that turns the scabs on my knees into symbols. They are only scabs, just like those behind a cat's ear that I pick at lovingly, being careful not to pull them off intentionally, but secretly hoping they will fall off on their own accord. Or there may be a sore on my mouth that I tongue all day and it doesn't mean a thing either, only that I am fascinated with it. Whether I got it from an infection, or an infliction doesn't matter. It is only what I do presently which creates memory.

But what "lets" memory? Not a photo album or a plot. Not languaging and loving. It's something beyond discursive knowledge and the plethora of other precise words which I can continue to string together when I really want to talk about the motivation of me running my index finger up and down a woman's back every night in order to feel her flesh pimple. I can say how ecstatic experience is mystical and point to William James and his assertions that the mystical experience is always ineffable and noetic, when it's easier to say I almost died last night making love, or "letting love" until my stomach hurt so bad and my blood pressure was so high that I hallucinated and had fearful dreams all night, that the post-exhaustion of lying there in silence was transient and fleeting, that it could pass forever at any moment and I might never see it again. I was crazy, last night and three decades ago throwing music at walls, watching a vision of musical scales and notes full of letters echo out like ripples, expanding or contracting.

I remember reading Crazy Horse had his vision when he was a child. He dreamed he went where there was only the spirit of things, the real world behind this one. Everything we see in this world is said to be a shadow of that one and to glimpse it is really something. Crazy Horse was on his horse in that world where they, the grasses and trees and stones, were all made of spirit and nothing was difficult. It all must have made sense and just floated there. His horse was still, yet it danced as if it was made only of shadow. When Crazy Horse went to battle, all he had to do was think of that world and he couldn't be wounded. I thought of the shadow world on the second story of the Shamrock Bar, cast from a light shining up from the center of the world and not yellow from above, I think.

And then we moved.

A Trailer Park.
Glasgow, Montana

Tell me, tell me where I'm going
I don't know where I've been.
Tell me, tell me, won't you tell me
and then tell me again.
from "Crystal Ball"
– *Styx*

“So we were leaving Texas because we weren't going anywhere and nobody had a job and your Gramma and Grampa left us because they were sick of being parents and wanted to find an escape. I was dating a half-retarded redneck named Junior and we decided to pack everything up in Texas in a big U-Haul and caravan with Hector and Ally who drove the old Chevy Impala up to Glasgow, Montana where your Gramma and Grampa had another trailer bigger than this one. Since Junior hated Mexicans, it was perfect that Hector and Ally were in another car. I don't know why I was moving. I think that it wasn't good for us there in Karnes City. That is all I can say about it. I'm not too good about using images and stuff like you. I can tell you it was raining and the drops were 'fat like me' is what Junior told me, and that was supposed to turn me on I guess. I just felt afraid maybe, and I wanted something different and thought that Montana might help.

"You weren't very happy in Karnes City, no matter what you think. It was obvious by your whining and acting up all the time. I remember there was a slow kid a couple of trailers down and you guys used to make ramps and jump bicycles all the time. One day you had a big board and a stack of cinder blocks in the middle of the road. You put the board on the very edge of the cinder blocks so that when Cain's bike, that was his name, do you remember?—anyways, when his bike hit the board it collapsed and his front tire smashed into the cinder blocks and he fell off his bike and got hurt pretty bad. Then I had to stick up for you because his mother was really pissed and crying. I should have whipped your ass but I didn't have the energy. I wanted to do that kind of stuff to people too, you know, hurt people you care about, but I didn't really have the energy for that either. I could gossip about Patti Anne and how she sucked off Victor Attanasof behind the bar in thirty seconds while her boyfriend was in the bathroom, but I would never smack her upside the head for it. Is this the stuff you want? Do you want me to really tell you everything? I don't know if I can do that. You want a specific story? Details? O.K. Why Junior?

"About the only thing he could do good was make love. Well, fuck. He was an idiot, but I didn't have anybody. Sometimes I'd close my eyes and imagine I was with somebody who really mattered. You know, somebody who could put up with the family and scrub the floor once in a while. Somebody who could figure out bills and save some money. Junior was fun, but he couldn't really help out with anything. He dug ditches for a living. What the hell can you do with those skills but dig your own grave? And that's what he was doing. He was in to amphetamines you know, speed, and that helped his fucking, but it didn't help him concentrate on making a relationship work.

"Oh, a story? Well you hijacked a horned toad from Texas because you wanted to start a revolution in the North by introducing a new species. You had some wild ideas back then. I told you that he'd freeze, but I didn't really know that. Hell, maybe it would have worked, but you would have needed two. You only brought one. You said that it could mate with a toad from the North and then the chances of a species that could survive would be greater. You were always thinking like that. It was something you know. You wanted to be a scientist. I was so proud of you too—I forgot the story again. Oh, well, you had this horned toad hidden under some chairs in the back of the U-Haul. And let me tell you something for once—that thing was really a lizard and everybody just got the name wrong because Aunt Ally told me that one time. She's one of the smartest you know, and I have no clue why I remember that; I guess it's just because I was thinking that was some useless knowledge to have, but she had it.

"So, we made it to Denver after driving twelve hours to stay with Dan Wall and his Hispanic girlfriend and she caught you sneaking into the U-Haul. You turned around with the toad and she started crying. You thought she was afraid and then she hugged you because she was crying about missing Mexico because she hadn't seen a horned toad in a long time, at least not in the city. And you hugged her and she cried some more. I was watching it all from a window and I bet you don't even know it happened. Did it? I don't even know sometimes. You know, we are not that different even though you'd like to think it. I don't know what really happened most of the time. My memory is so full of fear and things that I hoped had happened that I mix it all up. The names get screwed up. What I saw in a magazine might make its way into a memory and end up with me thinking that it was a moment in my life.

"So the story—well that was it. I forgot to talk about colors and stuff. Give me a chance, will yah! O.K. So we get to Montana where we would be for less than two weeks. It looked like the moon there you know. The whole city was like a pit. Our trailer park was all dirt and in the distance was a big dirt mountain full of gouges where the rain would run down. When we pulled into Glasgow I remember there was a double rainbow and we had some hope about things—like finding jobs. Gramma and Grampa where already somewhere else because your Grampa was a right-of way agent for a pipeline company, meaning he had to convince people all over the country to let his company dig up their land and put a pipeline there. He'd work a day a week and spend the rest of it having picnics and stuff. It drove Gramma crazy because he just didn't want to work. He was always talking about quitting "the system" is what he called it. Nobody in the family was very good at keeping jobs. Who wanted to work when there was so much living to do! Chad, it was the late 70s and all we had was memories of what could have been! I was still trying to make something happen but I didn't know what. It was about being a peace activist or something. I guess the way I lived was my activism. But I didn't think much of that stuff. I mean I had burned my bra and read *Our Bodies Ourselves* and shit like that. I didn't want any wars, but at that time I was too into making sure I wasn't alone. I was making sure we had some food and I had a little pot and booze money to make things happen. I don't know what I'm saying really. Is this what you had in mind? You just want me to keep talking? O.K.

"Well I think I said something about the double rainbow. It might as well have been a double noose to hang ourselves with because those two weeks about killed us. Ally and I had it in us to get Hector and Junior to find jobs while we tried to make that shitty trailer livable. Junior and Hector were no more mature than you were. You all would fight over toys for Christ's sake. Hector sat in the back with you a whole day making a city out of sand for your matchbox cars, only you came in crying because he wouldn't let you contribute to the city. What a fucker he was. We didn't get along with the neighbors either. You were trying to make friends with the kids, but their parents wouldn't let you play with *them* because they figured we were all too wild. Junior had that southern accent and Hector was Mexican. You'd go knock on doors and they'd shut up their homes and peek out the window to make sure you had left. Christ, I shouldn't have let you play with them, the little bastards. You see, even if the events don't really show it, I cared for you as much as I possibly could. I just didn't know how to show you. Sometimes it came out all sideways and stuff. But I loved to part your blond hair and press the little mole above your mouth like it was a button.

"So every day was something like what I just explained until the last day. You took off with Hector to make sure he was looking for a job, and Junior went off on his own. From what I found out later, correct me if I'm wrong, is that Hector got an application at a gas station and then spent the rest of the day in a bar bribing you with quarters so you could play pool if you promised to tell me and Ally that he applied at ten places. Well, he came home pretty shit-faced and you weren't a good liar. You just said he applied for some jobs over and over. 'Well, where?' I said?

"'He just applied for some jobs,' you said.

"'Gas stations? Grocery store? You must know.' And you kept saying the same thing and wouldn't look me in the eye. That was about 6 p.m. Then Junior comes home and he's shit-faced too. Ally and I were yelling at them both. I remember it was about to rain and the dirt cliffs in the distance would start flowing and mud would rush through the trailer park and take us with it. I don't know where you were, maybe out playing by yourself in the back. Do you remember that? Damn it was ugly there. It seemed like a city with no history. Just rock and, well, like I said—the moon. Maybe you were playing spaceman or Green Lantern, or something—you know, trying to save the universe and stuff. But the one thing that was interesting is that a rain changed the whole landscape and the city was different. The peaks in the distance weren't the same anymore. What was once the tallest was now the third or fourth tallest. It was really trippy how the earth could just change like that.

"So Ally and I were listening to music really loud because we were pissed and all the windows were open and the whole trailer park could hear everything. Rain was coming in the windows and we didn't give a shit because the furniture all sucked anyway. I didn't even decorate that place. It wasn't worth it. I guess I was waiting for a rain like this. I'm doing good now with this story I think; it's what you wanted, right?

"So we're listening to Styx really loud, 'Crystal Ball' was on. We were pretty stoned too because we had a little pot left, but it didn't mellow us out. You were out back, you know, playing spaceman again and I guess with some magic wristbands I had pinned around your tiny wrists. They were pretty small, smaller than other boys and I knew you had my bones, even if you didn't have my looks. *Styx* was singing, 'Tell me, Tell me,' and I said 'Yeah, tell me, I want to know fucker—What's your future? Where's your job?' I was talking to Junior and then Hector said to me, 'Fuck you fat bitch.' Then Junior tried to make up for the day by acting all chivalrous and called him a *wetback*. 'Swim back across the Rio Grande you fucking wetback,' he said. And that is when the macho pushing started and Ally and I became invisible, drowned out by the music and the alcohol.

"Those fuckers started pushing us and we were screaming and they couldn't hear a thing. They could hardly stand up. It wasn't like Ally and I were afraid, we could have easily pushed them over, but it was as if they would never stop running on low batteries. And we couldn't read them you know; we didn't know what they would do because when you get that drunk and are still able to stand, those batteries will run forever, just like that drizzle of rain that had been falling for hours. So we unplugged the stereo and walked outside.

"By that time you must have heard them two going at it because you were on your way in and I picked you up and ran straight across the street to the neighbors we never met. So we're in front of the neighbors with the rain coming down all over us with screaming in the background and I just said to them, 'It's time to let us in.' So they did.

"It was a middle-aged couple with a teenage daughter and a little boy about your age that you tried to play with once until his mother called him away. The man of the house was bald by choice and said, 'come in' and when we got into their trailer they had already set up extra chairs for us. The chairs were set up near the front picture window. All the trailers had those big windows spread across the front like a movie screen. Wouldn't you know the window was positioned right toward our picture window. We didn't have curtains in our house, but the neighbors did. They were lace so you could see through them from the inside but couldn't from the outside. It was perfect for us because we didn't want them bringing the trouble over where we were. So we just watched. All of us.

"There were seven of us in front of that window watching the rain come down. The cliffs started to crumble, and Hector takes off his belt and wraps it around his fist. Junior was motioning him to come on. The little kid who was your age started screaming, 'Make them stop!' And so did the teenage girl. The adults didn't listen and just kept watching. Hector and Junior would duck out of view a little and then come back. You know, I think we all sort of liked it. It was like watching animals fight on 'Wild Kingdom.' We all acted like it frightened us, but we knew that these things had to happen and we were learning. The rain and mud were gathering in the dirt streets—see, now I am sounding like you a little bit more. I can see the details and stuff—so while the water was rising we were staring at that because Hector drifted away back into the trailer to get a better belt.

"He for sure got something better, an old rusty gun, and you started smiling and laughing and everybody was worried for sure in the trailer because they thought that you had gotten some kind of shock or something and that you would never be the same again because you were so freaked out. The other kids really started screaming because this was the climax, what they all had been waiting for. This made the movie worth it.

"Hector didn't aim the gun; he just held it up in the air with one hand. Junior was motioning with his hand and fingers for him to 'bring it on.' I don't even know how he could see with that fat rain dripping down his Coke-bottle glasses. It was getting hard for us to see the details too because the rain was thick on the picture window. In the distance the streetlights lit up the cliffs that were changing. You know, those peaks sort of looked like a heart monitor. It was all about Hector taking aim now. We were actually hoping you would start crying so that things would seem more normal if you can imagine that.

"So we thought you had totally lost it until you started shouting between your comic gasps that it was a pellet gun and there were no pellets because you and Hector were looking for some all day. Well, it wasn't quite funny, but there was a sense of relief and the bald man of the house had enough and put on his shoes, grabbed an umbrella and stepped out into the night right into a mud slick and fell on his ass which pissed him off. He got up, swam across the alley, grabbed the pellet gun from Hector, hit him over the head with it, and dragged Junior back across the street. Hector fell to his knees, exhausted, with the rain flattening his hair and exposing his humongous Mestizo head. The rain eventually washed him away. Junior was taken into the house and thrown into the shower by the bald man.

"We all returned the chairs to their proper places and the rain let up a little since there was nothing more to wash away. It continued to sprinkle a little until the bald man put the three of us in his car at 2 a.m. and drove us to the edge of town and dropped us off. Something was finally right because when we stepped onto the highway and stuck our thumbs in the air the rain stopped."

And then we moved.

Planet's Resort.
Iron River, Michigan

My my, hey hey
rock and roll is here to stay.
It's better to burn out
Than to fade away.
My my, hey hey.
from "My My, Hey Hey (Out of the Blue)"
– *Neil Young*

My thumb was getting sore as I sat on a sleeping bag with my arm stretched over highway U.S. 2 as Mother and Junior smoked cigarettes 50 feet behind me out of sight in the ditch. I was the one getting most of the rides. I knew it too. It was the pity factor. People just weren't used to seeing a little kid in overalls and long blond locks hitchhiking. I just thought of it as sticking my thumb up the ass of the stars and that kept me occupied. The headlights reflected off my head as if it were a bright yellow yield sign, only round instead of triangular. With yield signs it's up to you to decide if it is necessary to slow down. I thought if only my hair was red or better yet, black, because then in my Green Lantern mythos, I wouldn't be the source of my own weakness. But with yellow hair, a majority of people slowed only a little and the speed was too great to stop totally once they were close enough to realize that it was a boy in bib overalls with his thumb stuck into the ass of night, and they kept on going wondering if they should turn around. And sometimes they did.

That's what we were all hoping for. They never turned around for Junior so he didn't have to stick out his thumb, which was just fine with him because he hated working. Maybe they turned around for Mother, but that was the only time I wasn't useful getting rides because when they would see me on their loop back, they'd change their minds and take off again, leaving us a puff of exhaust and a memory of what might have been if they would have only picked us up and then we'd be a little closer to what we would have to call home yet again—Iron River.

We were hungry most of the time since Junior hadn't worked a day since we left Texas. We had a loaf of Roman Meal bread and some peanut butter to get us from Glasgow to Iron River. Since we left in the middle of the night we didn't have time for Gramma to wire us money, or check the Greyhound bus or anything like that. It was literally fight or flight. Junior could have fought soon-to-be uncle Hector and then be forced to live with him in the trailer in Montana and make continual problems for all the mutants and minorities and oil riggers at the trailer park, or he could have fled in the middle of the night with the best piece of ass he ever had and the biggest obstacle to it—me. And so with my thumb stuck in the ass of night, I dangled from the sky as semi-trucks raced by and I blew back and forth like a chime in the tailwind of truckers fleeing the scenes even faster than us.

An Indian somewhere in North Dakota did a U-turn through six lanes of traffic, squealing his tires and everything. We got in and were up to our knees with beer cans and cigarette ash. I slid down the vinyl like an eagle feather slides through the hand of someone with fear in their heart, and was buried in the cans. He drove a couple of miles and then Mother insisted we had reached our destination and we got out. I tore off a piece of the ripped and frayed green vinyl for a memory and stuffed it in the chest pocket of my bib-overalls that I wore proudly. There were countless rides because most of them were just locals who were curious so they picked us up at the city limits of one town and dropped us off at the limits of the other. Wolf Point, Poplar, Bainville, Ray, Ross, Stanley, Palermo, Tagus, Minot, Rugby, Pleasant Lake, York, Leeds,

Devils Lake, Lakota, Mapes, Niagra, Arvilla, Crookston, Mentor, Bagley, North Pole, Bemidji, Cohasset, Warba, Swan River, Floodwood, Hermantown, Superior, Bessmer, Ironwood, Watersmeet, Beechwood, Iron River. The names stretched out like a long tongue that lapped the edges of history and spoke many languages before it burrowed into the soil and settled six feet under.

Our last ride took us about six hours. We were picked up on the Duluth-Superior bridge at the far western point of Lake Superior. A young guy who had just ran a marathon picked us up and was still fresh with adrenaline and eager to tell us his story. It was refreshing for once to sit back and hear someone tell a different story that had to do with training and discipline and sport. After all, wasn't that our story? The guy told us of the psychological preparation involved. He said that the strength wasn't even the half of it. It was mostly about convincing your body it could do something it was incapable of. Like taking a good beating with blows to the face, or screwing for a whole weekend.

* * *

The marathon runner dropped us off right at 711 Roosevelt. Molly had moved in and was being bitchy because she had put a little money into the house and didn't want it to get fucked up. "God no, you're not living here with that fucking redneck. Holy shit, Kate! He's retarded!" The house was still getting fucked up. The front steps were cracked in half and the porch that stretched across the front was sinking into the ground. I think Molly had fixed a leak in the sink. The apple tree that I had suckled as child was split through the center and had lost some branches.

She was with her new boyfriend, Shane. She sketched him nude in her Rolling Stones tongue shirt. Her Mexican boyfriend couldn't take the winters and had gone back to Texas. The exoticism of large stadium shows with Blue Oyster Cult, Supertramp, Rush, and Danny Soliz at her side was gone. She settled back into the radio and blond-haired, blue-eyed boys. They screwed for whole weekends until her belly swelled up with life and Shane's neck swelled up with death. Cousin Hope would be born and Shane would die of lymphoma.

Mom contacted Greg who was really happy to see me and I just didn't know how to act toward him because it had been a long time since I'd seen him and he was excited about playing father. He asked if I got the bike he sent me for Christmas and I told him the birds stole it. I told him I saw Charlie McCarthy die in a tree, and the moon, an Indian chief, the Alamo, and a shitload of Mexicans. I just kept talking because the father thing was new to me and I didn't know if I needed one. He said it was O.K. if I called him Dad, and I said "O.K. Greg," and it sounded about the same to me so I always stuck with that. He called me "Wonderful" and "Sunshine" most of the time anyway instead of son, so no big deal. He really wanted to help out so his Dad, Reynold, set us up with an A-frame on Sunset Lake at what was called "Planet's Resort." What a perfect name, I thought. In exchange Junior had to mow the lawn once a week and work on digging a trench for a new sewer pipe since that was the other thing he was good at.

It was spring and the trees were a green like never before. The sun must have been at a different angle from Texas and Glasgow. Or maybe it was the minerals in the ground that the trees sucked up their fat trunks like the alcoholics sucked up beer with fat straws until their complexions turned green. Mostly Junior would spend the day digging a little while, and then screwing, and then digging and screwing. Sometimes he would get confused and stand over Mother in the bed with his tool, or lie in the ditch face down.

I spent most of my days playing around with a little tool kit that came in a treasure chest about the size of a cigar box. It was the one thing Mother splurged on when we got back to Iron River. It had a broken top and was in a clearance bin at ACE Hardware. I figured out how to fix alarm clocks and toasters. Once I even fixed the lawnmower by cleaning the sparkplug. I wasn't really happy about that one though because I liked the tall grass, how it bent into the lake and naturally turned into waves. The animals would hide in that waving tall grass and turn into fish by the time they reached the lake.

We were located outside of town a bit and I didn't get to see other kids much again. I didn't really feel comfortable finding LittleMan either. I missed my Mexican friends, even if my memories were fat lips and blows to the gut. This is how it was with Mother when she was away from men too long. You start missing things you never thought you would have, things that you thought could have killed you but were still better than the sensation of being alone and having nothing to think about.

In the afternoons I'd follow Junior to the dock with a couple of dozen worms and a broken fishing pole I found in the rotting woodpile behind the other A-frame. At sunset the bluegills would bite at anything simply because they were bored too. We would fill up a plastic pail and then just leave them there most of the time to stink and rot. I wanted to throw them back but Junior always had plans to fry them and never did.

Once I caught a bluegill the size of a hubcap and I was sure I could make it into the *Reporter*, probably right next to somebody like Larry Hiekala. Then people would know the little boy with a good grip. I threw it in a bucket and took some of the ice that had been thrown over a half barrel of beer that was cooling for an afternoon party so I could keep the fish fresh until the morning. Junior took a swig from his St. Pauli Girl, looked at the label for a second, and finished it off, throwing the bottle next to the others. He looked at the fish and he looked at the pile of bottles. "Hell, I done downed another 12 pack!" he said, "I'm gonna have to switch to tappers." And then I forgot all about that fucking fish.

* * *

The shadows of the pines on the shore stretched across the yard and were long like the lanes of a running track. I ran down alone back to the house to tell Mother something, but I couldn't remember once I got there. People were already arriving for the welcome back party. I could smell the chemicals of the black charcoal briquettes and starter fluid in the air. Over the grill, the air was dizzy with the heat of a weak flame; the faces of Patti Ann, Rosanna, Patti Kolowsky, and the others shimmied. Some of the guests had brought their dogs and they ran around the resort chasing each other. I was drawn to them and, since there were no other kids around, I ran with them like I had done in Florida. All over the shadow tracks in the yard, we ran and ran until there was nothing on our minds except for running more and sucking in as much oxygen as we could in order to get higher and higher as the sun sank lower and lower. We waded into the water and I panted until I hyperventilated and feared a common fear that I would die.

There were many guests now. Junior came strolling across the front yard where I was rolling around with the dogs.

"Where the hell is that other grill, boy? We got to make some more chow for these Yankees. Where's those fishes we caught today?" He looked over near the dock where the still life of a bucket of fish, a rusty grill, and a pile of empty beer bottles was painted. "Hell, I got a jackpot!" He put his arm through the wire handle of the fish bucket and carried it with his elbow. He would never cook those fucking fish. With his free hands, he lifted the grill up just over his head as if he were some athlete, which he sure wasn't. Junior strolled across the lawn looking like he was blurred by the heat of the grill, but he wasn't. He was just "pig drunk" is what Mother would say. The dogs and I looked on and growled at that pig so he'd get out of our play area. As Junior swayed past us he made a motion like he was going to throw the grill at one of the dogs for absolutely no reason and the dog cowered and yipped and ran away from me.

"What did you do that for?" I said, looking him in the eye, "It didn't do anything to you."

"That's a Yankee dog," he slurred with his weak speech. Then he walked past an empty A-frame away from the lake until he was at ours, which was full of people now. They were pouring out the doors and windows. I walked to the dock and the dogs followed with their heads low. The sun was going down over Sunset Lake and it was really something. It deserved a name like that. The purples and reds swirled from somewhere under the horizon and poured the placenta of night all over everything.

Soon it was too dark to run around so I reluctantly left the dogs and strolled over to the party. The lake smell was peppered with wet soil. The scent of fried fish and burning newspaper was off and on, but it wasn't from our party. The grill and fish sat in the front of the house right where Junior had left them. Rotting and rusting. I walked inside the house.

Rosanna was sitting inside the front door at the kitchen table with her dirty-blonde hair spilled over the table and her bobble head trying to find the rim of a plastic cup of beer. The A-frame floor plan was a big square divided into four areas. Two areas on one side of the square were bedrooms, and the two areas on the other were a kitchen and a living room. There was a small bathroom between the bedrooms that had a shower and no tub. There wasn't a lot of room anywhere, but I had my own bedroom. Now it had become the room where the people with the really good pot who didn't want to share any with the others came. Rosanna couldn't really walk by now so she just sat there and was playing with my toolbox.

"Hey kiddo, what do you do with this thing?" she asked.

"I fix stuff."

"Yeah, can you fix alarm clocks?"

"Yeah, I bet I could. What is wrong with yours?"

"It keeps going off every morning," she laughed, "just like it's supposed too, but that's no good. Maybe you just ought to throw it on the ground a couple of times or kick it around a little." Her clothes hung over her loosely and I could see the silhouette of her large nipples at the end of her teats through the sheer cotton fabric that was embroidered with spirals. Her animalness was really showing as she belched and swayed and I knew what "pig drunk" was.

"Yeah," I said with a false grin. I never did figure out how to act when I realized what the alcohol did, how it stirred and slurred the being. It was like the transformation from a sober solid to a liquid. It was a melting process. But if I described it this way, that would mean that when Rosanna, for example, was sober, she was ice. But ice can't be a normal state. Even though she behaved as ice, her being was really liquid. Her normal state was the drunkenness. Come to think of it, that is a good way to describe the whole lot of them, because that's what Junior was like most of the time. And I guess if you just keep drinking you turn to a vapor and there's not much to you anymore. That was that.

I was sitting with Rosanna staring at her dripping out of her chair when Junior wafted in through the door like vapor on a current of lake air with the stench of rotting prize fish. Through the bottle cap glasses, his eyes looked like an incision on a carp's belly viewed under a microscope.

"Where the fuck is my Yankee bitch?" he growled to Rosanna. I was right there but it didn't matter. I never mattered to that guy and I am glad he didn't give a good shit about me because if he had shown me any attention in public, I would have been embarrassed.

Rosanna just shook her head "no" and it shimmied like Jello as it continued to turn from solid to liquid. For no apparent reason, Junior cuffed her upside the head and the Jello splashed all over the place and stuck to the sides of the cupboard and ran down slowly. I ran to my bedroom and opened the door to flee another scene. A smoke poured out. It was sweet. I always preferred that sweetness to the thick stench of alcohol that festered in the mouths of the likes of Junior As the smoke cleared, I saw Mother with her lips pressed to John Frizo. She was blowing him a shotgun, meaning that she was simply shooting the smoke from the joint she held backwards inside her mouth into the mouth and lungs of John. Though it looked intimate, it was a harmless gesture, but not in the fish gut slits of Junior. He was over my shoulder with his mouth gaping open. I could smell the dead fish and festering rot emanating from his scraggly moustache and dirty pants. He pushed me out of the way and ran through the sweet smoke to Mother. He yanked her arm right out of its socket and dragged her into the kitchen. Frizo just stayed where he was and exhaled. Then he lay back on the bed and enjoyed his buzz.

In the kitchen, Rosanna was on the floor leaning against the pine cabinets. A couple of guys had gathered around her and were trying to figure out what had happened. Then Junior came in dragging Mother as if she were an overstuffed ragdoll. I followed behind and sneaked past them toward the door but didn't leave.

"Man, what the fuck is going on?" one of the guys said.

"Ain't nothing. I just want my woman, and I want her in a bad way so I'm taking her."

"What the fuck are you talking about, Junior? Let go of my fucking arm. What the hell is the matter with you? Look at you. What are you fuming about? I was just blowing a shotgun in there," Mother pleaded.

"I'm gonna blow a shotgun off right here," he said with a threatening fist held up to the air. "What the fuck are you guys looking at?" he said to the others trying to pull up Rosanna.

"Man, you're gonna have to relax, and pull that pecker-of-an-arm out of the sky," one of the men said.

"Ain't no way."

"You're hurting my wrist, let me the fuck go," Mother said impatiently.

"Yeah, you're scaring the kid," somebody noticed. Actually, I was just uncomfortable with the rot and decay that festered all around. If I could have witnessed the same event passively from a clean seat in an arena, it would have been just fine. But being confined to the same space was just too much. This time I had fear in my heart and it was beating really fucking fast and I couldn't catch my breath, but I hid it best I could because I was all Mother had again and it was gonna be just us, like it used to be, and I held on to that thought.

John Frizo floated out of the bedroom and saw Junior's fist stuck to the air and grabbed it nonchalantly for no apparent reason. Mother slid from Junior's clutch and grabbed me by the shoulder on her way out the door. I grabbed my toolbox off the table and smiled at Rosanna. A couple of guys stepped in front of the door to prevent Junior from leaving. We jumped right into a car that was parked out front and locked the doors. Junior pushed his way past the guys which wasn't a problem because they were more stoned than drunk. He jumped on the hood of the car with his fist drawn back like the rattler in Florida that was poised to strike when I came upon it in a field while I was searching for an arrow I had shot straight up into the sky just to see if I could make it go out of sight. I wanted to shoot the car straight up into the sky out of sight too, but I knew it would come crashing down in some field and Junior would still be there, poised to strike.

He struck the window but it didn't shatter, didn't even crack, but I saw his knuckle bust open like a grapefruit.

"Where the fuck are the keys! Where the fuck are the keys!" she kept saying while Junior tried every window and the rind of his knuckles was peeled back more and more. I opened my toolbox and pulled out a screwdriver. I stuck it in the steering column and jiggled it a little until I could turn it completely in the ignition and started the car. Then we took off down the dirt road with Junior on the hood. We took a sharp right turn toward Iron River and he flew off into a ditch that he had dug.

"Rot in hell you fucker," Mother yelled.

"Learn how to treat animals, fucker!" I yelled, and Mother didn't seem to care.

That was the last time we ever spoke to Junior, but not the last we saw of him.

* * *

The Jack-O-Lantern Bar was run by Mimi Tarnovsky and had those black strippers from Detroit performing every weekend. The strippers stayed upstairs in the rooming house that used to be for the immigrant miners. After fleeing Sunset Lake with the sun, we had to find a place to hide out from Junior. Mom called around a bit from the local gas station, looking for a place to stay. She was a little hysterical and crying, and then Mimi tapped her on the shoulder. She was buying a pack of cigarettes and asked Mother what the hell she was blubbering about. Mom told her.

Mimi said enthusiastically, "Never mind that redneck. He won't think to look for you at my place. What the hell would you be doing hanging out with a bunch of black strippers? I'll take care of you Kate. Your mother wouldn't have it any other way."

We parked the car a couple of blocks away at my old school, Central Elementary, which had been recently shut down because of asbestos. We jumped shadows and entered the back door. Mimi had a single bed made up for us. The sheets were stiff and the pillow was hard. We had to share the room with a couple of the black girls, but they worked most of the night, and usually found other places to stay. It was pretty late so Mother set me up in bed. She found an old radio for me to take apart and put back together. She wasn't in the mood to deal with anything so she made her face and headed downstairs for a couple of stiff drinks in a bar populated with a bunch of stiff men.

The radio was only AM. I could tune in stations from Canada and some of them were in French. I was lulled. It had been only a couple of months since I had left Texas. I closed my eyes—the Mariachi bands were singing there and I wouldn't understand a word of it. Abel Soliz's mother was yelling at us but to me it could have been praise. Even though I wasn't an alcoholic yet, I was a melancholic. It was more comfortable to be lost in a foreign culture than it was to be cloaked in what was supposed to be my own culture. So I lost myself in the French programming and pulled the blankets over my head in case somebody came upstairs.

* * *

I always hated waking up alone in a strange bed. The bass of the disco music downstairs was shaking the bed. The dust and skin cells of a 100 years of immigrants was being disturbed and it was thick all over the room. I couldn't stop sneezing. So I did what one is supposed to do when they feel uncomfortable. I went to Mother. I walked out the door and down the steel fire escape stairs. I saw an entrance on the side and a couple of garbage cans. Between the cans a massive shadow was bouncing around hysterically and there was a whimpering like the sound of an injured wolverine. And then the animal spoke a primitive English and said "Yes! Suck it. Suck it." I wasn't naive then. I remembered Mother feeding off of Craig Kalavala in the living room behind City Market which was about 500 feet from where I was standing. I had to say "excuse me" because they were blocking the door. When I did, the massive black shadow of her hair turned around and there was still shadow, except for the whites of her eyes. She was even blacker than shadow and could hide simply by closing her eyes. I envied her for that.

"What ya need sugar? What ya doin' here all by yo self?"

"Hey, don't stop!" the man moaned with anger and frustration.

"You shut yo mouth for a minute. You'll get watz comin to you," she retorted, "Now you sugar, you go on in quick-like and see Mimi. She'll help you."

"I think she already did today. Well, sorry to bug you. Thanks. If you need anything fixed just let me know. I am staying upstairs for a little while."

"Beat it!" the man said.

"That's what I'm gonna do if you don't finish pretty soon!" I heard the shadow-woman say as I pushed open the heavy door and it squeaked loudly. The sound was immediately drowned out by the liquid of the music pouring out into the reality of night. It was too hot for anything to be solid and behaving.

I had to fight my way through the dance floor to the bar. I saw Mother at the end furthest from the main entrance. She was there just in case Junior thought to look and then she could duck down and escape out the back. I went up to her and tugged on her shirt.

"Chad!" I still loved to hear my name uttered by her. Her short "a" was much shorter than my Scandinavian influenced drawn-out "a." Hers was tinny like a star plucked from the sky and thrown into a pan. Mine was more of a thud, like a soft slice of moon-cheese dropped into a pot.

"I was alone up there and it was real dusty and I kept sneezing. I fixed the radio though."

"You can't hang out down here. I'll tell you what, I'll be up in an hour, and I'll even bring a visitor." She smiled, but her eyes were like "two festered assholes," Aunt Molly would have said.

"I don't want any visitors. Where's Junior?"

"He won't find us. I'm done with that prick. We can find someone else. So, I got some visitor I told you!"

"But I don't want a visitor." She wasn't listening. Mimi walked out from behind the bar.

"Kate, this isn't the place for him." Over my shoulder one of the black girls was tossing her bra around her index finger and deflecting cigarette smoke with her hips. "And there is a redneck at the other end of the bar. Is that your man? He can hardly speak, but it sounds southern."

Mom cautiously stood up on her tiptoes and came down quickly, all the way to the floor so the bar concealed her.

"Yeah, that's him."

"Well, Kate, come with me to the bathroom. Chad, you crawl back out the door and go straight upstairs. I'll send one of the ladies over to keep that pin-dick occupied. If he raises any trouble in here I'm gonna cut off his balls."

I looked around for a couple of seconds. There were stuffed fish on the walls with their lips parted as if they were perpetually gasping for air. They too were caught in the liquid of reality. Someone grabbed my hand and tugged me. I took the bait.

Back outside at the trashcan it was me and the black lady again. No man this time.

"Hey Sugar, it's time for you to get back up them long steel stairs."

"But I'm all alone up there. Will you come up there? I can tell you some stories." I tried to convince her.

"Sugar, that's what they always say. Ya know, everybody wantz to tell stories but they just end up makin' their own story with me to tell to someone else. I haven't heard any stories but I bet I'm in a lot. You don't know it now, but it costs money for my stories."

"Do you want to trade?" I asked, "I can fix something for you."

"I don't know if you can fix what I've got, Sugar. I've got a big ol' machine and it runs and all, but no matter what, it just ain't tuned right. I figured out how to drive it in any condition. So you go on and drive yo machine up those stairs and think of a story and put me in it."

"O.K.," I said, "but I like you." She kissed me on the forehead and said it tasted sweet. I unhooked myself from her hand and swam upstream.

I turned on the radio and fell into a dream. It was brightly colored. Actually, it was cartoons. Abel was in it. He was, for no apparent reason, an armadillo in full armor. There were all kinds of dogs, but they were about the size of mice. All the typical relationships among animals were distorted because of the atypical sizes of some. Mother was a hamster. Gramma was a raccoon, but her mask was red instead of black. Molly was a chinchilla the size of a small dog. Ally was a field mouse. Hope, well she was a mole and couldn't see very well. But the thing is that the dream really had no plot. There was no real conflict. Everyone was perched on a blade of seaweed under a freshwater lake and they swayed back and forth as they stared into a distance. Above the water, stars started to swirl and shimmy in the heat of the night. Planets were flying retrograde. Then the water started rippling above on the surface and currents started to shimmy the grass to and fro and everybody was struggling to hang on. I guess that was the conflict. No one fell.

I woke up and stared at the ceiling. It was hard to breathe with dust and water in my lungs. The bed jumped. Mom was back with a visitor and they were pounding the dust and dead skin cells out of the mattress. John Frizo was pounding the memory of Junior out of her and filling her up with lumberjack pride. I floated on my seaweed at the bottom of a lake. Or was it just a flooded field?

Mother put all four of her hamster feet in the air and squealed. I took out a piece of frayed green vinyl and rubbed it to my lips as if it were seaweed.

And then we moved.

Dober Location. Caspian, Michigan

Goodbye everybody – I've got to go,
gotta leave you all behind and face the truth.
Mama, ooo – (anyway the wind blows)
I don't want to die,
I sometimes wish I'd never been born at all.
from "Bohemian Rhapsody"
as sung by The Chipmunks

I was on my back legs with my front paws in the plastic hands of G.I. Joe, staring at him with my beautiful black and bulging Syrian Hamster eyes. The boy held each of us firmly in either hand and made us "play human," forcing us to jig on an old record that he used as a dance floor. His innocence led him to be somewhat torturous. He seemed convinced at times that I liked water. After singeing my yellow hair with a match in a failed attempt at darkening it, he would place me in a large pot full of tap water to see if I could swim. I tried to run in it as if it were a fluid wheel, only to get a lung full of water. But when it was all over, he would pat me dry with a soft cloth and fluff my hair in front of the forced air heating and I felt royal again.

For two weeks I ran around the perimeter of the living room counter-clockwise trying to reverse our predicament and make it grand like the first day when the mother returned home from treatment with chocolate gifts and a golden glow on the fat of her cheeks like I had only seen on well-rested animals when I daydreamed about living outside of captivity while running on my wheel. Once I had escaped The Cage and was making my counter-clockwise rounds, I found the boy curled up next to the heater with a blanket covering his entire body and the vent in order to trap the heat in. I could curl into the arch of his naked foot without him knowing.

It was winter and the forced air heater kicked on every five minutes and I ran to it dreaming of again being nestled in fresh pine shavings with a family that was in order. Mother and child were trying to catch me and I let them believe they were close. Sometimes I would gnaw on the TV stand to make noise, or dodge out from the shadows to catch their eye and initiate a chase. I might nudge the collection of empty liquor bottles in the corner for a familiar chime. Then the two would bond and come together with the common goal of capturing me so they could put me back on the wheel to run for hours as they wondered at the rhythm of the wheel. I'm not pissed about it. My imagination is active and on that wheel I was crossing continents, running through sweet vernal grass and meadow barley, wooing females with golden complexions all the way.

I am an animal in the most animal sense. I live to eat and shit and piss. That is what I want you to believe, but since I'm discussing this, it's hard to deny that I reason and have motives. Mother and child needed me. While in The Cage I had tried to take care of myself the best I could because I knew they couldn't. I had stashed a supply of food in a corner. I licked the hair around my ass and genitals for hours until it was pristine. I shoveled my waste—which was minimal since feedings had ceased—into the corner opposite the food. I gathered the few clean pine shavings I could for a fresh bed to prevent sickness and control stench because a cleaning was long overdue.

Occasionally there had been the visitors that noticed the stench and freed me from The Cage briefly. They lofted me into the invisible paws of air then patted me all over and my thick angel hair stood erect and I wiggled my whiskers a million times faster than usual. But then they would toss me around like a used rag, and I tried to revel in it. I had to be happy for that boy.

And when all the tossing and bashing was done, I crawled to him because that is what he had hoped for. He had resorted to animals because he saw human language failing all around him and knew—on a good day—that what really counted was something as simple as a scratch behind my ear or a fingertip on the belly.

He loved animals so much that even his favorite eight-track had become a choir of Chipmunks singing Christmas standards. In a high-pitched, high-speed strained voice, Alvin, the lead Chipmunk, sang "Christmas, Christmas time is here, time for joy and time for cheer."

Once there was a guest who was to play the mother for a night and she laughed and laughed with the boy as they listened to the other Chipmunks—Simon and Theodore—explaining that they had wanted hula-hoops and planes for Christmas. Her eyes were like mine, black and bulging, after she had taken a paper square of blotter acid with a picture of my cousin, Mickey Mouse, on it. I knew it all after living in that house—how people rolled joints and snorted amyl nitrate and cocaine; I was observer-in-residence, and somehow I cared about everything.

The mother for the night was more a child than the child she watched though she was at least ten years older. She looked in The Cage and tilted her head in amazement. She felt like she was communicating with me and she simply wasn't. She was only affirming to me that I had to make a big change. She took off my lid and picked me up. This night, when I was free in the paws of air and cradled in the hallucinating woman's hand who was watching the boy's legs grow and root into the second story floor as he stood in front of the eight-track and pressed rewind again and again trying to make Christmas come, I had it in me to stay out of The Cage because I figured I could take care of mother and child better than they took care of me. This was the day I planned to save my life in order to save another. I had a good two months left before The Cage would become uninhabitable and my hair would become wire with dried urine, the same amount of time mother and child had to make another change before their complexions turned piss yellow, the color of the stench and ambiance of Dober Location—the "good" location—which was anything but good, regardless of what the Slavic immigrants had said a hundred years earlier while standing on this same floor.

I had heard these stories and more while I ran and ran on that blasted wheel. I was full of empty history and curses, soap opera dialogues and rock and roll; the sounds of human sexuality, and long drawn out telephone calls while the boy was away at school about things he wasn't supposed to know but knew better than anyone. The mother was rapidly disintegrating, faster than me. The yellow of the beer and liquor had filled all the way up past her forehead now and was dulling her hair. Every conversation was now about "this," and every thought the child had at school was about "this" too, though it manifested itself in inappropriate playground love and violence behind the hedges when no one was looking. "This" was treatment. I heard the story first hand again and again on the telephone until finally the phone simply stopped working and the mother left for three weeks. "This" had happened. By that time I had only a little more than a month before The Cage would be uninhabitable.

This was the story: Mother came to in an emergency room and started screaming, "Let me go you fuckers! I'm not staying here!" The fluorescent rails on the ceiling probably ached in her eyes as they often did in mine when, because my stench was so rank, The Cage was moved from the living room to the kitchen sink and the bright rails of light hung from the bottom of the cabinet and prevented me from sleeping. For three days they piled dishes around me.

"Who the hell brought me here?" she continued.

"You brought yourself here," an orderly said, irritated. "You signed the papers. You said you needed help and wanted to go to treatment; now we are getting ready to transport you to treatment." And so it was that the mother was so ill she had to go to treatment yet again. She convinced the hospital to let her go home on the condition that she would check herself into treatment within a week. So she had a week to stare at the admittance papers and feel the numb between her interactions with the family and stew in the uneasiness of her decision. My tamed animal discourse keeps me from being overwhelmed with animal emotion that might keep me from reasoning for a family who needed me. If I had to tell the story boldly I would say she got shit-faced again, screwed the wrong people, pissed off half the town, left her son with no one, and had lost the capacity to take care of even the smallest animal.

The night before she left for treatment A-Man-Worth-Mentioning came over drunk and made love to her all night.

In the morning the child and I were loaded into a loud beast and moved to the aunt's house. The breeze between the beast and the house provided respite from the stench. The smells outside were incredible. There was frozen water everywhere and it was fat and white. My eyes were wide and let in all the sun they could to feign warmth. The child was in a one-piece winter suit with a scarf wrapped around his neck twice and then over his face, around his ears, and one final wrap over the top of his head and then back in on itself like a long strip of gauze. The mother dragged her legs, fighting the magnetic pull of the house. Once she got into the beast and slammed the door, the force was broken and she collapsed onto the dashboard. Tiny drops of mud formed from dashboard dust and tears. They slid down the dashboard and pooled onto the floor, mixing with the melting snow from her boots that she wore with no socks.

The aunt was Molly, and her boyfriend, Shane, looked worse than the whole lot of us. His yellow was mixed with hues of black and green.

We walked into Molly's living room which was messy with charcoal sketches of nature and skies and other landscapes with absolutely no people.

"What is that? Jesus Christ it stinks," she exclaimed while looking at The Cage held in the boy's dainty grip. It never occurred to her to wash me up a little. I hadn't really planned on ever being able to live in a cage free of stench and disease again anyway. And so the plans I had created while being tossed in the air by the hallucinating mother for a night became definite. If the mother ever made it back, I would leave The Cage and live among mother and child freely in the Dober Location house and we would all nest together. I would keep everything clean, from the floor to desire.

Regardless of what Molly thought of me, she was young and beautiful and smelled wonderfully most of the time—cream rinse and sweet tobacco, at least when those smells sneaked through my stench. It never occurred to her to clean The Cage or provide me with some food or water, but I hadn't counted on that in my cage-arithmetic anyway. She never looked at me long enough to read my lips, which mouthed "thank you for taking the child away from that," but she must have felt it because she provided him with pastels and watercolors so he could create great works of art that I would have pasted to the plastic walls of The Cage if I could to aid me in my fantasies. I would run into blue clouds and twirl off the blue walls. Or he would paint a Ferris wheel and I would ride it for hours, effortlessly without having to run. Once he painted the mother, himself, and the Man-Worth-Mentioning, and scribbled a black spot on the floor and labeled it me. In his picture I was already free.

After three weeks, with only one week of cage life left, the Man-Worth-Mentioning picked the child and me up and brought us to the mother who was waiting with chocolates and gold for us at Dober Location. That man loved the boy and was still figuring out how to do it properly. He had come to visit each weekend at Molly's in that really loud beast that sputtered and died in front of the house, and then entered with wonderful grains, fresh vegetables, and words for the boy.

For the first couple of days the mother was different, or maybe it was my delirium from the lack of fresh air and water. The condensation that I licked from the sides of the plastic would simply not do anymore. It tasted of salt, perhaps because of the little urine I had. My food supply was long gone. But what worried me most was the familiar shake that the mother began to acquire after her third day home.

The phone was fixed and it began to ring again. The voices dragged her down as if she was a drop of dirty liquid traveling down a dashboard or the sides of a plastic cage, a liquid unfit for even the soil. Her complexion risked green or black as she wondered at the empty liquor bottles and remembered the stories associated with each. They dazzled and sickened her simultaneously and the only way to break her was to draw her attention to something completely different.

And for the boy, the changes were manifesting themselves is subtle ways. He had pulled out the magnetic tape inside his eight-track and put it back into the cartridge backwards so that The Chipmunks sounded more like the screech I made in my younger years, months ago when I was stirred by the partying and blasts of cigarette smoke from spectators that hovered over me wondering at my exceptional strength on the wheel. The art he had created at the aunt's was hung on the wall upside down and he started to read his books from back to front. He would kiss my genitals rather than my nose. The mother was sure to fill the bottles in the corner and the people were sure to come again with their nicotine breath and fumbling hands. And the child would again take to having a perpetual chill that I couldn't mend from The Cage. My lungs were heavy and I wheezed. My only hope was to get the child to play human with me.

With all the strength I had left I stretched on my hind legs as he moped past The Cage. I wiggled my whiskers and flashed my yellowing teeth. I massaged the plastic with my tiny feet no bigger than pollen bursts trying to get his attention. I spun around twice and the child bent down to me.

"You stink! Want to dance with G.I. Joe?" The lid of The Cage lifted off like darkness does when it succumbs to the splayed hand of morning. The child's hand, the same size as a fairy's, wrapped around my belly and I collapsed into the curve of his lifeline. I surrendered to comfort briefly before the tension of change set in. And before he could stand me on my hind legs to tango with G.I. Joe, I played animal for once and sunk my teeth into the fat of his index fingertip enough to startle him. I was dropped to the ground on my side and bruised my ribs. I had to do it. I was anything but angry. I was in love. In love with what could be the progress and possibilities of a family. My motivation was purely gallant though I had drawn blood with my incisors. I could feel the stench lifting off from me on descent. I could feel the energy of the child's pain and hear his screams for his mother. The sound waves of the mother's footsteps drifted over me like thick rings of smoke. We were all alive and feeling. The blood was pumping in our veins and we all had a goal. Mine was to defy time and science, mother and child's was to capture me. This was the unity I sought.

* * *

For the first couple days they were really diligent about it. They were moving furniture, leaving food out, saucers of water, clean pine chips in a corner. It was good for me, but what mattered most is that they were working together toward a common goal. But I wasn't sure how long they could maintain an interest. For a couple of days it worked perfectly. The phone was ringing and the conversation was always the same, "I have to stay home tonight because Chad and I are trying to catch that crazy hamster."

Often I would jump up into the springs of the couch and be completely out of sight. This downtime was important because mother and child would sit together on the couch and play tacticians. "The next time you see him try to scare him into the bathroom. This morning I sealed the holes in the floor with duct tape and plugged all the drains. There is nothing for him to hide behind." I'm not sure why they even cared if I was back in The Cage. They just felt it wasn't right to have me running around.

I knew the desire wouldn't last forever, so that is why my motion was consistently counter-clockwise. In my mad animal science I thought perhaps if I ran perpetually I could freeze time or even turn it back a couple of days; the moment would stay and there would be no more alcohol and neglect and the pictures on the wall would turn right side up again. The Chipmunks would sing and mother would stay golden like the healthy animal she was. I was confident that I could defy time and science because they were the constructs of reasoning mammals, and I wasn't one in their eyes.

After a week I was well fed and for the most part my stench was gone. My legs started to cramp from the constant running. The shag carpeting was like thick, tall grass. My heart was aching from the pounding, yet it was full with unconditional love and a hope that only animals have. Call it ignorant, but I knew it would work. If the pain got too great I would stand on my hind legs and massage my chest with my front feet. On straight stretches I would close my eyes for micro-sleeps. I was losing weight so I could run even faster, though my joints were weaker.

But after ten or eleven days, mother and child showed disinterest in me. The phone conversations didn't mention me and she began planning for the weekend. I heard her talking to the mother-for-a-night again.

I stepped up the progress on week two and started my nervous gnawing at the tables on my counter-clockwise rounds, trying to get their attention. I chimed the empty bottles together and they half-heartedly tried to catch me. I let them closer and even contemplated letting them catch me.

It occurred to me that maybe I was running too fast and that I had turned time back too far. Perhaps now mother and child were at a pre-treatment moment.

At that juncture I had the option of turning around or continuing the counter-clockwise laps. Turning around may have progressed time with different results. It was possible that the mother might not make it to treatment, or even worse, not even make it out of the bar to the emergency room. The other option was to continue rolling back time. I was weak and frail, but I thought that if I were to increase my radius the time would go back even faster.

There was a small hole where the television cable came into the house. I gnawed at the edges of the hole so I could fit through and make it outside to run around the house. The first couple of laps I had to tunnel through the snow, but after that it was easy. The extreme cold wasn't a problem because I was generating a lot of heat. My joints felt like they needed butter. I wasn't able to check on the progress back in the house, but by my hamster math, I figured I had turned back a year.

I widened my radius to all of Iron River. I ran through Cannon Mine past pine trees and across the frozen water pits. I swam across the Iron River and dodged deer and traffic on highway U.S. 2. Main Street was dark except for the neon in the window at TJT's Nirvana Bar. Aunt Hope was inside, trying to convince Bruno he wasn't the Messiah. I had faith mother and the boy were leaving Montana and driving backwards to Texas and then backwards toward Michigan to another treatment center.

After two laps around Iron River, I went for the whole county. I ran through all the Quad cities: Stambaugh, Gaastra, Caspian, Iron River; through Amasa, Crystal Falls, and Beechwood. Sunset Lake was frozen over and the A-frames at Planet's Resort were in order except for a bucket of frozen Bluegills. I was really picking up speed now and blisters were forming at the back of my knees because of the chaffing from overextending each stride. It didn't matter though, because mother and the boy were in Stevens Point with the Man-Worth-Mentioning. He was reading to the boy, who lay in bed with heavy eyelids lucidly dreaming about Orpheus and Euridice, Star Sapphire, and the Green Lantern.

I was really moving now and went for the whole peninsula. I swam almost three quarters of the way in Lake Superior, Lake Huron, Lake Michigan, and the Sault Locks, and ran down the ice on Brule River the rest of the way. The pads on my feet were totally raw and I started to dream too and placed myself in a scene for warmth: I was at the feet of mother and child, who were in an orange grove sitting in the shade with hollowed weeds stuck into oranges. I could see a car traveling backwards all the way from Florida to Iron River.

The cans of beer were being filled and sealed and returned to the stores and factories. All the marijuana was being shoved into plastic baggies and returned to the Latin American countries it came from.

I spiraled out and lapped the whole state of Michigan in an hour. Eddy Plunket was sucking gas out of a car and a night bear was crawling out of a window on Third Street, scaling down the asbestos siding. Smoke was being sucked into a grandmother's ivory cigarette holder and Aunt Ally was pouring cereal back into a box and Tang powder was pouring out of a glass of water. Aunt Molly was putting her breast back in her shirt.

If I lapped the entire continental United States I was sure that everything could begin again and progress differently. I dipped my paws that were worn to the bone in two oceans. Crossing the Florida Peninsula, I stumbled on a brilliant ring of aluminum foil with a green pebble. I slipped it onto my neck and drew from its power. Maybe in eleven years if events would progress differently I would have a clean cage decorated with brilliant watercolor scenes, full of wheels and fresh shavings, brightly colored tubes that I could nestle in contently with no worry in my heart. I would be free to be unreasonable.

* * *

I think I have managed it. I am at the beginning. I see the grasses disappearing into the soil of fertile fields. There is a sunset at the door of a house so yellow I can smell it. I am massaging my chest now. It hurts but I beat it like the proud animal I am with my slender blistered and bleeding claws. My wheeze is a growl, but with this ring around my neck I strike one last superhero pose. I am a portrait of accomplishment. I am drifting off. I have made it back to the foot of the stairs and I step over the threshold of the good location and lay me down to sleep. The ring slips off my neck and tumbles into the snow. My heart is slowing and has an ache I mistake for love. My eyes are closed. I smell good. I am crawling back into the womb with child. Mother pulls us in. The black is like black. The hour is zero.

* * *

And then they moved.

Afterword

1308 Ninth Street.
Iron River, Michigan

So what becomes of all the little boys,
who run away from home,
well the world just keeps gettin' bigger,
once you get out on your own,
so here's to all the little boys,
the sandman takes you where,
you'll be sleepin' with a pillowman,
on the nickel over there.
from "On the Nickel"
–Tom Waits

July 2003: Mother, Aunt Molly, and I are sitting in a tiny cabin on the Paint River in Upper Michigan 10 miles outside of Iron River, which has been converted into a tattoo parlor. It is part of a complex of three cabins and two trailers which Aunt Hope and her husband, Alvin, own. Aunt Molly lives in one cabin with her son, Spyder. Hope lives in the main cabin. Mother has one of the trailers for when she visits, and Rosanna, a long-time friend of the family, has the other. The interior of the tattoo parlor is exposed logs. Pictures of tattoos Molly has done on others, mostly her daughter and other nieces and nephews, are all over the walls. There is a computer, some furniture situated around a woodstove, and a tiled area about 5'x10' which is a restricted area where she does the tattoos. In the restricted area there is an antique electric Dentist's chair. The cabin has a small kitchen and a bathroom as well. It is summer but the night is cool. A boom-box is playing Tom Waits for most of the evening while Mother is chain smoking. My shirt is off and I am smoking. Molly has just shaved my lower back. I straddle the dentist chair.

Mother: (*to Molly*) . . . I told you I got really bad choked the other night!
Molly: Yeah and you were crying! Oops! (*as if I wasn't supposed to know.*)
Mother: Yeah, and I was crying (*under her breath*).
Molly: Alright Chad, is this too big?
Chad: No.
Molly: No! He hasn't even looked for Christ's sake.
Chad: Yeah, I looked at it before, I don't think it's too big Mom, did you see it?
Mother: Uh-uh. Let me see. Oh! (*Cautiously excited.*)
Chad: What do you think?
Mother: I think you could have chosen better looking lettering. Isn't there a different style?
Chad: No, it's Greek.
Mother: It doesn't look very straight. Look at it Molly.
Molly: What do you mean it doesn't look straight? It was done on the computer!
Mother: I'm telling you, Molly. . . .
Molly: Jesus Christ! It's just the paper Kate!
Mother: Well look, that "K" looks a lot lower than that "U."
Chad: You know I want it solid, right?
Molly: Yep.
Chad: So I'm thinking right…well, pretty low. See where my pants are right now? That's where the middle of the letters should be; half in, half out.
Mother: You don't have any glasses over here? And what about coffee-flavored brandy?
Molly: Everything's in that white cupboard. Here, we're gonna have to put it on you while you're standing up so it looks best.
Chad: Hey Mom—

Mother: What, baby? (*Molly puts a tattoo stencil on my lower back.*)

Chad: So, why did we move into Ninth Street house?

Mother: (*from the kitchen pouring brandy*) Because I bought it. Patti Kolowsky got her real estate license.

Chad: Yeah?

Mother: Yeah, and she sold me a house.

Chad: Why did you decide to buy it?

Mother: Because she said I could.

Molly: She said I could. Ha! Can't you do better than that? O.K., come here, Chad.

Chad: Well, why did she say you could?

Mother: Well, she said, "Kate, you know you could probably buy a house," so we went looking at houses and I. . . .(*she has returned and looks down at me fidgeting with a mini-disk recorder*) Oh.

Chad: I'm, I'm listening. Just making sure it's recording. And?

Mother: Oh! So we went looking at houses, about six or seven, and as soon as I walked into that one I knew that was it. Well it was beautiful old brick; story and a half. It was on a dead-end road known as Lovers' Lane and it was the last house on the right and it had a magnificent front porch. The reason that I bought it is because when you walked in it looked wide open. Just so big and open and there were 144 windows on that front porch—there was a gross of windows on that front porch.

Chad: And why did you decide to buy a house at that point in your life? What time of your life was that?

Mother: I was working at Riverhouse, you know with the mentally disabled adults, and—

Chad: Had you gotten out of treatment?

Mother: I hadn't been out of treatment very long.

Chad: Where were we living before?

Mother: We were living down there in Dober, in munchkin land where I could wash the dishes and dry them and put them away and never move. That's how big the kitchen was.

Chad: That place is abandoned now. That's where I had that hamster I loved and found him frozen at the bottom of the stairs.

Mother: Oh, I remember! That thing stunk! And he got out and we couldn't catch the little fucker. I was FUCKED UP then.
Molly: Oh that house? Yeah. When weren't you fucked up?!
Chad: So when you moved there were you just alone?
Mother: Uh-uh. Actually when I bought it I was alone and not really involved with anyone, but in the process I got re-involved with Big Tom and we had talked about getting married and stuff. Well, he lived there long enough for me to get completely moved in and then I kicked him out the same day.
(*Molly is loading the needle with ink and laughing.*)
Chad: Why?
Mother: Because he went by, and I'm not against getting things out of the garbage, but he stopped and brought *Dean Mandrell's* garbage—garbage five times over—for my living room furniture. I mean, we had to prop it up with books; it was filthy; it was gross, and he set up this nasty couch and this nasty chair and I already had the TV and stuff in there and he sat down on that nasty chair and said, "this is where I'm gonna be spending a lot of my time," and I thought, "no you're not." So I said, "I don't think this is gonna work out." He got really mad and I got scared. He called me a selfish bitch—
Molly: Oops, don't let your pants come up and touch it.
Chad: Can I see what it's gonna look like?
Mother: Turn one of those lights on so he can see it really good. That top one would work great.
Mother: It's not gonna take long for her to do that.
Chad: (*I have my back to the mirror, doing my best to turn my head to see my lower back in the mirror.*) She's probably gonna give me a hassle.
Mother: Who, Gingi?
Chad: Yeah, that's O.K. So—
Mother: Don't even tell her, let her discover it.
Chad: Oh yeah, I'm not gonna tell her. So, I don't know. Keep going. So then what happened on Ninth Street?
Mother: So I kicked him out and since I bought that house through FHA they gave me $2,500 to fix up some stuff in addition to my loan. I had an account set up at the lumberyard.
Molly: Here, turn that way, just move your ass over here a little.

Mother: Anyways, Stan Sweet did a lot of work, I did a lot of work. I sanded the floors and redid the kitchen. And I don't recall how long I had been living there, but Greg was working for Trebessi's at the time out there on U.S. 2 taking care of their three retarded boys. And so I was calling and talking to him one day and I don't remember if it was him or if it was me, but one of us suggested something about us having dinner together or something like that. I don't know, I got that old feeling again and got all excited and the next thing you know we're moving in with each other again. But he didn't really want to put any time or energy into that house because it wasn't his so I just worked my ass off there and in the process I got politically active and interested in whole foods.

Molly: Yeah, nuts and berries!

Chad: Yeah, I remember Molly would come over—

Molly: Yeah and I'd say, "Got anything to eat?" Most of that stuff tasted like dirt.

Mother: Everybody said I was a natural vegetarian cook. Non-vegetarian people even liked my cooking, like Hope was crazy about my crepes and my sauces. I even made stuff like this, I made a green been and tofu thing, tofu stroganoff it was called, and Molly has to admit she liked it. And she liked my lentil soup and my bran muffins.

Molly: Yeah, that shit was good.

Mother: I used to make bran muffins all organic and put a quarter slice of pineapple in the pan. We ate that and lentil soup until it was coming out of our ears. I learned how to make bread and made our own tofu, our own yogurt, our own granola. So when Greg and I got back together and working on the house and stuff and he was at the Trebessi's and then his dad owned the Shamrock Bar you know, and Greg started managing it and I said, "I'm sorry but I can't have anything to do with it." You know, how excited would you be if you just quit doing heroin and I started selling it? You know, I wouldn't be around it. I did do some cooking. And I was going to aerobics twice a week. We had political meetings at our house.

(*Molly is testing the tattoo gun.*)

Chad: Aerobics twice a week? Holy Cow, how much did you weigh?

Mother: I weighed about 145.

Chad: So that was the best shape you had ever been in? Damn, how much are you now?
Mother: About twice that! And you had a fort in the woods, and then do you remember the incident, I think you wrote a poem about it, about the snow owl that dragged that animal across our yard and it left really strange markings? We saw that thing a lot. It must have lived up the road.
Chad: When we were washing dishes we would always see it.
Molly: (*I am in the chair now with my ass half exposed and Molly is bent over my back with the tattoo gun buzzing.*) Are you ready? I'll start out with a small line. Does it hurt?
Chad: No. Cat scratch.
Mother: And Carol lived next door with her ex-husband, remember Bill with the thick glasses? I see him all over town. And so she finally got rid of him and uh, Carol was not a very pretty woman, she was very attractive though, and had really nice skin and always took good care of herself and always looked nice and stuff, but she was a little bit snooty. But she never was with me. She was real good to me. She'd watch you when I worked at Riverhouse. I ran into her son Bill at the fair last year. He came right up to me and said, "Can I get my picture taken with you, man," and then he had somebody take our picture. And then he said, "I always said that if ever I saw you again I'd say thank you so much, you are one of the most important people in my life." He said, "I was a very tormented soul and you were extremely accepting and patient with me and I just really want to thank you for loving me unconditionally." I said, "Well I did love you unconditionally, Billy." He said, "I know you did and I am thanking you for it!" Cause I spent a lot of time with him. He would come over and just visit with me. He came out you know! Then we had that big tree removed when we lived there. When you walked down the stairs to the right around the back of the house there was a big old widow maker they called it. And it was dead.
Chad: Ouch! Ugh.
Mother: (*Mother cowers*) You see, I'm not gonna be able to take this—That's what they call a widow maker! (*Responding to the buzz and cry of pain*) You see, that's what's making me hurt now. So listen—Porky Rye and Joey Nordic—I bartered with them for pot, to cut that tree down. And Chad, they were like

monkeys. I've never seen anything like that in my life. Those boys knew what the hell they were doing and that was like a big deal because that was a very dangerous tree . . . Do you remember when I used to put my bed in the summer out on the front porch? Greg and I didn't make it because he was drinking a lot and running around with little Joni.

Chad: Greg was still drinking then?

Mother: Oh yeah.

Chad: You know, yesterday we were driving through Crystal Falls and he said, "Do you want to stop and see Joni quick?" And I said, "No, I'm sorry you know, but she's just"—ouch! Augh—"she's not very healthy and it kind of depresses me hanging out with her." Wow, no tattoo's hurt this bad before.

Molly: Yep, it's the most painful part of your body. The most sensitive, that's where all your nerve endings are.

Chad: Well that's fucking great! (*Mother laughs*) Especially if Gingi gives me a hassle. I'm gonna say, "Hey, listen, this fucking hurt you know!"

Mother: So then Greg and I didn't work out and uh. . . .

Chad: Listen. We were really poor for a while. I remember stuff happening and you crying because—

Mother: I'm getting to that part. I'm just trying to think about what happened next 'cause when he first left I was still working at Riverhouse and I stopped and started working at the chalet and then the gas got turned off and all we had was that wood stove. I remember one time it had gotten so cold that we moved everything downstairs. Do you remember that? And we just had that kitchen, dining room and little hall. Stan and Caroline stopped over one time on a weekend morning and I heard them pull up. We didn't have a phone, we didn't have lights or anything and I ran out there and I remember it specifically. Oh my god, I had on long-johns, boots, a flannel shirt, a flannel nightgown and my second-hand long mink coat and I ran out there crying, "You guys have got to help me, please help me, we are freezing to death here!" And what I had been doing was getting all this shit wood that just wouldn't work and then so I wound up getting coal, and every night we'd be putting that coal in there.

Chad: Fucking 1980s and we're burning coal in Iron River.

Mother: Fuck. Well, and then Mark Patterson came into my life and he rescued me financially.

Chad: Wasn't he the guy that died in the plane crash?

Mother: Yes, he was a pilot. And so I got it back together that way, and then I had a few little problems there with drugs and stuff, but I never did start drinking. And then I—

Chad: Wait wait wait, what kind of drugs?

Mother: Oh, I was doing a little tripping and smoking weed, but anyway I finally got my shit together and the house was looking good, I was looking good, and Grampa was living up there at Roosesevlt and I had known Ron Smeltzer for years and years and there was never any attraction there. We were always just friends. And he spent a lot of time with Duke. So then I started seeing Rod Smeltzer and he came back one weekend because he was living in Wausau and I said, "What are you doing back so quick?" And he said, "I came to spend some time with you." Well that was that and we slept together and that was really magical and he didn't drink or anything and—

Chad: Well why didn't he drink or anything? I know why! You see, I remember something that was weird to me. I remember when I was a little kid living on Ninth Street watching TV and it was the news and it said something about how someone had tried to hang himself in the Marquette jail because he had gotten busted and was really down.

Mother: Yes, he was busted for cocaine.

Chad: He tried to kill himself and it was right there on the news.

Molly: And he stole a truck.

Mother: Yeah, he stole a truck

Chad: And then you were dating this guy six months later and I was like, wow!

Mother: Well that was after he had gone to prison and gotten cleaned up and stuff.

Chad: Well for sure, but that was pretty profound for me as a little kid to make that connection, and then this guy's my mom's boyfriend!

Mother: That's why when he starts getting on me I say listen, you take care of your own shit and I'll take care of mine. I know what's going on. I started seeing him and I continued to see Mark Patterson, but as a friend. Until he died.

Chad: There were a couple of other guys too who you were messing around with. I remember Shel.

Mother: Oh yeah, I was on and off with Shel for many years.

Chad: Man, that was weird too. You were brother and sister!

Mother: Yeah, but only by law! We were all screwing those boys one time or another.

Chad: Anybody else?

Mother: I dated that one young guy from Riverhouse. Jim, the gay guy.

Chad: (*To Molly*) Do you almost have the outline yet?

Molly: Outline?! It's almost done.

Mother: I went out with a lot of guys there. Do you remember that one Harley guy from Alpha named Chris? Oh, and the mailman too.

Chad: You filled it in too? It's all black?

Molly: Yeah, I just have to fill in a couple of spots.

Chad: It's all filled in?

Molly: Yeah, I just have to touch up a couple of spots.

Chad: Well damn, that was quick! Let's get some more!

Mother: And I had a lot to do with Silvio on Ninth Street. And just before I had started with Rod Smeltzer, Silvio had moved to Seattle and I wanted to go with him and he, that's one of the things he says today, is that he should have taken us and he didn't, so—

Chad: And you still see Silvio?

Mother: Well, until a year or so ago and then I just asked to get him out of my past and it seems it was answered. You know it seemed every time I came up here he was here and when he is up here and he hears I am here he comes right out here.

Chad: Yeah, I never liked him.

Mother: Yeah, I know, I'm surprised you haven't written a lot of stuff about him. Was he mean to you or something?

Chad: He wasn't interested in me at all. You know maybe it was because that one time—I did write that poem about it, you know the time when you just dropped everything and pretty much forgot about me and you took off with him and went to the bluegrass festival and left me?

Mother: You see, well that's where you are wrong because I didn't leave you. (laugh)

Chad: Well, I felt like it though.

Mother: I'm sorry you feel like that but I really didn't, Chad. I didn't you know, and we didn't go to the bluegrass festival, we went to Flint.

Chad: Well, not in my book!

Mother: I know! Well, I have memories too that are wrong.

Chad: So if you think about the most significant thing at Ninth Street, what was it, if you really think about it? What do you remember? Something must have popped into your head already.

Molly: Shane died.

Mother: Oh, Yes, Shane and Moosey—Little Hope Allen.

Chad: That's another thing, I have a memory of Shane coming up the hill looking really bad.

Mother: They spent a lot of time there with us. Hope Allen came there when she was ten days old because Bruno had a problem with Shane.

Molly: Yeah, I wouldn't let just anybody watch her.

Chad: Bruno didn't like Shane?

Mother: No, he was mad at him for the way he treated Molly when she was pregnant. And I always liked Shane, though. That's another thing Mark Patterson did is he just really gave to me so I could help out Molly and Shane. I'd pay for their hotels and I gave her money for food and gas and everything and it was all Mark Patterson. Hell, they weren't even 20 yet.

Chad: Shit. You know, it's as if Mark didn't even exist for me. I don't even remember what he looked like. You completely own that story. I guess it is meant just only for you. How did he get all that money? Was he a commercial pilot?

Mother: No, no. He was running pot from Colombia.

Chad: No shit?

Mother: Yeah, and he was stashing it in the attic and I was selling it for him. He would come over with those big old green canvas Army bags full of it.

Chad: Are you shitting me? I know you were always dealing a little pot, but I didn't know I was sleeping under pounds and pounds of it! Well, glad you didn't get busted. And you found out about Mark's death from the news, right?

Mother: No, I found out from my neighbor because when I told her I was going to live with Rod Smeltzer she said, "What about Mark?" Because it wasn't odd for Mark to come and go and be gone for a month or two, and I said, "What do you mean? Mark is gonna be my friend wherever I am and we will always love each other because we do." And she said, "Kate, don't you know?" I said, "Don't I know what?" She said, "Kate, he's dead." Well, I...I was really freaked out. And I remember he said something about a deal going bad or something and I think those Puerto Ricans did something to his plane.

Chad: I thought you said they were Colombians?

Mother: Oh yeah. I'm getting a little loaded. So, of course I went to Duke. He was living alone then at 711 Roosevelt because he had "quit the system" he said and stopped working, started smoking pot, and turned his Mercury Gran Marquis into a cab.

Chad: And Gramma?

Mother: Oh, she wouldn't have that. She left town and went to Peoria to be with her sister and find another husband. So anyway, Rod Smeltzer was there that time too.

Chad: Was Rod cool about you mourning over Mark?

Mother: I was just really upset and I wanted to be by my dad.

Chad: I remember it all a little. So how did you meet Mark Patterson?

Mother: I met him years and years ago at TJT's and—

Chad: Cool, (*looking in the mirror*) looks good. How about those love handles on the sides. Can you get rid of those?

Mother: Maybe she can do some shading Chad. Now stand over here so I can get a good look at it. Well that didn't take long at all. Oh! Cool Chad, Wow! That is so cool. OOH, it puffed right out too, didn't it!

Chad: Well, it fucking hurt.

Molly: It's supposed to.

Chad: So what else happened there? Well, Molly did tell me her most significant thing, but you never told me your most significant thing. What else do you remember?

Mother: Let's see, I broke up with Tom, I broke up with Greg, I screwed all those guys I was talking about before, Mark died, Shane died....

Chad: Let's see, that was the time when you told Greg he couldn't see me anymore.

Mother: Yeah. Because he called welfare on me.

Chad: Yeah?

Mother: He swears he didn't.

Chad: I don't think he would lie about it. I'll ask him.

Mother: You don't think he would lie?! It got so bad between us that one time he pulled up on the hill there, and I was mad at him, and he had the window rolled up and was sticking his tongue out at me and I was trying to bust the fucking glass. I never had anybody push me to the fucking edge like that, Chad. He used to push me to the fucking edge. Oh yeah, so the next thing I know—

Chad: So why did he call welfare on you?

Mother: Cause he said I wasn't taking good enough care of you. I was working and leaving you alone until ten o'clock at night. He pissed me off about the welfare thing really bad because they came to my fucking house—you know if they wanted to get shitty I could have lost you. I not only wanted to keep you away from him, I wanted to kill him. But anyway, fortunately Caroline, well, a lot of her special ed kids had to deal with social services so the person that came to see me was the same person that Caroline always worked with and professionally he liked her because she was a very good teacher, you couldn't take that away from her—and she told him, "Kate is the only person I know who I would allow to babysit my children," and that was the truth, "and you've gotten into the middle of a domestic dispute." And I never heard another word about it, but I had had it with Greg. The man from social services came to see me and I wound up talking and crying to him for three hours about what had happened with Greg because by that time I felt like I was going crazy cause I had a new job at Happy Italians and all of the sudden Greg's new girlfriend was cooking in the kitchen and I felt there was a conspiracy against me and I was such a nervous wreck because I was like, "what am I gonna do?" I got a bald spot the size of a quarter on my head. She was coming here to work and Jeanette, the owner, said, "well I will cover your back." So I told Greg he couldn't see you anymore and then Reynold came to see me and he said, "Please don't do this to Greg, Chad is the only thing in his life that he has ever been responsible about."

Chad: Hey, got some tobacco?

Molly: Oh, Christ, you need papers and everything?

Mother: He said, "If I did the picking up and dropping off, would it be acceptable?" And I said, "Yeah, I don't want him coming to my house, I don't want him calling my house . . . ." So for a while that worked and then Greg kind of dropped it all after a while but he was still sinking his teeth into me sometimes and nibbling. You know he had his new little girlfriend and everything.

Chad: Who was the girl he was seeing?

(*Enter Aunt Hope and Rosanna*)

Hope: Well, everyone went to bed, but we came over heretoparty.

Chad: Good, you can hear her stories.

Mother: Look at his tattoo!

Hope: Yougotitdone already?

Mother: Bend forward so they can see it.

Rosanna: What does it say?

Chad: It says "insert here."

Mother: No it doesn't, it says "Gingi."

Chad: No it doesn't!

Rosanna: Oh, I think that's an "e."

Chad: So this is Gingi's real name. Her name is Euridike, which is Greek. This is her name, ευρυδικη in Greek. It's also the name of a goddess and there are poems and plays written about it and music has been set to it and stuff.

Hope: Alright Professor. What'dittakeyou, about ten minutes?

Molly: About 15.

Hope: Was that all? So, whatisit about this girl? God, you like those dark girls. What color are her eyes?

Chad: Brown. And there is a distance in them I want to travel to.

Hope: Huh?

Rosanna: Heavy. You know you should make it last longer if you get paid by the hour.

Molly: That was a freebie for my nephew.

Hope: You know, I'm not getting that "sister" tattoo the four of us talked about tattooed on my foot because it's the most sensitive place onyourbody so I'm having it put right here between my bra on my chest.

Mother: Well then you will be showing everybody.

Hope: I know, but I won't have to show my tits all the time, I can just show my tattoo.

Chad: She's telling stories about Ninth Street for the final chapter in this book. I'm letting her tell her part of the story for this one house. Do you remember the Ninth Street house?
Mother: Yeah, that's where Hope and Bruno broke up. That was another big thing that happened there.
Chad: What the fuck was it in 1980? Everything fell apart. What the hell was Ally doing?
Molly: (*cleaning up the studio space*) She was back in Texas having Maria and living in a hotel room with a bunch of whores while Hector was drinking all the money Gramma sent them.
Hope: Well, Bruno and I were already done. Ninth Street is where I met Alvin because I remember going over there and hearing Vicky Frangello bitchaboutAlvin and a month later I met him.
Mother: Yeah, because when she first met Alvin her kids stayed with us a lot.
Hope: Yeah, that's when Greg Banks stooduponthechair and ran from a mouse. God, we should'veknownhewas gay. He was a fairy just like all of us!
Chad: Yeah. Who would have thought that he would end up with a Polish queen?!
Hope: Um, did you put this in your book, that I tried to get you away from your mom?
Chad: I talk about it a little, I think. Lansing.
Mother: That's when she thought I was gonna give her my kid!
Molly: Hello! She tried to do the same thing with me by taking both my kids!
Hope: Well my sisters were fucking up at the time and I wanted to take care of their kids.
Mother: When he was two years old I was not fucking up. He came to visit you and you didn't want to let him go.
Hope: I know, but youusedtoleavehim with Bruno and me.
Mother: Yeah but he wasn't!—
Rosanna: But he was really good at holding joints at parties.
Chad: Did you hear that one?
Rosanna: I was gonna turn you in to welfare once.
Chad: Did you hear that one?
Hope: So that doesn't sound very responsible.

Mother: He was still in diapers.

Molly: That's when you were really, really, really, partying.

Rosanna: Yeah, passing joints when he was still in his diapers at parties.

Mother: Oh yeah, yeah. If there was a kegger he would carry the pitcher around and fill the beers.

Hope: And that one time in the welfare office….

Mother: Oh my god, we're at the welfare office and I'm rolling my own cigarette and he says, "Is that a joint, Mom?" just as Mr. Rommetti, the social worker, was walking by. I sealed his entire mouth with both my hands and pretended I was trying to get him to spit out a penny or something.

Hope: Got any beer here?

Mother: I think there is one in there.

Molly: Is there?

Hope: Busch Lite? Budweiser.

Rosanna: I forgot you smoked.

Chad: Only at night.

Rosanna: Can you roll me one of those? I'll pay you a buck for it.

Chad: You don't have to give me a fucking buck.

Hope: I am quitting though. I feel like I want to quit and I haven't felt that way in sometime so I'mgonnaquit. And I am excited about it.

Rosanna: I just want to not do what everybody else is doing and be good at doing that.

Mother: (*To herself*) So what else about Ninth Street?

Rosanna: Was that in Alpha?

Chad: No, that house is gonna have to be in the next book!

Hope: No Rosanna, we're talking about Ninth Street. Iron River.

Rosanna: Oh there, where the mailman used to come.

Chad: Yeah, weren't you dating the mailman?

Rosanna: Yeah, I think you were, that's why I said it.

Hope: I knew she was screwing him because her mail used to come fasterthaneverybodyelse's!

Molly, Hope, and Rosanna in unison: Special delivery!

Mother: Well it is weird how I met him because I had never seen him before until I worked at Happy Italians and somebody said he was the mailman and

I asked if he was my mailman and he asked where I lived and I told him 1308 Ninth Street and he said, "You're Rebecca Faries? I always wondered what Rebecca Faries looked like."

Molly: Hah! He knew her by her name!

Mother: And then I was his. I was a sucker for a good line.

Hope: (*listening to the music*) Thisiscool.

Chad: Yeah, it's Tom Waits.

Mother: And, well, you know I was wild on and off all my life. If you are saying I dated a bunch of men, well yeah, I did. But then as soon as I met Ron I stopped seeing everyone else.

Chad: You never cheated on Ron?

Mother: No.

Rosanna: I've got a really neat picture of them.

Hope: The mailman had really sexy teeth.

Rosanna: In the picture you're sitting on a porch in Alpha.

Hope: Still to this day he's really sexy. Well, he's my mailman now!

Rosanna: You had a cute scarf on your head, and you looked cute and Ron was looking good.

Mother: (*Everyone is beginning to ignore Rosanna respectfully.*) But that was another house. Well, back to Ninth. I don't think there was really anything else.

Hope: You know she made the best crepes! That's when you lost all that weight. Those crepes that she made with cauliflower and cheese and no white flower! EverytimeIwentoverthere I said, "Kate please make those things for me."

Chad: Well, why don't you start doing that again?

Mother: That's when I was running around with those liberal hippy girls, you know. Maggy and Janey Murphy.

Molly: They were so fake, though.

Hope: Kate was the only true person.

Mother: Maggy was O.K. She's with Rick Slate now, you know.

Chad: I just saw them at a party and he quit drinking, didn't he? He must have looked 20 years younger and they were just radiating.

Mother: Did he still have his beard?

Hope: Ohmygod Chad, he was the wildest.

Molly: He scared me once, He just came over here and said, "I'm sexually attracted to you and I would like to...."

Hope: Oh Chad, he'd walk intothebar and had super-glued his wallet to his ass, completely naked, and ordered fourteen cases of beer, thenhesat on the hood of the car and was being driven around while he was naked.

Mother: And had a dick as big as a Michelob bottle!

Hope: Then we walked into Amasa one night and he was naked and just had a pillowcase over it because he said his clothes were dirty. Then him and Alvin ate some mushrooms and Alvin kept his clothes on, but they swam across the river and went all the way up to the Hemlocks and Rick neverputathingon.

Mother: What other men (*to herself*)...? Mark Patterson, Silvio, the Mailman, Shel, Stan, Jim, Greg, Ron...oh!—Bobbie from Chicago. He was a TV repairman. He was very handsome, Bobby from Chicago, and everytime he came to town, you know I spent a lot of time with him. And Chad woke us up one morning for breakfast, and he had made us breakfast, and it was fried braunschwager with eggs and toast and juice and everything, and it was really good. Fried braunschwager for breakfast. He liked Bobbie because, well, you know why Chad liked Bobbie? Our TV was broken and he fixed it. That's why you made him breakfast. You were so happy. Yep. Bobby from Chicago.

Chad: Shit, I thought that was Roosevelt!

Mother: No, no, no. Ninth Street.

Chad: Well, got that memory wrong too.

Mother: You better let us write that book for you!

Chad: Well, what do you think you all are doing right now!

(*everyone, except for Molly and me, is getting pretty stoned and drunk*)

Hope: The only three boyfriends that I even remember what they looked like were Jimmy Swanson—

Molly: He was pretty.

Rosanna: I went out with him one night.

Molly: Only one night?

Hope: No personality.

Rosanna: He was too frickin' stuck on himself.

Hope: Best lay I ever had though.

Mother: We were just talking about your brother the other night, Rosanna. I used to go out with Rosanna's brother at night sometimes and we would have fun and stuff. But one night I was at his house in Caspian and we were eating Quaaludes and drinking his homemade beer and I got so fucked up I admitted myself into treatment and I woke up in the morning and said "what the fuck am I doing here?" and they said, "Hey, you called us!" I said, "I did not!" They said, "Yes you did!"

Rosanna: And you missed my wedding!

Hope: Rick Slate and Don Jones, but whenIwas just talking with Strawberry about all those guys—Teddy Loraine— in Battle Creek, I don't remember!

Mother: You don't remember Blake Putt?

Hope: Nope, not whathelooks like or nothing.

Mother: Teddy Loraine and Blake Putt were…wow— Fabulous!

Rosanna: Johnson? Don't you remember Johnson? Don't you remember we used to wake him up in the middle of the night and screw him until all hours of the day?

Mother: Johnson who?

Chad: Feeling young, Molly? This was before your time! You were a little kid!

Hope: That was Johnson, Johnson Lindwall.

Molly: Ohhh, I remember.

Hope: That was the first man I ever kissed after Bruno because I had never been with another man for ten years.

Rosanna: This is a really weird thing (*on the side while Hope is telling the story of Bruno*), this guy Johnson, I used to wake him up and he would open his door and we would just go and go until all hours of the day and all he did was fuck.

Hope: And Bruno freaked out and left me and I never kissed anybody for those eleven years, and he did allthetime. Molly used to catch him allthetime with women.

Rosanna: And I would come back again.

Hope: (*Laugh.*) Even when I was in the hospital giving birth to little Ally!

Chad: Johnson Lindwall? That's who you're talking about? I remember Johnson Lindwall. He killed his cat by shooting a pistol at the ceiling because he thought it was a squirrel running around upstairs! He used to come to Gramma's all the time. He was older than all of you, wasn't he?

Mother: Yeah, he's my age.

Hope: You see I'd gooverthere because Bruno was in Tomah at the VA hospital and I'dsay, "I'm comin'overthere," and I'd get drunk and not make it overthere, but when I finally did he had 12 long-stem yellow roses, and by the time I got there they were kind of old and I said, "Wow thesearereally pretty!" And he said, "They were for you, about three days ago." And he bought my kids a Christmas tree and he put one up for himself because he'd never hadaChristmas tree.

Rosanna: (*Incoherent.*) All I gave him was sex. (*Everybody is acting as if she isn't there*)

Hope: We were really really serious. He carved and for Christmas I got him this set. Yeah, he loved me.

Rosanna: He loved me too. (*everyone still ignoring her*)

Chad: What's he doing now?

Hope: He's married. He's filthy rich. I can almost count how many people I'vedonein my whole life.

Mother: Well, I can't.

Chad: Really, so you're not like her, Hope?

Hope: I only had three months to do it.

Mother: Well she was married for 11 years.

Hope: Kate took care of my kids for three months.

Chad: And you were just out screwing?

Hope: Yeah, prettymuch. One time I stayed in bed for three days when we were down in Caspian.

Rosanna: I don't even want to talk about my sex life.

Hope: Kate remembers that guy on Ninth Street, what washisname? (*whispers to herself*) Is he dead now?

Mother: Oh, Bushy! Remember you and me and Kevin Nordic?

Hope: No, not Bushy. He'sstillalive. No. Umm, one of Mimi Tarnovsky's sons—Tony?

Molly: Oh yeah! Not Tony, Jerry. Hairy Jerry.

Mother: He's still alive. Tony's dead, though.

Hope: Yeah, Jerry, I stayed in bed with him for three days.

Mother: Yeah, I remember I stayed in bed with Tony for three days too when we lived in the house that Greg lives in now. That was where I had my first real orgasm and every time I go to that house that's what I think about.

Chad: You know what? I just realized that there is a house I forgot to write about.

Molly: Oh! New chapter!

Chad: Oh well, it will be a lost chapter. But I don't have any memories of it.

Mother: Which one? Can you add something at the end?

Chad: Well, I already added Shamrock and that orgasm house you just mentioned.

Hope: Chad, you need to hurry up and get done with this book because Iwantyoutowrite my book. I'll put it on tape for you because there is shit you never even heard of that's happened in my life. I told a woman once when I was really drunk. She was—

Mother: I was there.

Hope: She was—

Mother: At Kevin's funeral?

Hope: She was a reporterorsomething and she wanted to write it, she said, "Can you remember everything?"

Mother: She also told you that you had to stop letting people walk all over you but you don't remember that part. So which house did you miss?

Chad: With Eddy Plunket. That house that was behind the Heartbreak Hotel.

Mother: Oh, we only lived there a month.

Hope: I lived there too.

Chad: But we lived there!

Rosanna: Oh, that little teeny house!

Chad: Greg was saying that everybody lived there.

Hope: Yeah, everybody that lived there broke up. That'swhereBruno was hanging out at Pike's Bar and I caught this women giving him a blowjob in the car right out in front of our house and I went back to the house and threw everything I owned out the front door.

Mother: You see, I did the same thing to Eddy. I did the same thing. And then I had to clean it up. I thought, "I will never fucking do that again."

Hope: And then mom came over and I chased that woman with a pool stick and momwashelpingme.

Chad: Gramma was helping you?

Mother: I remember that.

Hope: Yeah, she was the wildest. I was 17 and working at Pike's.

Chad: So mom, did we go from there to Lincoln?

Mother: No, we went to Battle Creek from there.

(*Rosanna gets up.*)

Hope: (*Under her breath after Rosanna goes to the bathroom*) You didn't know that Bruno was screwing Rosanna when I was giving birth to Little Ally?

Chad: Is that what she was talking about? I thought she was talking about Johnson Lindwall or something?

Hope: She was talkingabouthimtoo, but I knew about Bruno.

Chad: Did she tell you?

Mother: Everybody knew. Somebody said something to me the other night about if I screwed Bruno back then. I said, "No! Hell no!" He didn't like me because I was out there partying and I knew what he was doing—sneaking and hiding from me all the time.

Molly: I caught him once and he said "If you tell on me I'm gonna kill you," and I told on him right in front of his face. He dove at me and I jumped behind the chair.

Hope: Hewasmean and crazy. Vietnam shit.

Rosanna: (*enters*) Who was mean?

Hope: Bruno. Fucking crazy. I remember that. I don't remember a whole lot but then whenIstarttalking I remember. He got really crazy in Minnesota. He had jars and jars of cocaine and 115 poundsofpot—

Mother: —In the bathtub.

Hope: No, upstairs in the spare bedroom, and the cats used it for kitty litter.

Rosanna: The pot or the coke?

Molly: He locked himself in that room for a month?!

Hope: He read the Bible.

Mother: She snorted the coke.

Chad: I remember that a little, the Jesus days.

Hope: We were starving. 30 miles from International Falls in Minnesota.

Chad: I remember visiting you somewhere and it was like a trailer or a pre-fab or something.

Mother: We visited her once there in Minnesota, we did.

Chad: You fell through a porch or something and another time grease splattered into your eye.

Hope: That was in Harvey, Michigan.

Chad: Could have been. Yeah, that trailer park!

Rosanna: (*Almost completely incoherent.*) I used to see you guys walking around a lot.

Hope: First he wenttocollege and he lived in that cement building.

Molly: Oh yeah.

Mother: Married housing, the old married housing near where we ended up living.

Hope: And then he went to school when he wanted to. AllIremember is he never really worked a lot and he just slept.

Chad: Did he even finish?

Mother: No, not when he was with Hope.

Hope: Now he did! He's with his professor. He'sajournalist.

Chad: He's sharp. I had some good talks with him.

Hope: (*Nonchalantly.*) Hethoughthewas Christ for a while, or the chosen one.

(*Pause.*) He got up in the middleofthenight after he hadn't come down for 30 days and said he hadtogo catch a fish. (*Pause and then Chad laughs heartily.*) And that's when I sent the note with the kids to give to the bus driver. It said, "Help me! Call this number!" My kids were dehydrated. I had lost 35 lbs. ButIwasdoing all kinds of coke. I did almost all of it. And I chopped up all the Vitamin C because the mafia in Chicago wasafterus.

Molly: And you were replacing it with aspirin!

Hope: Yeah, I was replacing it with aspirin and Vitamin C. (*laugh*) And then they came after us. But then Bruno was so fucking crazy that they leftusalone. That's when he was hearing helicopters and shit and he went to the Vet hospital and they puthiminTomah. Betty Rosetti and Stan Sweet came alltheway out there to International Falls with a big pot of spaghetti and got me. And allIremember was the kids eating and puking because they were so dehydrated they couldn't keep anything down.

Mother: And they bought you a bunch of groceries and stuff.

Chad: Betty and Stan Sweet?
Mother: Yeah, Stan said he was sitting in the bar and Betty, Bruno's Mother, came in all upset and he said, "I'll take care of it." And he did.
Hope: We were fucking starving in International Falls. I went to the grocery store before the block froze on the car and charged abunchofgroceries because I knew I couldn't pay them. Frozen meat, oatmeal, popcorn. Allofour water froze. Our cat froze solid on the back porch.
Chad: Well the kids were pretty young so they didn't remember much, Gene wasn't even born was he?
Hope: Yes he was. And I couldn't afford diapers so I just keptem'in a playpen with newspapers and keptchanging them. After that we moved back to Iron River and then Bruno gottajob in Coleman, Wisconsin, and Jason started kindergarten in Neenah.
(*indefinite silence*)
Mother: How is your back feeling baby?
Chad: It's a little sore.
Mother: Oh, I almost had to leave, she hurt him a couple of times and I said "I'm not gonna be able to take it."
Molly: You know what it was, the middle letter that was on his spine.
Mother: Well, Chad, stand up there in front of them and take off the plastic just for a minute so they can see it. There you go, turn around and show them. Cool! Isn't it!
Hope: Oh, it's cool. What the hell is it?
Chad: It's Gingi's real name, Euridike, in Greek. I hope she doesn't kill me. I thought I told you this before?
Hope: I'm getting kindaloaded. What does Gingi do anyway?
Chad: She is a communist Dallas Cowboy Cheerleader with an alter ego named Star Sapphire.
Hope: Howdoesshe do that in Czechrussia or wherever she's from?
Mother: Hope, he's lying. You're fucked up.
Molly: So what are her powers?
Chad: Actually she was just an oak nymph. I'm the one with the powers. I have a beautiful song and woo her. And I have a magic ring.
Hope: You sure y'aren't stoned?

Mother: Green Lantern! I remember that stuff. You were in to him. That was weird.
Chad: Fuck, I've been sober over 15 years now! She's a Slovak national and ethnic Hungarian. She is still a grad student. We met when I was a Fulbright Fellow finishing up my Ph.D. in Budapest. I don't know if it's gonna work, though.
Hope: Well why'dyouget a tattoo then? Hell, I'm having fun telling stories! Why isn't it gonna work?
Chad: Bad role models, I guess.
Molly: Bad role models. Hah!
Rosanna: I want to talk about screwing.
Chad: I'm ready for another tattoo. Orpheus looking back.
Molly: You want a piercing? Come on, just a little spike through your eyebrow.
Chad: I have to piss.
Pause. Chad goes to the bathroom. Tape recorder is still on.
Mother: (*Quietly so I couldn't hear.*) And yesterday I was so bummed out.
Hope: Why?
Mother: Well, it's just because lots has been going on and I got loaded the other night and cried and cried, and almost choked myself. You know, my friend Eric is dying of AIDS, my marriage sucks, Chad is moving back to Hungary, and everything was coming to a head and then I woke up yesterday and you know how you are full of remorse and self-loathing—and I had a hangover, and I was just bawling and crying because I had left Chad out here and told him I was running into town to go to the store and didn't come back until 4 a.m. and he was crashed outside by the fire-pit waiting for me. Then the phone rang at 9 a.m., and it's Dale, "I just called to tell you how much I love you." And I remembered feeling the same way on Ninth Street, before that call—I was so down and everything was totally fucked and all I wanted was a phone call like that. Hell, we didn't even have a phone.
(*Chad enters and hears the tail-end of the talk.*)
Chad: So what did you do about it on Ninth Street?
Mother: I smoked a joint and found an old telephone receiver and started to pretend I was talking to someone. I talked for a long time, kind of like we did tonight.

Chad: And then what?

Mother: And then I hung up the receiver and waited for someone to call.

Chad: But you said the phone was turned off.

Mother: It was.

Chad: So what did you do?

Mother: I waited for it to ring until I was out of pot and couldn't wait anymore.

(*Indefinite silence. Rosanna's eyes are like two festered assholes.*)

Molly: What time is it anyway?

Hope: Lookatthe clock—it's flashing 00:00.

Rosanna: Guess we have no time....

Mother: ...Or all the time in the world! Molly, you got a phone here?

Molly: No.

Chad: Good, let's just sit here and wait for it to ring. No one move.

Acknowledgments

Excerpts from this book have appeared in *Verbsap*, *Post Road*, *KNOCK*, *The Emergency Almanac*, *Pilvax*, *Conte*, and *r.kv.r.y. quarterly*. Portions of this story were also told during my raconteuring with the "Unchained Tour of Georgia."

The production of *Drive Me Out of My Mind* was supported by the Antioch Media and Publishing Center in Seattle.

Printed in the U.S.A. by Lightning Source on acid-free, 30% post-consumer content recycled paper.

Emergency Press participates in the Green Press Initiative. The mission of the Green Press Initiative is to work with book and newspaper industry stakeholders to conserve natural resources, preserve endangered forests, reduce green house gas emissions, and minimize impacts on indigenous communities.

BOOKS FROM EMERGENCY PRESS

Strata, by Ewa Chrusciel
ISBN 978-0-9830226-0-2, Paperback, $15.00

Various Men Who Knew Us as Girls, by Cris Mazza
ISBN 978-0-9753623-8-9, Paperback, $16.00

Super, by Aaron Dietz
ISBN 978-0-9753623-9-6, Paperback, $16.00

Slut Lullabies, by Gina Frangello
ISBN 978-0-9753623-7-2, Paperback, $15.00

American Junkie, by Tom Hansen
ISBN 978-0-9753623-6-5, Paperback, $15.00

IMPATIENCE, a Poem in 52 Pieces by Scott Zieher
ISBN 978-0-9753623-5-8, Paperback, $15.00

Touched by Lightning, by Ernest Loesser
ISBN 978-0-9753623-4-1, Paperback, $15.00

Six Trips in Two Directions, by Jayson Iwen
ISBN 0-9753623-2-1, Paperback, $15.00

The Border Will Be Soon, by Chad Faries
ISBN 0-9753623-3-X, Paperback, $15.00

VIRGA, a Poem by Scott Zieher
ISBN 0-9753623-1-3, Paperback, $15.00

EMERGENCY PRESS
www.emergencypress.org
info@emergencypress.org